Other Books by
Joyce Carol Oates

Do With Me What You Will
Marriages and Infidelities
The Edge of Impossibility:
  TRAGIC FORMS IN LITERATURE
Wonderland
The Wheel of Love
Them
Expensive People
A Garden of Earthly Delights
Upon the Sweeping Flood
With Shuddering Fall
By the North Gate
Anonymous Sins (POEMS)
Love and Its Derangements
  (POEMS)
Angel Fire (POEMS)
Scenes from American Life:
  CONTEMPORARY SHORT
  FICTION (EDITOR)
The Hungry Ghosts

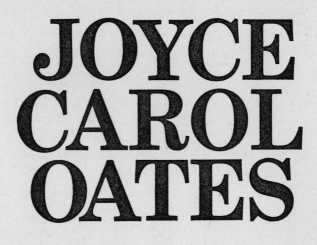

JOYCE
CAROL
OATES

NEW HEAVEN,
NEW EARTH:

the visionary experience

in literature

The Vanguard Press, Inc.

New York

for my mother and father,
Caroline and Frederic Oates

Ah no, I cannot tell you what it is, the new world.
I cannot tell you the mad, astounding rapture of
its discovery.
I shall be mad with delight before I have done,
and whosoever comes after will find me in the
new world a madman in rapture.

—D. H. Lawrence, *New Heaven and Earth*

Evil does not exist; once you have crossed the
threshold, all is good. Once in another world, you
must hold your tongue.

—Franz Kafka, *Diary* (1922)

CONTENTS

ACKNOWLEDGMENTS These essays have appeared, in various stages of transformation, in the following journals: "The Art of Relationships: Henry James and Virginia Woolf," in *Twentieth Century Literature*, October, 1964; "The Hostile Sun: The Poetry of D. H. Lawrence," a two-part essay, in *American Poetry Review*, Nov.-Dec., 1972, and *The Massachusetts Review*, Winter, 1973, and as a separate publication by *Black Sparrow Press*, 1973; "Anarchy and Order in Beckett's Trilogy," in *Renascence*, Spring, 1962; "The Nightmare of Naturalism: Harriette Arnow's *The Dollmaker*," in *Rediscoveries*, ed. David Madden (Crown Publishers, 1971), and reprinted as the "Afterword" in the Avon reissuing, 1972; "The Death Throes of Romanticism: The Poetry of Sylvia Plath," in *The Southern Review*, Fall, 1973; "The Visionary Art of Flannery O'Connor," a two-part essay, in *Thought*, Winter, 1966, and *The Southern Humanities Review*, Summer, 1973; "The Teleology of the Unconscious: The Art of Norman Mailer," in *The Critic*, Nov./Dec., 1973; "Out of Stone, Into Flesh: The Imagination of James Dickey," in *Modern Poetry Studies*, Summer, 1974; "Kafka's Paradise," in *Hudson Review*, Winter, 1973–74. To all these journals and their editors, thanks for permission to reprint are due.

PREFACE

To some artists there falls the difficult task, one perhaps imposed upon them by the vast "tide of emotions" Yeats envisioned as underlying individual roles, of standing between two worlds—one the visible, material, "real" world, the other a world no less real, but not physically demonstrable. There are some mystics—perhaps those who have experienced the very highest consciousness available to man—who never create art at all and who, if they communicate their vision to others, are compelled to speak directly. Not for them the self-consciousness of the artist, who distances himself from his audience *and* his vision through the medium of his art—no, these mystics con-

3

front others in the flesh, directly, since their ineffable vision is not distinct from their own personalities. Once one has crossed that threshold of which Kafka speaks, once one has directly experienced the divinity and unity of the universe, "evil" (or division) is eradicated, and "all is good." There is only affirmation. There is not even affirmation, but only existence. And one must "hold one's tongue."

But eternity is in love, after all, with the productions of time. And if the visionary individual does hold his tongue, in the sense of not personally recording his experience, others will record it for him; other artists will interpret that firsthand experience in the light of their own unique personalities. And so, out of the spontaneous mystical experience of the individual, we have, gradually, inevitably, the intellectualization of that experience—religion, philosophy, science, formal art, civilization itself. Walt Whitman said that the poetry he wrote was incidental to his life; and Lawrence often made the point, emphasized by those who were close to him, that his true art was his life, the living of his life. But the mystic in our time often chooses to be the analyst, the recorder, the intellectually curious observer of his own experience; and by this attempt to synthesize both worlds, or to explain poetically why the two worlds (the "physical" and the "spiritual") are not two at all, but one, he may create an art that is very disturbing, because it is so foreign to ordinary experience.

Such artists are passionate believers in the authenticity of their visions, and whether they know themselves as thoroughly as did Blake and Yeats, or whether their need to express themselves is largely an unconscious one, they inherit roles that are basically religious, and their art is

4

only the means—the "vehicle"—by which they communicate their truth. Like gnostic intermediaries, like translators, they try to bring metaphors from one system to another; they try to affirm a world most people never notice, or notice only to proclaim that it is "fallen." Some take the time to be exquisitely accomplished artists—like Virginia Woolf—and some, possessed by the excitement of creativity, write so quickly that—like Lawrence, like Rilke near the end of his life, like most writers at one time or another—they seem to experience an impersonal force, a blossoming, a flowering of the energies of life itself. Such artists, having experienced what seems to them an incontestably suprapersonal spirit that speaks through them, generally affirm all manifestations of this spirit and see the ordinary world's division of it into "good" and "evil," "objective" and "subjective," as fallacious. They often demonstrate a willingness to sympathize with forces outside the range of the ego, or the collective ego of civilization; and since "aesthetics" is an invention of civilization, they may at times harshly criticize those to whom art is higher than morality. Though he is one of the finest artists of our time, Lawrence is first of all a visionary, and then an artist, when he claims that the essence of true human art is a form of sympathy, a way of allowing the artist to give expression to the depth of his religious experience.

In the East, the "way" of the mystic is not antithetical to the "way" of the intellectual; nor are mystical experiences and intellectual achievement necessarily superior to ways of love or ordinary work. One chooses a pathway according to the inclinations of one's personality, and the pathways are not in competition. In the West, however, our difficulties are obvious: there is no truly felt communal acknowledgment of unity, the pathways are taken as ends in themselves, the differing personalities are not recognized as differing but as curiously and arrogantly at variance . . . even at war. Those who have glimpsed the "new heaven," "new earth" are seen to be, and often passionately declare themselves to be, the enemies of those to whom the only reality is what is in accord with tradition. Given the assumptions of our culture, such conflicts are not tragic but only natural. We seem to live in a culture in which conflict between individuals is a programmed necessity.

And what art has flowered out of this conflict! Would we surrender the torturous art work of our religious writers in exchange for the harmony they envision? Did Kafka not truly delight in the labyrinthine hells he created as he transcribed metaphors from one system to another? When exceptional individuals integrate the warring elements of our culture in themselves, and experience in themselves the evidently "tragic" personality of the epoch, we have great art. When the warring elements are not quite seen as parts of an individual psyche and when some are projected outward into the world, we may not have great art, but we will always have very exciting, combative art—at times an incredibly sophisticated "artless" art, as in Samuel Beckett, a despair beyond despair, at the point at which it turns into comedy.

Not all mystics are reconciled to the world order as it is, but most are forced—even against their conscious "intellectual" wills—into affirmation of one kind or another. The artist's original role in society was one of simple affirmation, of imitation, of instruction; only when he experienced himself as a unique individual, apart from others, could his art become critical or destructive, and such a realization of one's identity, the shock of perceiving one's own specific identity, coincides with the possibility of the tragic experience. Before tragedy as an art form could develop as consciously and beautifully as it did, before the assumptions of its vision could be shared by a community, the artistic individual as an individual had to experience this growth of perception, this isolation. That it must be seen as a necessary growth, an evolution, a blossoming of the spirit, and not as an evil "fall," is part of the visionary experience.

It is my belief that the serious artist insists upon the sanctity of the world—even the despairing artist insists upon the power of *his* art to somehow transform what is given. It may be that his role, his function, is to articulate the very worst, to force up into consciousness the most perverse and terrifying possibilities of the epoch, so that they can be dealt with and not simply feared; such artists are often denounced as vicious and disgusting when in fact they are—sometimes quite apart from their individual conceptions of themselves—in the service of their epoch, attempting to locate images adequate to the unshaped, unconscious horrors they sense. However, most of the visionaries included in this study are really quite affirmative—all but one or two strongly affirm the life force itself and the artist's relationship to it, and I see in the most despairing of these writers, Sylvia Plath, a furious impatience with the limitations of the ego (which she called the "mind"), a raging self-disgust that, had it not ended in suicide, might have cleansed her of those impurities of her era she had absorbed, and allowed her the visionary experience she sensed was a human possibility.

7

This book has only the most lyric kind of chronology; ideally, it should begin and end with Kafka, whom I first read over twenty years ago and whose extraordinary grasp of the "paradise" that is mistaken as "hell" allowed him to create such terrifying and beautiful works of art.

1
THE ART OF
RELATIONSHIPS

*Henry James and
Virginia Woolf*

Art does not reproduce what
we see. It makes us see.

Klee, "Creative Credo"

The "realistic" imagination draws back from the work of Henry James and of Virginia Woolf, for it finds in their fictional worlds no evidence of the natural, physical, biological world out of which everything arises. Their people are spirits without personal bodies; they inhabit time and space in a ghostly manner, and in the indulgent complexities of their subjectivity the supernatural seems never distant. Indeed, there is something supernatural about these fictional worlds, which exist without appetite or pain in a glimmering, shifting mosaic of aesthetic considerations. And they are strangely limited. Typical critical judgments are those of E. M. Forster in *Aspects of the*

Novel (James's premise is that "most of human life has to disappear before he can do us a novel") and of Walter Allen in *The English Novel* (Woolf is a "novelist of very narrow limits. . . . [Her characters] tend to think and feel alike, to be the aesthetes of one set of sensations").

The charge is that the characters of both novelists do not experience the range of life as it is really lived; moreover, they seem to inhabit worlds in which questions of social strife, of evil and suffering, of religious doubts, even of something so necessary to life as work, are ignored. It is felt generally, even by admirers, that in the novels of James and Woolf the aesthetic sensibility has so constricted life as to distort or pervert it, taking into account little of the richness and the vulgarity of the real world. It is not my suggestion that James and Woolf are similar in many important aspects; surprisingly enough, they seem quite clearly unrelated in matters of form, since James prepares forms quite as rigorous, though not as visible, as the plots of the traditional novel, and Woolf seeks to discover, along with her characters, design in the free flux of life; thematically, James is obsessed with the moral education of pastoral creatures—whether princesses or hardy Adamic voyagers from America—while Woolf is concerned with the necessary though doomed attempt to forge out of daily life a meaning that will somehow transcend it.

They are related, however, in their creation of subjective worlds that seek to define themselves in relationship to the larger, "real" world, the process often bringing with it annihilation, as in *The Voyage Out* and *The Wings of the Dove*. They are related most clearly in their use of minute psychological observations, Woolf casting about much more freely and inventively than James; and in their deliberate, unhurried, at times relentless faithfulness to these observations. What is most interesting about their art, however, is that it seems dehumanized to the ordinary intelligent reader. One cannot abstract from their worlds characters who are able to survive in an alien environment, as it would seem one might with other novelists—Dickens, Austen, Twain, Joyce. But this apparent weakness, however, may be seen as a necessary part of their literature.

One need only think of representative novelists—Thackeray and Conrad, for instance—to see that the vision of reality accepted by James and Woolf is severely different. For Thackeray and Conrad, unrelated though they are in most respects, reality is set and may be defined objectively, as history; for James and Woolf reality is a subjective phenomenon—more accurately, an endless series of subjective phenomena that may or may not be related. The secret lives of other people remain secret; one cannot penetrate into them, and the few flashes of rapport between people are perishable and cannot be trusted. Even the dead are mysterious. Milly Theale and Mrs. Ramsay influence "reality" after their deaths, but their effect on others does not bring with it any sudden understanding on the part of their survivors. Human essences, shrouded in mystery, are forever one with the single existing moment in which they are expressed—they cannot be abstracted out of it, they cannot be summed up, understood, even forgotten. If, in modern art, it is a truism that things do not exist and relationships alone exist, this observation will work well in explaining the literature of James and Woolf. Their concern is primarily with the mystery and beauty and tragedy of human relationships, not with the depths of reality that constitute individual "personality."

13

The creation of characters as ends in themselves, complete without functioning in a social or psychological equation with other characters, implies a metaphysical basis that is apparently not available to, or not chosen by, James and Woolf. Their metaphysics has in common the suggestion that man gains his identity, experiences his "life," in terms only of other people—other intelligent consciousnesses with whom he can communicate. Moreover, an individual's "reality" as an individual is determined by these relationships, which are entirely temporal and, especially in Woolf, undependable. The older sense of man defining himself in terms of God or of country or of family "history" has been replaced in James and Woolf by the sensitivity of the modern secular intellectual who admits of no reality beyond that experienced by the mind.

I

James's great myth is essentially the myth of the Fall: to James, heir of his Puritan ancestors as were Hawthorne and Melville, the fall is unfortunate in that it brings with it the mortal taint of decay as well as the "education" that is supposed to constitute a kind of minor, compensatory victory. One needs, then, to define James's world as essentially pastoral: an extension, into a more recognizable social *donnée*, of the blighted Eden of *The Turn of the Screw*. The paradise of innocence is carried precariously within a series of virginal heroines who are rounded, humanized descendants of Hawthorne's Hilda rather than Richardson's Clarissa—American purity typifying a spiritual purity that extends to mythic proportions, rather than being a reality, an end in itself as it is in the English novel. So we have Isabel Archer, the betrayed child Maisie, the children Miles and Flora, Maggie Verver, Milly Theale, and Fleda, who loses the spoils of Poynton because she is "too good" to compete for them. We also have Lambert Strether, the ambassador from Woollett, Massachusetts (innocence hardened into sterility, banality), to Paris (intuitive life hardened into sordidness), who is a widower, has experienced his only child's death, yet is seen to be unfulfilled until he comes to terms not simply with the richness of life Europe appears to offer but with the devastating underlying suggestion of evil this "real" life hides. In *The Ambassadors* (1903) James refines experience so that it takes on the quality of thought rather than life, leading Forster to make the remark I have already quoted; at the same time, James develops to perfection the art of narrative by point of view, third-person restrictive, telling the story only through Strether's limited, though expanding, consciousness. The novel may be defined as a minute recording of an education into the reality of the self and the world entirely through the hero's deciphering of his relationships to other people and their relationships with one another. One is reminded of music cast into visible forms: of the dance, the changing and rechanging of partners, not, as in Austen, the gravitational pull toward "truth" and the "good," which are one, but the relentless pull toward knowledge. One cannot feel that Strether can be imagined apart from the novel; his psychic environment defines him, becomes him. For a man of Strether's sensitivity, by no means rare in our time, it is the consideration of what is not immediate that blights or undermines the present: "The obsession of the other thing is the terror," he says. Is the reality of this world of endless qualifications less legiti-

15

mate than the reality of violence in the American novel, the one so committed to the mind, the other so committed to the body? James was surely influenced by the transcendentalists in his understanding of and insistence upon the legitimacy of psychic experience as total reality in the face of opposition by such critics as H. G. Wells. In an important sense all art is pastoral, its exclusions being at least as significant as its inclusions. For James the technique necessary to investigate reality to its depths is so precise, so fine, that the range investigated must be limited. The Jamesian technique cannot effectively be fused with the novel of action, nor is there any reason why it should be or why, failing its involvement in "total life," it should be considered somehow incomplete: dehumanized or, as Forster puts it, castrated.

In James as well as in Woolf there is the suggestion that art controls life, that the demands of the "architecturally competent" novel must alter the free flow of life and that, in Woolf especially, the exquisite epiphany becomes an end in itself rather than a means of illuminating character: as if the novel were a novel only of "character" in the old-fashioned sense. If James's most satisfactory and perhaps most Jamesian work, *The Wings of the Dove* (1902), is considered in some detail, however, it will be seen to give us what must surely be the most exhaustive attempt ever made of rendering the sensitivity or reflection of a tragic experience. It is the experience that matters; the aesthetic achievement is secondary. The plot of the novel sounds legendary: a dying American heiress, Milly Theale, is betrayed by her "lover," Merton Densher, who is in love with another woman. This woman, the beautiful and powerful Kate Croy, has directed the love affair in the hopes that with the mar-

16

riage of Milly and Densher, and Milly's expected death, Milly's fortune will come to them and complete their lives. Milly learns of the plot, her death is hastened, but she wills her money to the young man just the same: by this act forcing in her betrayers a moral sense so violent as to change their lives. Milly reminds us of the passive victims in Dostoyevsky—the saintly, the weak, the helpless, who possess paradoxically, as Dostoyevsky thought, the greatest power in the world. It is Milly's submission to her "fate" that secures her power; but it is not a perverse masochistic submission as Dostoyevsky's women sometimes exhibit—for instance, the suicidal Nastasia Philipovna of *The Idiot*—so much as a Christlike surrender of the self to the sins of others, in this way bringing about a moral transformation in the sinners. Not that James was Christian, or even ostensibly concerned with religious problems. But the movement of the novel, its very rhythm of sacrifice and moral self-realization, the theme of the power of selfless love—all are unmistakable parallels with the religious experience, whether Christian or tragic in the Greek sense. Milly embodies the symbolic roles of the Adamic innocent and the savior, the transition from the one to the other being precipitated by her encounter with evil; she is the dove whose wings spread to enclose the soiled, to carry her innocence away into the safety of death (the dove as soul), the dove of the 68th Psalm, as R. P. Blackmur has noted: "Though ye have lain among the sheepfolds, yet shall ye be as the wings of a dove that is covered with silver wings, and her feathers like gold." Above all, Milly is a sacrificial victim. "Why do you say such things to me?" she appeals to Kate in an uncharacteristic moment of weakness.

Kate replies:

17

"Because you're a dove." With which [Milly] felt herself ever so delicately, so considerately, embraced; not with familiarity or as a liberty taken, but almost ceremonially. . . .

As if it were the function, the fate, of innocence to be victimized: the necessary doom of the innocent to accept sins against themselves. If Milly feels herself guilty of a weakness, it can only be her intense desire to live, that is, to love and be loved, and this "weakness" she overcomes through her complete obliteration of self. It is the passivity of the lover who truly loves, who does not, in Shakespeare's words, alter when he "alteration finds" but continues to love in the face of betrayal. The little American heiress gains tragic dimensions only through James's technique, for the situation itself is hardly tragic.

Is it not, crudely synopsized, a working out of the conventional fear Milly has at the beginning of Book Three when we first meet her—the fear that the two lone women, touring Europe together, "were apt to be beguiled and overcome"? Precisely: but the brute experience itself is not what is important. It is Milly's consciousness of her experience, and the consciousness of sin on the part of Kate and Densher, that make the novel great. It is an education, a growth of the moral sense in all involved, that is the "reality" of the novel. Milly is the instrument by which we are shown the tragic knowledge of the relationship between life and death, life being fulfilled only through death (knowledge), the dove becoming the symbol—and James makes us see the rather trite image in the actual process of *becoming* symbol—of death-in-life, life-in-death. The Greek *ate* is here defeated, for the assimilation of evil by the innocent, the refusal to continue the power of evil by passing its suffering along to others, are affected by Milly's silence: in the clichéd sorrow of Mrs. Stringham's remark, "She has turned her face to the wall." The beauty of the spirit overshadows the "talent for life" of Kate Croy, Milly's opposite; the power of the dove overshadows that of the panther.

Virginia Woolf comments on *The Wings of the Dove* in her diary entry for September 12, 1921: ". . . And then one can never read it again. The mental grasp and stretch are magnificent. Not a flabby or slack sentence, but much emasculated by . . . timidity or consciousness. . . ." The truth being, of course, that the novel must be read "again," that a first reading cannot be more than superficial. The timidity and consciousness Woolf objects to are the very material of the novel itself: without the technique we have something rather like a Restoration comedy, except for the uncomic ending. What makes the novel seem emasculated or at least overrefined is its insistence upon the exploration of motives and judgments at great detail. Yet James is never obscure; each episode advances the "action," the action being the condition of relationships between the three or four main characters. James's power is an accumulative power. Only the reader who has earned, along with James, the experience of Milly's betrayal can appreciate the reality of this sudden realization of Densher's:

. . . he saw at moments, as to their final impulse or their final remedy, the need to bury in the dark blindness of each other's arms the knowledge of each other that they couldn't undo.

An impossibility: for the Jamesian education parallels the education of beast into human, amorality into morality.

The Golden Bowl (1904) continues the theme of innocence accosted by evil, or the world, the essential—and rather surprising—difference here being that where the earlier heroines were defeated because of their innocence, the young heroine Maggie Verver is able to achieve a victory by way of her innocence. It is most clearly the story of an education, more faithful to life perhaps in its refusal to surrender life along with "innocence," less effective as art than *The Wings of the Dove*, which tends to equate (one is reminded of *Billy Budd*) purity and life itself. It involves the awakening of a "moral sense" adumbrated in the earlier *What Maisie Knew* and, though the parallel is rather sinister, in *The Turn of the Screw*. The novel has had and continues to have a baffling critical history. Its difficulty arises partly from the technique James used—the story is Maggie's, but Maggie does not become a consciousness for us until Part II—and partly from the rich interweaving of suggestion, appearance, ceremony, and disguise that constitute the supposedly pastoral world of the Ververs. The proposition that *The Golden Bowl* is the last of a trilogy further complicates an understanding of the single work: one accepts the Blackmur suggestion that the three novels (the other two being *The Wings of the Dove* and *The Ambassadors*) constitute a "spiritual trilogy" but finds confusing rather than helpful the theory that the novels are the expression of a Swedenborgian mysticism inherited from James's father.

Essentially the story of a family, the novel's movement is determined by the changing of individuals into roles, the discovery of individuals that they are participants in a drama that has rich and threatening implications for them all. "No themes are so human as those that reflect for us, out of the confusion of life, the close connection

of bliss and bale, of the things that help with the things
that hurt . . . [the consideration of the] one face of
which is somebody's right and ease and the other somebody's pain and wrong": so speaks James in his preface
to the New York edition of *What Maisie Knew.* In *The
Golden Bowl* the ease and the pain are exchanged, as the
young heiress Maggie Verver learns to manipulate her
adulterous husband and stepmother, a woman her own
age, so that she is able to achieve a victory out of what
has been a sordid situation. The conclusion of the novel
involves, depends upon, a re-establishment of *order* not
on a moral level but on a social level, a preservation of
something rather like an institution—the institution of
marriage, of "love," of civilization—not of the individual.
If James's work contains any single great irony, it is the
irony of the imprisonment of the individual in relationships and forms precisely at the moment of his "illumination." James's people are usually wealthy, bathed in
riches as the lambs and children of Blake's pastoral are
bathed in sunshine, and they are wealthy for the same
reason that Shakespeare's tragic figures are kingly: their
economic freedom assures them moral freedom. As Lady
Agnes Dormer says in *The Tragic Muse,* "What freedom
is there in being poor?" What freedom, indeed? And
what freedom in being wealthy? It is her immense wealth
that sustains her innocence for Maggie, but perhaps such
moral innocence points toward a kind of decadence. The
Prince remembers reading, as a child, Poe's narrative of
A. Gordon Pym, the conclusion of which confronts the
voyager with a "dazzling curtain of light, concealing as
darkness conceals, yet of the colour of milk or of snow."
He feels himself confronted by a similar veil in the Americans: an innocence that is mysterious and ominous. It

21

is the force of Maggie's "whiteness," ultimately, that bends the lovers, the Prince and Charlotte, into forms; it is her innocence and her great wealth that make Maggie a prisoner. We witness here the buying and selling of souls. The Prince begins as an individual but ends as a unit: while he jests at the beginning about being a possession of the wealthy Americans ("a part of [Verver's] collection . . . a rarity, an object of beauty, an object of price"; "it was as if he had been some old embossed coin, of a purity of gold no longer used"), he becomes in reality a possession, just as his mistress Charlotte is subdued by the father, Verver, led around by an invisible rope, a "silken noose."

The reader feels constantly the mercenary shallowness of both the Prince and Charlotte, so that James's refusal to concern himself with the morality—and good taste— of the transaction is puzzling. That he does not do so seems clear by his complete absorption in the character of Maggie, who begins as a shadow, a pronouncer of the customary, proper remarks, and who ends as the "creator" of her world—she has nearly acquired omnipotence by the end of the novel. That her fight for her husband must be waged behind social forms makes the struggle more difficult and, for the loser, Charlotte, who never learns how much anyone knows about her adultery, more cruel. Neither Maggie nor James shows any remorse. Maggie is the victor, having surrendered a father and chosen a husband; she enters history; it seems perhaps a regrettable flaw that the man for whom she sacrifices her innocence is not worth her sacrifice, since a better man would not have betrayed her—would not have necessitated her education. The novel ends with Maggie's father taking Charlotte to America, leaving Maggie with her husband, whom she both pities and dreads. She has learned to deceive in order to impose her will upon the world:

. . . she reminded herself of an actress who had been studying a part and rehearsing it, but who suddenly, on the stage, before the footlights, had begun to improvise, to speak lines not in the text.

The unsympathetic reader may ask why Charlotte and the Prince do not run away together or why, at least, Charlotte does not leave her husband. But to make such demands is to fail to see the internal logic, the centripetal force of relationships that constitute the world of James's later novels. It is unthinkable that one can escape the bounds of the psychological world. One may speak of American City, but it does not exist; nor would these people exist apart from their relationships to one another. This curious transparency of character is underscored by the earlier *What Maisie Knew* (1897), which is technically limited to a concentration not only upon a single consciousness, the child Maisie, but upon a single concern of this consciousness, the relationships between parents and step-parents and lovers; Maisie becomes a point of view. A weakness of such pastoral is its inability to relate itself directly or, one might say, sanely with the real world: so the abandonment of Maisie by her irresponsible parents and guardians because she has learned to judge them morally leaves her on the edge of a precipice, on the brink of nothing at all. Like Miles in *The Turn of the Screw*, Maisie has pushed out to the very barrier of the world available to her, and James must break off the story if he is not to be forced to arrange for the child's death.

James must be understood, then, in his later novels

23

especially, as a creator of relationships; the actors—the fictional "characters"—come second. Though we may agree in part with his brother, William, when he criticized what he saw to be a "method of narration by interminable elaboration" directed to the strange goal of "arousing in the reader who may have had a similar perception . . . the illusion of a solid object, made . . . wholly out of impalpable materials,"[1] we must see that his apparent sacrifice of life to art is necessary for his vision of character *as* art. Like the medieval alchemists, whom he may resemble in other ways also, James transformed himself into a lifework, and each of his characters carries the transformation further. His main characters are artists, and the art they create is their own lives.

II

Virginia Woolf's novels, like James's, are characterized by an extraordinary blocking out of vast areas of life and a minute, vivid, at times nearly hallucinatory obsession with psychic experience. The intensity of her vision is so great that one feels the need to draw back from the particular, the subjective, to a detachment that will "explain" what is happening: a necessity Woolf admits in her use of techniques like the "Time Passes" episode in *To the Lighthouse* and the descriptions of sea and sky that introduce the various sections of *The Waves*. Her themes, unlike James's, usually have little to do with ethical problems. She dramatizes the mystery of life—the tensions between life and death, consciousness and unconsciousness, order and chaos, intimacy and isolation. Where earlier novelists chose as their technique a narrative structure that resembles the paneled murals of painters with a clear story to tell, Woolf uses a technique that reminds us of pointillism. Time, the necessary medium of human experience, is never violated; though the dreaming mind may cast itself back and forth in time, Woolf observes chronology faithfully. The technical problem is the difficulty of bridging the gaps from moment to moment, epiphany to epiphany; of being able, as is Lily Briscoe, to complete the vision being communicated to us. Woolf's art may be compared to Lily's view of reality:

She could have done it differently of course; the colour could have been thinned and faded; the shapes etherealised. . . . But then she did not see it like that. She saw the colour burning on a framework of steel; the light of a butterfly's wing lying upon the arches of a cathedral.

Here one has the impressionistic mode of art given shape by an a priori pattern, so that the two aesthetic views combine to give us the whole, the reality.

This tension between formlessness and form, the butterfly and the cathedral, provides the structural tone for Woolf's novels. The desultory wanderings and musings and attempts at relationships of *Between the Acts* are bounded by the acts of the pageant, the movement of English history itself, the romantic Isa gaining pathos from her juxtaposition to objective time; the rich soliloquies of the "characters" of *The Waves* gain something close to tragic dimension by their being bound, constantly, by the relentless passage of the sun across the sky. *To the Lighthouse* can be seen from a distance as a journey to a fixed point, the journey revealing to the sensitive child, James, the fact of there being two lighthouses, two "fixed points," two kinds of reality. Everything depends upon one's point of view and upon one's relationship, not only to the so-called objective world but to the minds of others. The desire to "be" is constant; the desire to *know* that one is, one exists, is superimposed on it; beyond this, there is the desire to establish one's "being" in terms of others—one thinks of Lily Briscoe's anguished question, "Could loving, as people called it, make her and Mrs. Ramsay one? for it was not knowledge but unity she desired. . . ." She says that knowledge is intimacy, and the strain toward the achievement of such "knowledge" runs through the minds of Woolf's people, providing a king of framework external to plot. In *The Waves* Louis thinks:

. . . if I do not nail these impressions to the board and out of the many men in me make one; exist here and now and not in streaks and patches, like scattered snow wreaths on far mountains . . . then I shall fall like snow and be wasted.

Yet it is also true, as Bernard says, that identity is an illusion:

'Who am I?' I have been talking of Bernard, Neville, Jinny, Susan, Rhoda, and Louis. Am I all of them? Am I one and distinct? I do not know. We sat here together. But now Percival is dead, and Rhoda is dead; we are divided; we are not here. Yet I cannot find any obstacle separating us. There is no division between me and them.

Balanced against the bitter dissatisfaction of Peggy in *The Years* ("Why do I notice everything?" she asks. "Why must I think?") is the strange, intuitive, half-mystical affirmation of life made by her aunt, Eleanor, the "Victorian spinster" who comes as near as anyone to being the center of the novel:

Does everything then come over again a little differently? she thought. If so, is there a pattern; a theme, recurring, like music; half remembered, half foreseen? . . . a gigantic pattern, momentarily perceptible? The thought gave her extreme pleasure: that there was a pattern.

The two impulses—toward identity and toward unity—are determined solely through relationships with others.

Yet the unity is always spiritual and, in spite of this, is always temporary. It should come as no surprise that Woolf does not concern herself with social questions in any but an incidental way, or that matters of a religious nature seem irrelevant. Like James, she has a "mind too pure to be violated by an idea"—that is, a mind too sensitive to be violated by the simplicity of single, dominating ideas. The terrible straining for unity, for obliteration of the self in the "knowledge" of intimacy, suggests a sexual overtone: indeed, one expects Woolf to use sexual relations metaphorically. But just as in James those who come on stage have been freed of economic bondage, so in Woolf they have been freed of their physical bondage; the passions James is capable of creating—in Densher and the Prince, in the unfortunate governess of *The Turn of the Screw*—would annihilate Woolf's world. There is no distinction between the relationships of men and women and the relationships of women and women, men and men, adults and children. Where the Puritan mind establishes tension by its exclusion of the physical life deliberately and systematically, Woolf excludes it incidentally; it quite literally does not matter. The child James stands by Mrs. Ramsay as she talks to her husband, who feels sorry for himself because he is a "failure":

. . . James . . . felt her rise in a rosy-flowered fruit tree laid with leaves and dancing boughs into which the beak of brass,

27

the arid scimitar of his father, the egotistical man, plunged and smote, demanding sympathy.

Though it is never anything more than "sympathy" that is demanded (one senses at first reading the discrepancy between metaphor and intention), this sympathy is enough to kill off Mrs. Ramsay. The tension in Woolf, however, is always between two or more spirits, two or more points of view.

Having eliminated the vast complex areas of social, religious, and sexual concerns, Woolf is able to address herself to the primitive—or at least fundamental—question, "What is real?" If Woolf's characters appear to us creatures paralyzed in metaphysical wonderment, hence unable to live, it must be remembered that at the center of her work is life itself: the London of *Mrs. Dalloway*; the young man Percival, envied and loved; the mother of eight children, Mrs. Ramsay; the "Nature taking part" in the pageant of *Between the Acts*. The paradox is Lambert Strether's in *The Ambassadors*. Only the sensitive can understand that nothing else matters except to live: "Live all you can; it's a mistake not to," Strether tells Bilham, who ironically does not need the advice. Yet the sensitive become by dint of their very sensitivity unable to simply "live," for they are committed to judgment and assessment and the establishment of order; and those who do no more than simply live cannot be conscious of the wonder of their experience.

To the Lighthouse (1927) directly addresses the problem of knowledge and experience. The tension between Mr. and Mrs. Ramsay is partly accountable to their representing, not at all perfunctorily, the traditionally opposed talents for knowledge and for life. Mr. Ramsay is a professional philosopher who spends his time thinking, as the artist Lily naïvely imagines, of a "kitchen table" when he is not present (the noumenal reality, the reality prior to and independent of experience):

The kitchen table was something visionary, austere; something bare, hard, not ornamental. There was no colour to it; it was all edges and angles; it was uncompromisingly plain. But Mr. Ramsay kept always his eyes fixed upon it, never allowed himself to be distracted or deluded, until his face became worn too and ascetic and partook of this unornamented beauty which so deeply impressed [Lily].

Mrs. Ramsay, by contrast, is immersed constantly in time. One sees her always busy—knitting, mending, comforting a child, writing letters on the beach, opening windows and shutting doors, hiding the pig's skull on the nursery wall with her shawl. Lily thinks, after her death, of Mrs. Ramsay's instinct for humanity:

And this, like all instincts, was a little distressing to people who did not share it. . . . Some notion was in . . . them about the ineffectiveness of action, the supremacy of thought. [Mrs. Ramsay's action] was a reproach to them, gave a different twist to the world, so that they were led to protest, seeing their own prepossessions disappear.

Moreover, Mrs. Ramsay is able by the magic of her being to make of the moment something permanent, to impose on the flux of life an order similar to the order of the artist. Her immortality, she thinks, consists in her kinship with others:

They would, she thought . . . however long they lived, come back to this night; this moon; this wind; this house; and to her too. It flattered her . . . to think how, wound about in

their hearts, however long they lived she would be woven.
. . . She felt . . . that community of feeling with other people which emotion gives as if the walls of her partition had become so thin that practically . . . it was all one stream.
. . .

Mrs. Ramsay, thinking herself ignorant in contrast to her husband, admires the "masculine intelligence, which ran up and down, crossed this way and that, like iron girders spanning the swaying fabric, upholding the world," but clearly Woolf wants to make a distinction between reason and understanding in Kantian terms: reason being limited, for all its power, and understanding or intuition being freed from its dictates.

These evidently opposing forces, knowledge and experience, intellect and feeling, the masculine and the feminine tendencies, work to resolution. Mr. Ramsay fulfills his obligation to the dead by going to the lighthouse with James and Cam ten years after Mrs. Ramsay's death, his achievement signaled by the overcoming of his children's hostility to him. Woolf wanted the sense of Mr. Ramsay's reaching the lighthouse and Lily's finishing her painting to be simultaneous (see *Diary*, September 5, 1926), so that the fulfillment of a gesture of love and of a work of art would be united: Mrs. Ramsay's memory having given Lily the vision necessary to begin the work again, Mr. Ramsay's journey having given her the energy to complete it. She draws a line in the center of her painting, a symbolic accolade to the lighthouse itself, to the stabilizing power of the fixed point. The completion of the ceremony carries with it the suggestion of life as art being somehow perfected, an idea puzzling when considered alongside Woolf's usual ideas of the flux, the claim of the still point upon this flux, the flux again, all of which suggest a kind of dialectic restlessness too great to be confined by art; see Bernard's despair in *The Waves,* near the conclusion:

My book, stuffed with phrases, has dropped to the floor. It lies under the table to be swept up by the charwoman when she comes wearily at dawn. . . . What is the phrase for the moon? And the phrase for love? By what name are we to call death?

If the conclusion of *To the Lighthouse* seems to us dissatisfying, the complexity of life delivered over much too glibly to the demands of art, it is only because Woolf has taught us the ravages of an indifferent nature in the middle section, "Time Passes." Here the lighthouse with its beam enters the deserted rooms, viewing the chaos of a world without human order as it viewed Mrs. Ramsay years before—Mrs. Ramsay so communing with it that she felt herself becoming the light, seeing her own eyes meeting her own eyes out of the light. The achievement of order, then, is brutal and imposed upon from without when it is delivered apart from love: the lighthouse as it is to James when he arrives in the boat, not the lighthouse as it is to him on shore. The motif of "We perished, each alone" is balanced by the earlier "And all the lives we ever lived/And all the lives to be,/Are full of trees and changing leaves. . . ." The isolation of identity dissolved into a kind of communion, in a crude sense the communion of death, in another sense the communion of sympathy: separate and doomed identity defeated by the completion of the journey and of the painting, for by these acts Mr. Ramsay and Lily are related to Mrs. Ramsay, Mr. Ramsay relates himself silently to his children and they to him, and Lily relates herself to Mr. Carmichael. This multipersonal representation of reality achieves a higher reality in proportion to its distance from old-fashioned naturalism. It is significant that Erich Auerbach ends his monumental *Mimesis,* a study of the "representation of reality in Western literature," with an analysis of a passage from *To the Lighthouse.*

The lighthouse as a final symbol remains an enigma because, like Melville's Moby Dick, it has been used to carry the burden of separate projections of meaning, the attempts of several individuals to come to terms with what is permanent within each of them in relationship to what is permanent "objectively"; the lighthouse carrying absolutely no connotations of good or evil, or a blend of both or neither, as Melville's whale does, but emerging instead as the fixed point of necessary order itself, ironic in that it can never be known except as a series of subjective experiences. It is the spiritualization of reality, once again the making immaterial of the "opaque," as Proust said. Arguments over the ultimate meaning of the lighthouse and the intention of the final pages are futile, since the novel is to be taken as a series of impressions in time, the final impression of unity being no more significant, perhaps, than Mrs. Ramsay's apparently basic feeling that there is no "reason, order, justice: but suffering, death, the poor." All depends upon point of view; Woolf shows the process of the mind in continual change, so that even those who are dead and ostensibly safe from further involvement are resurrected and given life again by their survivors.

The works of James and Woolf must evolve slowly because they deal with relationships, with ratios: the slow growth of man's assessments of himself and the world, "knowledge" in James gained through the relentless witnessing of others' commitment to action, "unity" gained in Woolf through the processes of the mind in its desperate attempt to transcend time—and itself. We are not able, as readers, to "know" Milly Theale until we know her as Kate and Densher have experienced her. Her death, like Mrs. Ramsay's, takes place in a moral vacuum—until the surviving witnesses explain her to us. The individual as individual does not exist, but is defined both to himself and to others in terms of the world about him.

In this sense both James and Woolf represent the furthest limits of the traditional English novel, their preoccupation with interior details corresponding to the more conventional preoccupation with exterior details; their basic assumption that the individual's identity is gained only through participation in a complex field of other individuals' consciousnesses corresponding to the heartier, more agreeable, but perhaps no less anxious assumption in Fielding, Austen, and Thackeray that human identity is achieved only by acquiescing to social judgments. But the field of inquiry of James and Woolf is, of course, much more aesthetically sophisticated; and for them "identity" can never be a fixed issue, a coming to rest in a marriage or even in death. In Woolf ethical problems seem to hang suspended, as if awaiting definition, and in certain works of James (*The Lesson of the Master,* as well as *The Golden Bowl*), the ambiguity of life is an epistemological rather than a moral problem.

But in the end we are somehow left dissatisfied. We recognize the wonder of their aesthetic achievements, yet we must admit that the melodrama of Dostoyevsky and Stendhal has the power to move us more deeply. Why is this so? Why, beneath the most polished and exquisite structures, do the visions of James and Woolf somehow elude us? Henry James emerges in his own life—the last turbulent year of his life—as more heroic, more vital, than any of his protagonists. He could create his own soul in response to a brutal historical challenge; and yet, within the context of the social world he had chosen for his fictional milieu, he could really not create heroic behavior at all. His intelligent heroes are invariably weak; his saintly heroines are victims; his forceful characters are selfish manipulators of others' lives. Henry James himself is superior to any of them. Virginia Woolf's exquisite sensibility allowed her to move further and further away from the material of real, turbulent, physical life, so that her finest writing seems to us always experimental, as if in the making, as if the author were writing tentatively, testing the element in which she existed mentally but not in which she existed as a total person. Their artistic achievements are among the finest in our language not because of their subject matter but in spite of it: this, it has always seemed to me, is what we have honored in them. That artists of such genius should address themselves to so narrow, so stubbornly monastic a vision must correspond to a repressed ascetic instinct within us.

The novel is perhaps the highest art form because it so closely resembles life: it is about human relationships. Its technique, page by page, resembles our technique of living day by day—a way of *relating*. James and Woolf are superb visionaries of the web of consciousness we often inhabit, the defining-by-others of certain forms of mental life. But they are preoccupied with the relatedness of the sensitive self to selves not finally worthy of them. The ceremony is awe inspiring, the generosity of the sacrifice saintly, but the gods themselves are disappointing. Hei-

34

degger has said that Western metaphysics (and all Western thought) is obsessed with beings rather than with Being. And to get beyond the dazzling complexities of beings to the transcendent/imminent Being itself is the real aim of art. The ambiguities of James and Woolf remain for us aesthetic pleasures, forms of near perfection made of ordinary human substance. It is necessary to see their art as a triumph of intuitive genius over the tragic limitations of the social, organized life. One can go no further in the alchemical Western feat of transforming material into spirit; their great novels are like the marvelous heroic couplets of Pope, accomplishments valued as much for liberating us into another way of writing as for their own beauty. After Pope, a certain technique of poetry—and therefore a certain technique of "seeing" —was finished. And after James and Woolf, after the experiment of the mind's dissection of itself and its dissociation from the body,[2] perhaps we are ready to rediscover the world.

2

THE HOSTILE
SUN:

The poetry of
D. H. Lawrence

I am that I am
from the sun,
and people are not my measure.

Lawrence, "Aristocracy of the Sun"

Virginia Woolf objected to Lawrence's art because, to her, he "echoes nobody, continues no tradition, is unaware of the past"—the very qualities that help to account for Lawrence's amazingly vital genius, though Woolf was surely mistaken in believing that Lawrence was unaware of the past. It was that past, the pastness of the past, the burden of history and tradition, that infuriated him; and he rejected as well Woolf's belief that the artistic act was neither easy nor joyous, but created slowly, torturously, "pulled through only in breathless anguish."[1] *Why* must art be painful? And, if it is deliberately conceived of as a negative human activity, how

39

can its products be anything less than death-affirming, despairing, an unnatural distortion of one of the most joyful of all human adventures, the mysterious flowering of the imagination into conscious forms? Surely Lawrence was correct in believing that the excessively self-conscious artist seeks to exalt himself over his subject; and that the highest role of the artist is to proclaim not his own ingenuity and superiority over other men but his sympathy with them—an effort that will demand a radical and disturbing individualism, that refuses to continue an intellectual or literary tradition in order to proclaim the impersonal and the divine within ordinary men.

The "impersonal and the divine" is existentially immediate, however; it does not require torturous effort in order to be expressed. If the artist allows his subject a certain measure of freedom, it will spring forth, not with a Joycean overdetermination but with the spontaneous flowering of nature itself. In Lawrence's poetry, more than in his prose, we see again and again this spontaneous discovering of Being, this recording of the explicit revelation. Not an abstraction, not an intellectual discovery or deduction, the beauty of the universe is, to Lawrence, a perpetual creation. Though to him the novel remained the one "bright book of life" because of its dramatic rendering of the complex interrelatedness of life, it is in his poetry—less read than his prose, and seriously underestimated—that his ability to show the unique beauty of the passing moment, even the passing psychological moment, is most clearly illustrated.

Lawrence's poems are blunt, exasperating, imposing upon us his strangely hectic, strangely delicate music, in fragments, in tantalizing broken-off parts of a whole too vast to be envisioned—and then withdrawing again. They are meant to be spontaneous works, spontaneously experienced; they are not meant to give us the sense of grandeur or permanence that other poems attempt, the fallacious sense of immortality that is an extension of the poet's ego. Yet they achieve a kind of immortality precisely in this: that they transcend the temporal, the intellectual. They are ways of experiencing the ineffable "still point" that Eliot could approach only through abstract language.

It is illuminating to read Lawrence's entire poetic work as a kind of journal, in which not only the finished poems themselves but variants and early drafts and uncollected poems constitute a strange unity—an autobiographical novel, perhaps—that begins with "The quick sparks . . ." and ends with "immortal bird." This massive work is more powerful, more emotionally combative, than even the greatest of his novels. Between first and last line there is literally everything: beauty, waste, "flocculent ash," the ego in a state of rapture and in a state of nausea, a diverse streaming of chaos and cunning. We know Yeats fashioned his "soul" in the many-volumned *Collected Works of W. B. Yeats,* quite consciously, systematically; Lawrence has unconsciously and unsystematically created a similar work. In part it is shameless; but there are moments of beauty in it that are as powerful as Yeats's more frequent moments. There are moments of clumsiness, ugliness, and sheer stubborn spite, quite unredeemed by any poetic grace, so much so, in fact, that the number of excellent poems is therefore all the more amazing. Ultimately, Lawrence forces us to stop judging each individual poem. The experience of reading all the poems—and their earlier forms—becomes a kind of mystical appropriation of Lawrence's life, or *life itself,* in which the essential sacredness of "high" and "low," "beauty" and "ugliness," "poetry" and "non-poetry" is celebrated in a magical transcendence of all rationalist dichotomies.

I   The Candid Revelation:
Lawrence's Aesthetics

Lawrence is one of our true prophets, not only in his "madness for the unknown" and in his explicit warning—

> If we do not rapidly open all the doors of consciousness
> and freshen the putrid little space in which we are cribbed
> the sky-blue walls of our unventilated heaven
> will be bright red with blood.
>
> ("Nemesis," from *Pansies*)

—but in his lifelong development of a technique, a fictional and poetic *way* in which the prophetic voice can be given formal expression. It is a technique that refuses to study itself closely, that refuses to hint at its position in any vast cultural tradition—unlike that of Eliot, for instance!—and that even refuses, most unforgivably to the serious-minded, to take itself seriously. Richard Aldington, writing in 1932, contrasts Lawrence's delight in the imperfect with James Joyce's insistence upon perfection, and though Aldington seems overbiased against Joyce, his point about Lawrence is well made. Lawrence was not interested in that academic, adolescent, and rather insane human concept of "The Perfect," knowing very well that dichotomies like Perfect/Imperfect are only invented by men according to their cultural or political or emotional dispositions, and then imposed upon others. Everything changes, says Lawrence; most of all, standards of apparently immutable taste, aesthetic standards of perfection that are soon left behind by the spontaneous flow of life.

Therefore he strikes us as very contemporary—moody and unpredictable and unreliable—a brilliant performer when he cares to be, but quite maliciously willing to inform us of the dead spaces, the blanks in his imagination. Not a finer poet than Yeats, Lawrence is often much more sympathetic; he seems to be demonstrating in his very style, in the process of writing his poetry, the revelation that comes at the conclusion of Yeats's "The Circus Animals' Desertion" (a poem that itself comes near the conclusion of Yeats's great body of work)—the knowledge that the poet, for all his higher wisdom, must lie down "where all the ladders start,/In the foul rag-and-bone shop of the heart." Yet it has always seemed to me ironic that this revelation comes to us in a poem that is technically perfect—a Platonic essence of what a poem should be. By contrast, Lawrence seems to be writing, always writing, out of the abrupt, ungovernable impulses of his soul, which he refuses to shape into an art as studied as Yeats's. He had no interest in "perfection"; he would have scorned even the speculative idea of hoping for either a perfection in life or in art—he is too engrossed in the beauty of the natural flux.

But it is sometimes difficult for critics, especially tradition-oriented critics, to understand this. A healthy respect for the great achievements of the past should not cause the critic to be suspicious of what seems revolutionary and upsetting, contrary to his definition of "art" —on the contrary, such iconoclastic art should be welcomed, since it expands our grasp of what is known in ways that classical, "correct" art cannot. There is pleasure, certainly, in reading once again a "perfect" novella —in encountering a poet who demonstrates a marvelous facility with diction—but there should be pleasure, as well, in the raw, jagged music of voices quite contrary to our own, voices that even seem to us unlikable. Some of the academic prejudice against Lawrence may have been due to the lingering puritanism of aesthetics articulated by Woolf—that the artist *should* work very hard, that his work should cause him pain, not release in him emotions of a pleasurable nature. And then, as well, there are the many critics who, while sympathetic to the creative artist, yet do not exactly comprehend his necessary redefining of his craft. How else to account for R. P. Blackmur's judgment in the essay "Lawrence and Expressive Form" (in *Language as Gesture,* 1954) that Lawrence wrote "fragmentary biography" and not "poetry"? When a critic charges a poet with having failed to write poetry, one must certainly question his inclination to use a literary term ("poetry") in a restrictive and punitive way. In all cases the critic's definition of poetry, whether stated or implied, is always based upon his expectation of what poetry ought to be, based upon the past. Blackmur believed that poetry required what he called "the structures of art," and that these structures must be the result of a "rational imagination." Surely one may honor Blackmur's own conception of art without agreeing that this is always the case or that it has given us the art that has moved us most deeply. It was Lawrence's belief that the essence of art is, after all, its ability to convey the emotions of one man to his fellows—a form of sympathy, a form of religious experience. Had Lawrence attempted to write poetry to please men like Blackmur, had Lawrence the "craftsman" managed to silence the "demon of personal outburst," his unique nature would have been violated. Admittedly, it is extremely difficult for the critic to avoid punishing his subject for not being a form of the critic himself, a kind of analogue to his ego! There is a slightly paranoid fear, perhaps connected with political and social prejudices, that chaos will come again if rules established in the eighteenth century are violated; and having begun as a monastic labor, the role of the academic to keep order, to insist upon hierarchies, to be continuously *grading*, is one that coincides far too easily with a puritanical fear of and loathing for the processes of life that most artists celebrate.

For Lawrence, of course, life predates art, and art predates any traditional form. He is fascinated by the protean nature of reality, the various possibilities of the ego. Throughout the entire collection of poems there is a deep, unshakable faith in the transformable quality of all life. Even the elegiac "The Ship of Death" (written as Lawrence was dying) ends with a renewal, in typically Lawrentian words: ". . . and the whole thing starts again." Like most extraordinary men, Lawrence is concerned with directing the way his writing will be assessed; the ambitious are never content to leave the writing of their biographies to others, who may make mistakes. So he says, in a prefatory note of 1928, "No poetry, not even the best, should be judged as if it existed in the absolute, in the vacuum of the absolute. Even the best poetry, when it is at all personal, needs the penumbra of its own time and place and circumstance to make it full and whole." Surely this is correct, and yet it is a point missed by most critics—and not just critics of Lawrence—who assume that their subjects are "subjects" and not human

45

beings, and that their works of art are somehow crimes for which they are on perpetual trial.

The critic who expects to open Lawrence's poems and read poems by T. S. Eliot, for instance, is bound to be disappointed. Lawrence's poems are for people who want to experience the poetic process as well as its product; who want the worst as well as the best, because they are infinitely curious about the man, the human being, D. H. Lawrence himself. If you love someone, it is a total engagement; if you wish to be transformed into him, as one wants to be into Lawrence, you must expect rough treatment. That is one of the reasons why Lawrence had maddened so many people—they sense his violent, self-defining magic, which totally excludes them and makes them irrelevant, unless they "become" Lawrence himself, on his terms and not their own.

He trusted himself, endured and suffered himself, worked his way through himself (sometimes only barely) and came through—"Look! we have come through!"— and he expects no less of his readers. Only a spiritual brother or sister of Lawrence himself can understand his poems, ultimately; this is why we strain upward, puzzled but yearning for an equality with him, if only in flashes. We need a violent distending of our imaginations in order to understand him. It is almost a reversal of Nietzsche's remark, to the effect that one must have the "permission" of one's envious friends in order to be acknowledged as great: Lawrence might have felt that one's friends must earn the permission of recognizing that he, Lawrence, *is* a great man.

There is a deadly little poem called "Blank" in which Lawrence says coldly:

46

"At present I am a blank, and I admit it.
. . . So I am just going to go on being a blank, till some-
    thing nudges me from within,
and makes me know I am not blank any longer."

The poems themselves are nudges, some sharp and cruel
and memorable indeed, most of them a structured streaming of consciousness, fragments of a total self that could
not always keep up the strain of totality. Sometimes Lawrence was anguished over this, but most of the time he
believed that in his poetry, as in life itself, what must be
valued is the springing forth of the natural, forcing its
own organic shape, not being forced into a preordained
structure. He is much more fluid and inventive than the
imagists, whose work resembles some of his cooler, shorter
poems, in his absolute commitment to the honoring of
his own creative processes. Picasso has stated that it is his
own dynamism he is painting, because the movement of
his thought interests him more than the thought itself;
and while Lawrence does not go this far, something of the
same is true in his utilization and valuing of spontaneity.
He says:

Ours is the universe of the unfolded rose,
The explicit,
The candid revelation.

("Grapes")

So Lawrence declares and defines himself, and the impersonal in himself (which he valued, of course, more
than the "personal"), in a word-for-word, line-by-line,
poem-by-poem sequence of revelations.

For Lawrence, as for Nietzsche, it is the beauty and
mystery of flux, of "Becoming," that enchants us; not
permanence, not "Being." Permanence exists only in the

47

conscious mind and is a structure erected to perfection, therefore airless and stultifying. Lawrence says in a letter of 1913, written to Ernest Collings, from Italy:

I conceive a man's body as a kind of flame, like a candle flame, forever upright and yet flowing: and the intellect is just the light that is shed on to the things around. And I am not so much concerned with the things around—which is really mind—but with the mystery of the flame forever flowing. . . . We have got so ridiculously mindful, that we never know that we ourselves are anything—we think there are only the objects we shine upon. And instead of chasing the mystery in the fugitive, half-lighted things outside us, we ought to look at ourselves, and say, "My God, I am myself!"

(*Collected Letters*, I, 180)

This is exactly contemporary with us: at last, men whose training has been scientific and positivistic and clinical and "rational" are beginning to say the same thing. Unlike Freud, Lawrence would assert that the so-called destructive instincts are really a manifestation of intellectual perversion, not healthy instinct. Lawrence's arrogant prophetic stance in "The Revolutionary" ("see if I don't bring you down, and all your high opinion/. . . Your particular heavens,/With a smash") is becoming justified.

Lawrence loves the true marriage of heaven and hell, illusory opposites; he loves to exalt the apparently unbeautiful. For instance, in the poem "Medlars and Sorb-Apples" from his best single volume of poems, *Birds, Beasts and Flowers* (1923), he says:

I love you, rotten,
Delicious rottenness.

> I love to suck you out from your skins
> So brown and soft and coming suave,
> So morbid. . . .

He sees these fruits as "autumnal excrementa" and they please him very much. Earlier, in a poem called "Craving for Spring," he has declared that he is sick of the flowers of earliest spring—the snowdrops, the jonquils, the "chill Lent lilies" because of their "faint-bloodedness,/slow-blooded, icy-fleshed" purity. He would like to trample them underfoot. (What is remarkable in Lawrence's "nature" poems is his fierce, combative, occasionally peevish relationship with birds, beasts, and flowers—he does them the honor, as the romantic poets rarely did, of taking them seriously.) So much for the virgins, so much for portentousness! It is with a totally different emotion that he approaches the sorb-apples, a kind of worship, a dread:

> Gods nude as blanched nut-kernels,
> Strangely, half-sinisterly flesh-fragrant
> As if with sweat,
> And drenched with mystery.
> . . . .
> I say, wonderful are the hellish experiences,
> Orphic, delicate
> Dionysus of the Underworld.
>
> A kiss, and a spasm of farewell, a moment's orgasm of
> rupture,
> Then along the damp road alone, till the next turning.
> And there, a new partner, a new parting, a new unfusing
> into twain,
> A new gasp of further isolation. . . .

These poems are remarkable in that they refuse to state, with the kind of godly arrogance we take for granted in Shakespeare, that they will confer any immortality on their subjects. As Lawrence says in his short essay "Poetry of the Present" (1918), he is not attempting the "treasured, gem-like lyrics of Shelley and Keats," though he values them. His poetry is like Whitman's, a poetry of the "pulsating, carnal self," and therefore Lawrence celebrates the falling away, the rotting, the transient, even the slightly sinister, and above all his own proud isolation, "Going down the strange lanes of hell, more and more intensely alone," until hell itself is somehow made exquisite:

> Each soul departing with its own isolation,
> Strangest of all strange companions,
> And best.
>   ("Medlars and Sorb-Apples")

In 1929, Lawrence says in his introduction to *Pansies*: "A flower passes, and that perhaps is the best of it. If we can take it in its transience, its breath, its maybe mephistophelian, maybe palely ophelian face, the look it gives, the gesture of its full bloom, and the way it turns upon us to depart . . ." we will have been faithful to it, and not simply to our own projected egos. Immortality, he says, can give us nothing to compare with this. The poems that make up *Pansies* are "merely the breath of the moment, and one eternal moment easily contradicting the next eternal moment." The extraordinary word is *eternal*. Lawrence reveals himself as a mystic by this casual, offhand critical commentary on his own work as much as he does in the work itself. He can experience the eternal *in* the temporal, and he realizes, as few people do, that the temporal is eternal by its very nature: as if a piece of colored glass were held up to the sun, becoming sacred as it is illuminated by the sun, but also making the sun itself sacred. To Lawrence the sun is a symbol of the ferocious externality of nature, the uncontrollable, savage Otherness of nature, which must be recognized, honored, but not subdued—as if man could subdue it, except by deceiving himself. The sun is "hostile," yet a mystic recognizes the peculiar dependency of the eternal upon the temporal; the eternal being is made "real" or realized only through the temporal. Someday it may be taken for granted that the "mystical vision" and "common sense" are not opposed, that one is simply an extension of the other, but, because the mystical vision represents a natural development not actually realized by most people, it is said to be opposed to logical thought.

There is a rhythmic, vital relationship between the eternal and the temporal, the one pressing close upon the other, not remote and cold, but mysteriously close. Lawrence says in "Mutilation":

> I think I could alter the frame of things in my agony.
> I think I could break the System with my heart.
> I think, in my convulsion, the skies would break.

Inner and outer reality are confused, rush together, making up a pattern of harmony and discord, which is Lawrence's basic vision of the universe and the controlling aesthetics behind his poetry. It is significant that when Lawrence seems to us at his very worst—in *The Plumed Serpent, Kangaroo,* much of *Apocalypse,* nearly all of the poems in *Nettles* and *More Pansies*—he is stridently dogmatic, authoritative, speaking without ambiguity or mystery, stating and not suggesting, as if attempting to usurp the position of the Infinite (and unknowable), putting

51

everything into packaged forms. When he seems to us most himself, he is more fragmentary, more spontaneous, inspired to write because of something he has encountered in the outside world—a "nudge" to his blankness, a stimulus he is startled by, as he is by the hummingbird in the poem with that title, imagining it as a jabbing, prehistorical monster, now seen through the wrong end of the telescope; or as he is by a doe in "A Doe at Evening," when he thinks:

> Ah yes, being male, is not my head hard-balanced, antlered?
> Are not my haunches light?
> Has she not fled on the same wind with me?
> Does not my fear cover her fear?

Questions, and not answers, are Lawrence's real technique, just as the process of thinking is his subject matter, not any formalized structures of "art." Because of this he is one of the most vital of all poets in his presentation of himself as the man who wonders, who asks questions, who feels emotions of joy or misery or fury, the man who *reacts*, coming up hard against things in a real world, both the creator of poems and the involuntary creation of the stimuli he has encountered—that is, he is so nudged by life that he must react, he must be altered, scorning the protection of any walls of "reason" or "tradition" that might make experience any less painful.

Typically, he is fascinated by "unissued, uncanny America" in the poem "The Evening Land," confessing that he is half in love, half horrified, by the "demon people/lurking among the deeps of your industrial thicket"— in fact, he is allured by these demons, who have somehow survived the America of machines:

52

Say, in the sound of all your machines
And white words, white-wash American,
Deep pulsing of a strange heart
New throb, like a stirring under the false dawn that pre-
cedes the real.
Nascent American
Demonish, lurking among the undergrowth
Of many-stemmed machines and chimneys that smoke
like pine-trees.

For Lawrence, America itself is a question.

II   New Heaven and Earth:
Lawrence's Transformations

In Lawrence we experience the paradox—made dramatic by his genius—of a brilliant man trying to resist his
own brilliance, his own faculty for dividing, categorizing,
assessing, making clear and conscious and therefore finite.
It seems almost a dark angel of his, this dreaded "consciousness," and he wrestles with it throughout his life,
stating again and again that we are "godless"when we are
"full of thought," that consciousness leads to mechanical
evil, to self-consciousness, to nullity. He yearned for the
separateness of an individual isolation, somehow in conjunction with another human being—a woman—but not
dependent upon this person, mysteriously absolved of any
corrupting "personal" bond. It is the "pulsating, carnal
self" he wants to isolate, not the rational self, the activity
of the personality-bound ego he came to call, in a late
poem entitled "Only Man," the "self-apart-from-God"—
his only projection of a real hell, a fathomless fall into
the abyss:

For the knowledge of the self-apart-from-God
is an abyss down which the soul can slip
writhing and twisting in all the revolutions
of the unfinished plunge
of self-awareness, now apart from God, falling
fathomless, fathomless, self-consciousness wriggling
writhing deeper and deeper in all the minutiae of
    self-knowledge, downwards, exhaustive,
yet never, never coming to the bottom. . . .

He uses his intellect not to demolish the mind's attempts at order, as David Hume did, but to insist upon the limits of any activity of "pure" reason—to retain the sacred, unknowable part of the self that Kant called the Transcendental Ego, the Ego above the personal, which is purely mental and sterile. So intent is he upon subjecting the "personal" to the "impersonal" that he speaks impatiently of tragedy, which is predicated upon an assumption of the extraordinary worth of certain individuals, and there is in his mind a curious and probably unique equation between the exalted pretensions of tragedy and the rationalizing, desacralizing process he sensed in operation everywhere around him: in scientific method, in education, in industry, in the financial network of nations, even in new methods of war that resulted not in killing but in commonplace murder. Where to many people tragedy as an art form or an attitude toward life might be dying because belief in God is dying, to Lawrence tragedy is impure, representative of a distorted claim to prominence in the universe, a usurption of the sacredness of the Other, the Infinite. Throughout his life he exhibits a fascination with the drama of the self and its totally Other, not an Anti-Self, to use Yeats's vocabulary, but a truly foreign life force, symbolized by the sun in its healthy hostility to man. It is a remarkable battle, fought for decades, Lawrence the abrasive, vitally alive individual for some reason absorbed in a struggle to deny the primacy of the individual, the "catastrophe" of personal feeling.[2] Why this battle, why this obsession? Why must he state in so many different ways the relatively simple thought here expressed in "Climb Down, O Lordly Mind"?—

> The blood knows in darkness, and forever dark,
> in touch, by intuition, instinctively.
> The blood also knows religiously,
> and of this the mind is incapable.
> The mind is non-religious.
>
> To my dark heart, gods *are*.
> In my dark heart, love is and is not.
> But to my white mind
> gods and love alike are but an idea,
> a kind of fiction.

Calvin Bedient in a brilliant study of Lawrence argues that his flight from personality had been, in part, an effort to "keep himself separate from others so as to be free to face toward the 'beyond' where his mother had become 'intermingled.' "[3] Because of this, his mysticism is "somewhat morbid." But the mystic in Lawrence is fierce to insist upon salvation, even in the face of madness and dissolution, when the merely mental might give way. It is significant that the delirious fever Ursula suffers at the very end of *The Rainbow* brings her to a mystic certainty of her strength, her unbreakable self; if it is deathly—she evidently suffers a miscarriage—it is not *her* death, not Lawrence's idea of death at all. Ursula's real or hallucinatory terror of the horses (that attempt to run her down in a field) is the means by which she is "saved," absolved of Skrebensky's child, which is to her and to Lawrence hardly more than a symbol of the finite, the deathly personal and limited. Nothing in Lawrence is without ambiguity, but it is possible that much that seems to us morbid is really Lawrence's brutal insistence upon the separation of one part of the self from the other, the conscious self from the unconscious, and both from the truly external, the unknown and unknowable Infinite.

In the cycle of confessional poems called *Look! We Have Come Through!* (1917) the most important poem is the very mysterious, yet explicit "New Heaven and Earth," which invites reading in a simplistic manner, as another of the love poems—indeed, Lawrence does more harm than good with his prefatory foreword and "argument" when he suggests that the sequence of poems is about a young man who "marries and comes into himself. . . ." Certainly the spiritual crisis Lawrence suffered at this time had something to do with his private life, with the circumstances of his elopement, but not all marriage is attended by such a radical convulsion of the soul. Lawrence's marriage, like everything else in his life, must be considered epiphenomenal in relationship to the deeper, less personal emotions he attempts to comprehend. This poem bears a curious resemblance to the very beautiful late poem "The Ship of Death," though it is about a mystical reaffirmation of life.

"New Heaven and Earth" consists of eight stanzas, the first stating that the poet has crossed into "another world" where unknown people will misunderstand his weeping. It is not clear until the very end of the poem that the "unknown world" is really the ordinary world, which he re-experiences as totally new. He has passed over into an interior dimension of the sacred; he has evidently experienced the kind of absolute spiritual conversion we find recorded so often in history—the undesired, perhaps dreaded rearrangement of all prior thought. But he must still talk about his experience in ordinary language, which the people around him will not understand "because it is quite, quite foreign to them." This is the problem for Lawrence, as it is for any mystic: he must use ordinary language, but he must use it to express an extraordinary event (unless he chooses, as Thomas Merton declares the poet must, to separate entirely his mystical life from his life as an artist). This might account for much of Lawrence's notorious impatience with and contempt for most of humanity, certainly for organized religion and morality, since there is nothing more frustrating than hearing people speak casually and glibly of experiences they have not had personally and, not having had them, do not understand their real meaning. Anyone—and today nearly everyone—can speak of the "expansion of one's consciousness," the "transcendental experience," the "mystic vision," until these terms become meaningless, mere commodities or linguistic ties. Yet anyone who has had such a vision is seared by it, his personality totally changed, and it would be impossible for him to revert back to an earlier, more "personal" self, even if he wanted to; one thinks of the certainty, the almost egoless egoism of Rousseau, who says that a topic for an essay competition catapulted him into another personality: "From the moment I read these words . . . I beheld another world and became another man."

For Lawrence the shattering experience of a totally new vision had no clear, single cause that he has recorded. It is rather a downward, deathly movement into despair, a psychopathological experience that seems in his case to have been characterized by an exaggerated sense of his own "self," the hard unkillable selfish kernel of being so coolly and affirmatively described in the short story "The Princess."[4] This sinking into despair sometimes takes the form of the ego's terror at dissolution—not of simple physical death, but of immediate psychic dissolution, difficult to describe if one has not felt it, and Lawrence elsewhere (notably in the chapter called "Sunday Evening" in *Women in Love*, but only at the beginning of the chapter—the very Lawrentian Ursula reasons her way out of it) explores this terror also. But the locked-in horror of the unkillable self seems to have been closer to Lawrence's own experience:

> I was so weary of the world,
> I was so sick of it,
> everything was tainted with myself. . . .
> . . . .
> I shall never forget the maniacal horror of it all
>   in the end
> when everything was me, I knew it all already,
>   I anticipated it all in my soul
> because I was the author and the result
> I was the God and the creation at once;
> creator, I looked at my creation;
> created, I looked at myself, the creator:
> it was a maniacal horror in the end.

It is instructive, Lawrence's quite casual use of the expression "in the end"; clearly, whatever happened to him was a kind of death, and he came to the end of one phase of his life. If he had endured in his selfness, like Gerald Crich of *Women in Love*, he would have lived out the rest of his life in his mind, this mind being, horribly, "a

bubble floating in the darkness." But of course Gerald
has not much of a life remaining to him; the world becomes so loathsome that he commits a kind of suicide,
not just in rushing out into the cold but in falling in love
with his exact counterpart, the life-fearing Gudrun. Gerald seems to recognize his psychic predicament but cannot cross over into another world—he is "mechanical"
man, doomed to die in a vacuum. The recognition of the
"maniacal horror" is not enough to force a conversion, as,
sadly, it rarely is:

> Life, friends, is boring. We must not say so.
> After all, the sky flashes, the great sea yearns,
> we ourselves flash and yearn,
> and moreover my mother told me as a boy
> (repeatedly) "Ever to confess you're bored
> means you have no
>
> Inner Resources." I conclude now I have no
> inner resources, because I am heavy bored.

The voice is, of course, John Berryman's, the voice he had
to endure inside his head, stating and restating the dimensions of that head, the recounting of experiences become
memories, only inside the head, the immutable imprisoning skull. And here is another voice, ultimately more
savage than Berryman's:

> . . . Is there no way out of the mind?
> Steps at my back spiral into a well.
> There are no trees or birds in this world,
> There is only a sourness.

This is Sylvia Plath (in "Apprehensions"); and elsewhere,
in her autobiographical novel *The Bell Jar*, she speaks
candidly of the horror of this sourness, the same stale sour

59

air breathed in and out, though she is a young woman with obvious gifts, an obvious "life" to live—yet doomed.

But Lawrence seems to have felt a basic revulsion for suicide, which is expressed in a poem in *Pansies* called "What Matters," where at the conclusion of a catalogue of sleazy thrills he says:

> After that, of course, there's suicide—certain aspects, perhaps,
> Yes, I should say the contemplation of clever suicide *is* rather thrilling,
> so long as the thing is done neatly, and the world is left looking very fooled.

But this is another of Lawrence's voices, itself cerebral and glib. In "New Heaven and Earth" the tone is awed, reverential, the language continually straining its boundaries in an effort to make the strangeness of his experience coherent. But he can only use generalized words, phrases, pseudodramatic actions:

> I buried my beloved; it was good, I buried myself and was gone.
> War came, and every hand raised to murder;
> very good, very good, every hand raised to murder!

He shares in the apocalyptic madness of the war, imagining himself as part of the era's murderousness, and then finds himself trodden out, gone, dead, reduced "absolutely to nothing." But, somehow, he then experiences a resurrection, "risen, not born again, but risen, body the same as before/. . . here, in the other world, still terrestrial/myself, the same as before, yet unaccountably new."

60

The deathly ennui is sloughed off, magically, and Lawrence finds that he is "mad for the unknown." A miracle has taken place, but it cannot be explained, only experienced:

> I, in the sour black tomb, trodden to absolute death
> I put out my hand in the night, one night, and my hand
> touched that which was verily not me. . . .

Perhaps the depth and passion of Lawrence's self-disgust were enough to get him through, or his religious notion that it is "the" death and not "his" death he awaits . . . ? In any case, a transformation occurs:

> Ha, I was a blaze leaping up!
> I was a tiger bursting into sunlight.
> I was greedy, I was mad for the unknown.
> I, new-risen, resurrected, starved from the tomb,
> starved from a life of devouring always myself. . . .

It is important to see that, in the seventh stanza, the poet touches his wife *after* his conversion; the wife herself, with whom he has lain "for over a thousand nights," is clearly outside the experience and outside the poem. He touches her after he is "carried by the current in death/ over to the new world," but, newly transformed, he will not be able to explain what has happened. He will be a "madman in rapture" and the poem ends with a celebration of mystery, the "unknown, strong current of life supreme," the core of "utter mystery."

Why Lawrence is one of the survivors and not one of the many who, confronted with this kind of despair, force their own deaths in one way or another, is a question probably unanswerable, since it brings us to a consideration of the ultimate mystery of human personality. Perhaps it is Lawrence's reverence for all life, even his own sickly and self-consuming life, that allows this experience —whatever it is—to take possession of him; he does not attempt a false possession of it. Lawrence, to be true to himself, to his deepest self, must allow the "drowning," the near annihilation, the sweeping of the soul back to the primitive "sources of mystery."

An earlier poem, "Humiliation," more clearly related to Lawrence's private life, suggests this same attitude— a reluctant but permanent acceptance of the power of something quite apart from him. It is painful, horrible, humiliating, but it is probably what saves Lawrence from utter despair off and on during his troubled life:

> God, that I have no choice!
> That my own fulfilment is up against me
> Timelessly!
> The burden of self-accomplishment!
> The charge of fulfilment!
> And God, that she is *necessary!*
> *Necessary*, and I have no choice!

(It is interesting to compare the idyllic lyricism of such poems as "Wedlock" and "Song of a Man Who is Loved" with the rhetorical frenzy of a poem like "Humiliation" —assuming, with Lawrence, that both attitudes toward his beloved are normal and must be expressed.) One is struck again and again by Lawrence's moral courage, his stubborn faith in the processes of life, the sweeping currents of life that at times force him on to new visions *even against his instinctive will;* he never loses the initial vision that makes incidental suffering bearable:

There are said to be creative pauses,
pauses that are as good as death, empty and dead as
　death itself.
And in these awful pauses the evolutionary change takes
　place.

("Nullus")

Such poems as "The Death of Our Era," "The New
World," "Nemesis," "A Played-Out Game," and many
others remind us of Yeats's dramatic use of the individual
poet enduring his age's spiritual exhaustion but transcending it through a mystical affinity for the age to come,
achieved only through some apocalyptic upheaval of civilization. In "The Hostile Sun," included in the generally
disappointing volume *More Pansies*, Lawrence speaks of
the terror of the sun, its opposition to man's finite consciousness, whose "thoughts are stiff, like old leaves/and
ideas . . . hard, like acorns ready to fall." The sun,
which is the source of all life, is too powerful, too savage,
for ordinary diminished men. Proper dread of it is a way
of honoring the unknowable in the universe, and the
unknowable deep in the self:

. . . we suffer, and though the sun bronzes us
we feel him strangling even more the issues of our soul
for he is hostile to all the old leafy foliage of our thought
and the old upward flowing of our sap, the pressure of
　our upward flow of feeling
is against him.

Understanding this hostility, man must retreat to the
calmness of the moon, to its strange sinister "calm of
scimitars and brilliant reaping hooks"; there, peace is possible. But peace for Lawrence usually signals a kind of

63

death, and the only noble human gesture is a brave affirmation of the sun's inhuman powers:

I am that I am
from the sun,
and people are not my measure.
("Aristocracy of the Sun")

In Lawrence's finest sustained sequence of poems, *Birds, Beasts and Flowers*, he honors the unknowable mysteries of other forms of life, some of them as disturbing in their ways as the sun itself. Lawrence is really unlike any poet one can call to mind in his utter absorption with the Other, which goes far beyond the kind of Negative Capability Keats demonstrated in his poetry. He is not trying to project himself into these creatures, nor is he trying, really, to interpret them. They remain alien, brute, essentially unknowable. They exist in their own absolute realms of being, separate from him, though they may become temporarily symbolic during the course of a poem, as in "Snake," where the snake's observed godliness is transformed into "that part of him that was left behind [convulsing] in undignified haste"—Lawrence's destruction of the god in the snake, hence the "god" in himself, for which he is ashamed.

"Humming-Bird" is an exotic, highly imaginative poem in which the poet envisions the bird in a primeval-dumb world, in an "awful stillness" before "anything had a soul,/While life was a heave of Matter. . . ." The humming-bird, apparently so fragile, is seen as flashing ahead of creation, piercing "the slow vegetable veins with his long beak." Man, seeing him today, is really observing him through the wrong end of the long telescope of time —in his original state he was enormous, a huge jabbing monster. This bizarre vision might have been experienced by any symbolist or expressionist poet, but only Lawrence could have rejoiced at the nightmare image he has created. And only Lawrence, in contemplating the energies of "The He-Goat," could have shrewdly observed the diminished egoism of that "black procreant male of the selfish will" enslaved to the female, and therefore to the herd. The mindless submission to one's own selfish will, though it appears to be an acquiescence to natural instinct, becomes only a mechanical frenzy, a domestication, when the true object of desire—the "enemy," the "Other"—has been removed. Thus the male goat has no natural enemy, being king of his herd of indifferent females; all the other males have been removed from his world, and he is left in this "sullen-stagnating atmosphere of goats":

> . . . Like a big ship pushing her bowsprit over the
> little ships
> Then swerving and steering afresh
> And never, never arriving at journey's end, at the
> rear of the female ships.

In a natural setting, in a world of combat, the male goat would break through this rancid hypnotic lust "with a crash of horns against the horns/Of the opposite enemy goat,/Thus hammering the mettle of goats into proof, and smiting out/The godhead of goats from the shock." A poem that is a hymn to higher consciousness!—in spite of its unusual subject matter, its relentless examination of the fenced-in life, the life of boundaries, domesticated procedures in which the herd (which happens here to be female) dominates the individual, hypnotizing him with his own lust, imprisoning him inside the routine, ceaseless ritual of "procreation." There is probably more shrewd psychological analysis in this little-known poem than in any number of books, and it would be fascinating to examine Lawrence's assumptions here—and in the companion piece, "The She-Goat"—along with the famous hypothesis Freud advanced in *Civilization and Its Discontents*. For here, and probably only here, in a domesticated animal herd, do we find the absolutely uninhibited id, never challenged even by another id of comparable strength but enjoying dominion over any number of sexual subjects; it is as if the rest of the world had been obliterated, all other rivals, all paternal figures, and the superego banished, forgotten. Civilization, Freud believed, is shaped out of the frustration of aggressive impulses: as men experience conflict between their own desires and the desires of others, the fruits of their difficult denials (their sublimation of primal energies) coalesce into what we call "civilization." Thus, civilization is abstract, a collective enemy that, in fact, has no identity. Whatever the beauty and surprising variety of culture, it is the product solely of the sublimation (or frustration) of basic instincts.

Lawrence, however, understands that the release from all restraints, all conflict with the Other, throws the individual back upon himself, his own instincts, and these become cruder and cruder, more and more routine, rancid, mesmerizing, in a way quite deathly . . . ironically enough, since the male goat is evidently fertilizing the entire herd. But he is being used, he is reduced ultimately to "a needle of long red flint he stabs in the dark" while the she-goat "with her goaty mouth stands smiling the while as he strikes, since sure/He will never *quite* strike home. . . ." Exactly: the male will never "quite" mate with the female, under these circumstances, because he is undefined, only a dark instinct, "devilish," "malicious," stupid. During the later years of his life Freud was struggling with large, philosophical issues, trying to determine the relationship of the individual to "culture" and what the future must be if each person, retaining his basic opposition to all other persons, was finally unable to overcome his aggression. Hence, the "discontents." But the larger discontent of civilization was, in Freud's opinion, its apparently inevitable desire for destruction, even for self-destruction (aggression smothered and turned inward); given such a basic proposition, the future must be exactly like the past—endless wars, endless bloodshed, as long as human nature is "human nature." But Lawrence seems to have intuitively known that it is not the presence of a restraining or alien "enemy" that destroys man; it is the removal of this enemy. When the Other is obliterated, the individual is also obliterated. It is ironic that Lawrence was known for most of his life as an "immoral" person, a writer of "pornography," when he seems to have understood the absolute need for sublimation of basic instincts. His admiration is for the ugly she-goat in the other poem, a marvelously individualized creature, really a personality in her own right. He is infuriated by her, he detests her as she pretends not to recognize him, then jumps "staccato" to the ground:

> She trots on blithe toes,
> And if you look at her, she looks back with a cold,
>   sardonic stare.
> Sardonic, sardonyx, rock of cold fire.
> *See me?* She says, *That's me!*
>
> That's her.

Then she leaps the rocks like a quick rock,
Her backbone sharp as a rock,
Sheer will.

One is impressed continually by Lawrence's uncanny instinct for what will bring out the best in him—or perhaps the worst: his gravitation toward conflict, drama, the stimulus that will "nudge" him out of his blankness. In his own life he had so many enemies—both personal and generalized—that he was saved from the dull contented domesticity of the he-goat; he admires the she-goat whom he really detests, or detests half-seriously, because this is a creature whose will is in opposition to his, a defiant cranky thing, rather like the Lawrence of the biographies. It may even be that Lawrence's ill health inspired in him a kind of stubbornness, a willful defiance of any routine accommodation of his problem. Not only would his diminution into a typical invalid, his restraining of the more iconoclastic of his prophecies, satisfy his enemies, but it would be too easy. He worships the sun, but not in any conventional neoprimitive manner—he worships it because it *is* hostile, inhuman, and unaccommodating. He was one of those unusual persons who exhibit a deep, unshakable faith in the inexplicable processes of life—or fate, or time, or accident—against which the individual must assert himself in a continual struggle. Yeats vacillates between a desire for inert perfection (the golden bird, Byzantium itself, the "tower" of all the poems, the heavenly stupor to which Plotinus swims) and an eager, excited conviction that such perfection would be really hellish (in the play *Where There is Nothing*, heaven is defined as a place where music is the "continual clashing of swords," and in the second of the Plotinus poems, "News for the Delphic Oracle," the

68

languid paradise of the dead is jarred by "intolerable music" issuing from Pan's cavern).

To Lawrence, man's ideal state in nature is alienation —not total alienation but a condition of disharmony that allows for the assertion of the personal self. He is not a Romantic, therefore, because he has no interest in regressing to a theoretical oneness with nature; he does not want to revive the primitive, as he makes abundantly clear in such stories as "The Woman Who Rode Away" —she rides away, after all, to her death. When an intelligent, civilized person tries to behave as if he "knew" nothing, he becomes grotesque, stunted, like the unfortunate Hermione of *Women in Love,* who is probably the most abused character in all of Lawrence, savagely criticized by her lover, Birkin, for wanting sensuality in "that loathsome little skull of yours, that ought to be cracked like a nut." A similar woman in the short story "None of That" is punished even more savagely for her pretensions. It is wrong, I think, for critics to assume that Lawrence is venting his sadistic hatred of such women here; some of his energies are sadistic, of course, but essentially Lawrence was exorcising unclean, muddled, pseudoprimitive yearnings in himself, for he does reserve his most passionate scorn for people who express ideas close to his own. Such critics as Blackmur and Graham Hough, approaching Lawrence as an academic subject, fail to see how the creative artist shares to varying degrees the personalities of all his characters, even those whom he appears to detest—perhaps, at times, it is these characters he is really closest to. What Lawrence declared in an early essay, "The Crown," holds true for all of his work: ". . . we are two opposites [lion and unicorn] which exist by virtue of our inter-opposition. Remove the opposition and there

is a collapse, a sudden crumbling into universal darkness."[5]

This faith in the necessary tension of opposites helps to
explain the rather abrasive "She Said as Well to Me,"
which begins as a love poem—and quite nicely, the reader
thinks—and then swerves sharply into something else
when the lover turns upon his admiring beloved and forbids her to caress and appreciate him: "it is an infamy."
Just as the woman would hesitate to touch a weasel or an
adder or a bull, she should hesitate to touch her lover so
complacently, she should not assume that she *knows* him
so intimately. (The title gains a deeper meaning, after
the angry lesson of the poem has been absorbed.) Man
should not be easy in his loving, he should not be easy
with himself, with nature; his inner sun is as hostile as
the external sun, as dangerous and majestic.

Lawrence believed in the totally spontaneous synthesis
of "spiritual" and "sensual" love, indeed, but this love is
not based on personalities, on anything personal, on what
anyone happens to look like, or to believe, or to *be*.
He is totally opposed to the waste of one's sacred energies with a crowd of people—he is a monogamist by nature (though he eloped with another man's wife)—and
extremely critical of anyone who failed to live up to his
ideal of permanent marriage. His "ideal" is at first highly
comprehensible, at least to a century somewhat liberated
from notions of shame or uneasiness about the physical
side of life:

> At last I can throw away world without end, and
>   meet you
> Unsheathed and naked and narrow and white;
> At last you can throw immortality off, and I see you
> Glistening with all the moment and all your beauty.

But the personal, private self, the self with a name, is to Lawrence a confining, a limitation ultimately deathly. This is what makes him so radical and so abrasive: his permanent love is based not upon the daily, glistening body; it begins with this body, but goes through it and transcends it, so that as the permanently opposed entities of male and female join, they create an inhuman, more-than-human equilibrium, whether they want to or not. . . . Therefore one marries only the person with whom he has experienced this "inhuman" love, which is not at all romantic love or perhaps even love at all. One marries, once. Lawrence's complete theology of love can be found in Birkin's many passionate speeches in *Women in Love*, which must be read, probably, before certain poems can be understood. The book of poems called *Look! We Have Come Through!* is a brutally honest recording of Lawrence's private experience, after he and Frieda have gone to Europe, leaving her husband and children behind; it is not a justification of this action—Lawrence never once indicates any interest in the husband or children, certainly no guilt—but it is a remarkable book, perhaps the first of the frank, embarrassingly intimate confessional books of poetry commonplace today. But Lawrence achieves his higher, transcendental experience through the intimate; he evolves out of the love/hate between himself and Frieda into an essentially inhuman sphere:

> We move without knowing, we sleep, and
>   we travel on. . . .
> And this is beauty to me, to be lifted and gone
> In a motion human inhuman, two and one
> Encompassed, and many reduced to none. . . .
>   ("One Woman to All Women")

71

The unconscious is valued as the unknown oceanic source of all energies, good and bad, and Freud's heroic —or Faustian—desire to supplant the id with the ego would, of course, be an "infamy" to someone like Lawrence. One must remember that Lawrence projected his incredibly strong sense of self onto everyone—he could not have comprehended the neurotic fear that one is not perhaps an "aristocrat of the sun," nor could he have truly sympathized with the agonizing terrors of the mentally unstable, that they have sinned and must punish themselves by assuming irrational burdens of guilt, in order to forestall actual punishment. The clinical psychiatrist or psychotherapist, faced with the terrible immediacy of disturbed human beings, cannot afford to acclaim —as the visionary all too often does—the spontaneous overflowing of the "unconscious." Because Lawrence had no idea of Freud's day-to-day contact with suffering humanity, and because the mystic is all too often reconciled with a "world order" that is in fact only his own projection of self, one must see that Lawrence was defending the sacred nature of those emotions he valued, and not all emotions. However, the Aristotelian-Freudian-"classicist" model of psychological health—that emotions be purged, refined, made totally conscious and therefore discharged of their power—is certainly a dubious one, and one may sympathize with Lawrence's detestation of the goal of psychoanalysis (as it is the goal of repressive systems of government): "Where Id is, there shall Ego be." Such a model assumes the malevolent nature of the "id"; from this it is a simple step to the assumption that this "id" is a natural enemy of "civilization." (And a simple step further, the projection of fears of "chaos" by the masculine consciousness onto all women—for wherever one encounters the Aristotelian-Freudian ideal of home-ostasis, in opposition to the Oriental or Jungian ideal of integration of opposites, one is likely to encounter a secret detestation of the feminine.)

In his deep, stark, stoical pessimism Freud is, ironically, a kind of romantic, and his puritanical overemphasis upon infantile sexuality is characteristic of the personality behind most "romances"—seen as illicit and adulterous, otherwise not exciting. To Lawrence this kind of dramatic exaggeration of one phase of erotic love—the sexually active phase—was truly obscene, as was the peculiar emphasis upon "knowing," "defining," categorizing human beings along a scale that tends to range from very sick to mildly sick, with the normal not an average so much as an unrealizable ideal. *Why* must so much of human behavior be classified as "neurotic" when in fact it is simply natural, given certain personalities and certain environments? The impulse to "make well" may be the most sinister of Western civilization's goals, and this perhaps accounts for Lawrence's angry outbursts against psychiatry.

What is known and knowable about oneself, then, is of little value. This accounts for Ursula's rejection and rather cruel denunciation of her lover, so typically Victorian and career oriented—poor Skrebensky, who would have been quite a daring figure in any other English novel, to have wandered into a novel by D. H. Lawrence! Ursula, like Lawrence himself, undergoes near death and near annihilation as a preparation for her tempestuous love for Birkin of *Women in Love*, Lawrence's explicit, heartlessly candid portrayal of himself in a dense, peopled world that does not always appreciate him. When Lawrence believes that he really *knows* something, him-

73

self, the results are usually catastrophic, sordid beyond belief. When the rich, vulnerable humanity of Birkin or Lawrence's bemused persona of *Birds, Beasts and Flowers* gives way to the absolute dictator Ramon of *The Plumed Serpent*, it seems even to the most sympathetic reader that everything is lost, that Lawrence the artist has been murdered by Lawrence the dogmatist, whose cruelty or self-righteousness might be traced back, far back, into Lawrence's early career as a teacher—a half-serious observation, but one that makes sense if Ursula's experience as a teacher in *The Rainbow* is studied. When Lawrence worships the Other, his writing is at its finest; when he attempts to usurp the position of the Other, forcing his dream of a metaphysical utopia upon a God-enchanted, exotic land (it would have to be Mexico—not even the vast rawness of the American Southwest could have accommodated Lawrence's mad fantasy), it is mechanical and forced, embarrassingly bad. In the Quetzalcoatl state, which is dedicated to a resurrection of the body on earth, to a reawakening of man's fierce rapport with the universe, the voice of the sane Lawrence—"I think every man is a sacred and holy individual, *never* to be violated" —would be outshouted by the dictatorial Ramon, who desires nothing less than to be "lord of the day and night," controlling even his subjects' dreams. So Ramon and Lawrence must become neoprimitive, resurrecting an ancient Aztec myth and inventing new rituals—the kind of behavior Lawrence usually scorned for its willful and Faustian desire to *control*. (After the egoistic fantasy of *The Plumed Serpent*, however, Lawrence turns to the very human and in a way very subdued world of *Lady Chatterley's Lover*, where a few of the totalitarian ideas of Ramon turn up in the natural aristocrat, Mellors, but are sanely diminished; for Mellors, like Lawrence, recognizes the presence of enemies that will not be conquered, only challenged, by the "bright, quick flame" of human tenderness.)

Even at its worst, however, Lawrence's imagination is fertile. His invective against machinery never quite becomes entirely mechanical itself, for in a perverse way he sometimes seems to share in the crazy energies of the machines, especially as they rush into self-destruction ("traffic will tangle up in a long-drawn-out crash of collision"—"The Triumph of the Machine"); and his retorts to Whitman and Jesus, among others, show how seriously he takes these apparently opposing points of view. It is clear that the simple act of writing was for Lawrence a triumph, a continuous triumph, an assertion of himself in which he could synthesize an extraordinary variety of selves—the "personal," the "transcendent-personal," the "sexual," the "social," the "artistic"—sometimes so excitedly calling attention to his foreground materials that we tend to forget that this *is* a form of art, perhaps the most sophisticated form of all. In both his fiction and his poetry Lawrence shows an awareness of the dichotomy of the illusions available to the imagination—the formal, structured work that exhibits content, and the exuberant, almost autonomous content that moves too fast to be structured.

Most of the poems, of course, are just as Lawrence judged them in "Chaos in Poetry": suffused fragments, visions "passing into touch and sound, then again touch and the bursting of a bubble of an image." But the finest poems achieve triumphs of both content and form, and bear comparison with the greatest poems in our language. "The Ship of Death" is a "deepening black darkening"

75

work of art that combines an intense, painful subjectivity and a mastery of objective form, the absolute conclusion of Lawrence's autobiographical work—one has only to imagine the *Collected Poems* without it to realize how terrible a loss this would be. (More so than the loss of "Under Ben Bulben," perhaps.) Here, at the end of his life, the very consciously dying poet composes a poem to get him through his death, just as, years before, he composed "New Heaven and Earth" in an attempt to express his mystical experience. Like the beautiful "Bavarian Gentians," "The Ship of Death" is a construction by way of the artistic imagination of the attitude one must take toward death—that is, toward *dying,* the active, existential process of dying. And here Lawrence is equal to the challenge, as he has been equal to the challenge of expressing the mysteries of life throughout his career. "The Ship of Death" is about a symbolic ship, but a small one; the images of death are terrible, final, but they are familiar and small as well:

> Now it is autumn and the falling fruit
> and the long journey towards oblivion.
>
> The apples falling like great drops of dew
> to bruise themselves an exit from themselves.
>
> And it is time to go, to bid farewell
> to one's own self, and find an exit
> from the fallen self.

The "fallen self" builds its ship, its poem, to take it upon this journey into the unknown, into oblivion; it rejects once again the self-willed act of suicide: "for how could murder, even self-murder/ever a quietus make?" The symbol of the small ship is exactly right, it is exactly true to Lawrence's personality, for it is stocked with small, unpretentious items, a very human, humble vehicle:

> Now launch the small ship, now as the body dies
> and life departs, launch out, the fragile soul
> in the fragile ship of courage, the ark of faith
> with its store of food and little cooking pans
> and change of clothes,
> upon the flood's black waste. . . .

(Just as Yeats declares as an *accomplished fact* his own death, and commands that his tombstone be made not of marble but of limestone quarried nearby.) But Lawrence's death journey ends at dawn, a "cruel dawn," out of which glows a mystical flush of rose, and there is some kind of renewal, "the whole thing starts again" as the frail soul abandons itself utterly to the Infinite: Lawrence's way of affirming again, and at a time in his life when he might be tempted to deny it, the absolute mystery of the Other, which cannot be guessed and cannot be absorbed into the human soul. It is a kind of sensuous stoicism, an intelligent paganism—if the "pagan" were to be joined with the artistic soul in having the consciousness required for the exertion of this will, this building of the individual's way into oblivion.

"The Ship of Death" goes beyond criticism, as it goes beyond the kind of poetry Lawrence usually wrote. A more characteristic poem—though not a lesser one—is "Fish," which exhibits an almost Mephistophelian sleight of hand, paying homage to the ineffable at the same time that the poet captures it. Here, content and form are perfectly joined. It is a remarkable kind of art, risky, chancy, characteristic of the best in *Birds, Beasts and Flowers,* an attempt at the kind of mimetic exercise

77

Birkin does in copying the Chinese drawing of geese in an early chapter of *Women in Love*. Lawrence stares down at the fish:

> Aqueous, subaqueous,
> Submerged
> And wave-thrilled.
> As the waters roll
> Roll you.
> The waters wash,
> You wash in oneness
> And never emerge.

Lawrence is not assessing his own relationship to the fish, or converting them into symbols of human emotions. He is trying, trying very hard, to get into the suchness of fish:

> No fingers, no hands and feet, no lips;
> No tender muzzles,
> No wistful bellies,
> No loins of desire,
> None.

Only the fish in their "naked element": "Sway-wave./ Curvetting bits of tin in the evening light." The poem becomes an incantation, an extraordinary feat of magic as the poet and his reader are transformed partly into fish:[6] "Water-eager eyes,/Mouth-gate open/And strong spine urging, driving;/And desirous belly gulping." The poem goes on in this manner—it is one of his longer poems— with the roll of the waves themselves, the merging of self into anonymity, into shoals of fish. These fish, "born before God was love,"

> . . . drive in shoals.
> But soundless, and out of contact.

78

> They exchange no word, no spasm, not even anger.
> Not one touch.
> Many suspended together, forever apart,
> Each one alone with the waters, upon one wave with the
> rest.
>
> A magnetism in the water between them only.

Lawrence sits in his boat on the Zeller lake and, enraptured, stares down at the fish, saying finally to himself *who are these? . . .* for his heart cannot own them. The reader has become half-transformed by the poem, in a conventional response to the language, and now he is shocked at the poet's sudden reversal, his dramatic statement:

> I had made a mistake, I didn't know him.
> . . . .
> I didn't know his God.
> I didn't know his God.

And now the poet is forced to recognize the terror at the "pale of his being," which is only human, which stares down into the world of fish and must realize the limitations of the human soul, the fact that there are "Other Gods/Beyond my range. . . ." He catches a fish, unhooks it, feels the writhing life-leap in his hand, and

> . . . my heart accused itself
> Thinking: *I am not the measure of creation.*
> *This is beyond me, this fish.*
> *His God stands outside my God.*

Calm and matter-of-fact as this statement is, it is really revolutionary; it is a total rejection of that dogma of the West that declares *Man is the measure of all things.* How contemptible Lawrence found such pronouncements, and how shrewdly he recognized the melancholy nihilism behind them!—for it was his life's pilgrimage to break through the confines of the static, self-consuming self in order to experience the unfathomable power that transcended his own knowledge of himself. Not "knowing" himself fully, he cannot "know" and therefore violate anyone or anything in nature.

One of our great prophetic books is *Women in Love*, which attempts to dramatize Lawrence's faith. However ironically its vision is contested by its plot, it is a work meant to impress upon us the need for men to join with other men in a mysterious union, an impersonal love, as they are conventionally joined with women in order to transcend their limited selves. Without this union and its transformation of the individual, the human race is doomed: but, since Lawrence does not believe in tragedy, there is nothing tragic about this predicament. Like most visionary artists, he celebrates the life force wherever it appears, even if it withdraws itself from the species to which he belongs. Here, in a passage at the conclusion of *Women in Love*, is the clearest statement of Lawrence's love for what may seem hostile, other, unhuman, but sacred—and it is a statement central to the visionary experience itself:

If humanity ran into a *cul de sac*, and expended itself, the timeless creative mystery would bring forth some other being, finer, more wonderful, some new more lovely race, to carry on the embodiment of creation. . . . The mystery of creation was fathomless, infallible, inexhaustible, forever. Races came and went, species passed away, but ever new species arose, more lovely, or equally lovely, always surpassing wonder. The fountain-head was incorruptible and unsearchable. It had no limits. It could bring forth miracles, create utter new races and new species, in its own hour, new forms of consciousness, new forms of body, new units of being. . . . To have one's pulse beating direct from the mystery, this was perfection, unutterable satisfaction. Human or inhuman mattered nothing. The perfect pulse throbbed with an indescribable being, miraculous unborn species.

3

ANARCHY
AND ORDER IN
BECKETT'S
TRILOGY

Granted that I am a babbler, a harm-
less vexatious babbler, like all of us.
But what is to be done if the direct
and sole vocation of every intelligent
man is babble, that is, the intentional
pouring of water through a sieve?

Dostoyevsky,
Notes from the Underground

Beckett's purgatorial world is accessible from any direction, since its center of gravity is so stable. Not so famous as his plays, but remarkable for their unity of vision and their examination of the aesthetic impulse from the inside, the novels *Molloy, Malone Dies,* and *The Unnamable* are among Beckett's most characteristic works. Here the perpetual babbling "I" speaks directly, frankly, and one can—as if accidentally—experience the process of a plot, or the unfolding of sequences of time that in a traditional novel would constitute a plot.

We are not in hell, because hell suggests a kind of permanence, a coming to rest. This is purgatory, and its basic metaphor is the isolated consciousness of an individual who is a writer of some kind, a creative thinker, withdrawn totally from the outside world. The usual preoccupations of the novel are forsaken here—character, continuity, setting, the evocation of interest, even the assumption that there may be an audience to interest. Instead, we have only the hideously self-conscious "I," in a Sartrean antechamber of the soul where one's eyelids are missing and man's fate is perpetual consciousness, the "pouring of water through a sieve" that Dostoyevsky's underground man saw, bitterly and spitefully, as the only activity for an intelligent man at this secularized, vulgarized point in history. Movement is not upward or outward but, as always in Beckett, inward to a primary zero: the natural, preferred condition of the human consciousness. The "I" here does not submerge itself in the destructive element of life—this would constitute a conventional "plot"—nor does it shape and reshape itself, achieving an "ego," an integrated personality—this would constitute a conventional "development" of character. The "I" instead forsakes everything except language and is obsessed with a frank, brutal, often dull, often astonishing consciousness of its own essence: if Beckett contains any gesture toward plot, this is it. Behind it the primary concern seems to be with the achieving and defining of a metaphysics, since without this framework the "I" can come to no ethical—and therefore human—level of existence. To understand the peculiar climate of Beckett's world, to the extent to which it is capable of being understood, it is necessary to see first how Beckett denies the accustomed means of understanding reality and, secondly, how he resolves the inevitable conflict within the central consciousness (this "central consciousness" is not really a fictional character, but only a stream of words) through the final balance and equilibrium of the writing itself. Beckett is concerned with the creation of a pure art: the transformation of existential properties and methods into an art of essences, bereft of the accidental and arbitrary. Traditional forms of comedy and tragedy are unrecognizable in Beckett, though the attributes of comedy—droll, absurd observations, preposterous happenings—and the attributes of tragedy—an endless dying, without religious consolation or redemption—occur on every page.

The doubt expressed by Beckett's talking character may not lead, as it led Descartes, to the expected affirmation of existence; identity remains forever the *x* in the equation. It is that which cannot be experienced. Beckett questions Descartes' initial proof of the primacy of consciousness, the certain existence of the "I," by having his character refuse to acknowledge the "voice" as his own, by believing instead—yet with that peculiar ironical sense of intentionally disavowing the inevitable, of insisting upon illogical contradictions that recur endlessly throughout the novels—that the voice and the words are from without, delivered with an intent to deceive, to convince him falsely of his own existence. He says in *The Unnamable:* ". . . they don't know where I am, or what I'm like, I'm like dust, they want to make a man out of dust. Listen to them, losing heart! That's to lull me, till I imagine I hear myself saying, myself at last, to myself at last, that it can't be they speaking thus, it can only be I, speaking thus. . . ." The realization of an identity, a single mode of being, is impossible because identity for Beckett has yet to be proved as necessarily continuous. The condition of Beckett's world reminds us, rather surprisingly, of the strange world suggested by David Hume in his

Treatise on Human Nature (about 1739), and his *Inquiry Concerning Human Understanding* (1740): here the observed concrete flux of the world, so confused and confusing in Molloy's story, has no absolutes to anchor it to a meaning that may be understood. Hume says in the anonymous "critical" essay, "An abstract of a Treatise of Human Nature," "No matter of fact can be proved but from its cause or effect. Nothing can be known to be the cause of another but by experience. We can give no reason for extending to the future our experience in the past, but are entirely determined by custom when we conceive an effect to follow from its usual cause. . . ." And, later:

. . . in no single instance the ultimate connection of any object is discoverable either by our senses or reason, and that we can never penetrate so far into the essence and the construction of bodies as to perceive the principle on which their mutual influence is founded. . . . It will be easy to conceive of what vast consequences [the above] must be in the science of human nature if we consider that . . . these are the only links that bind the parts of the universe together or connect us with any person or object exterior to ourselves. . . .

As we examine Beckett's world further, the striking parallel to Hume will become more evident.

The dimensions of space are the illusory; one travels finally only within the ambits of his own "region"; and the imposed artifice of time is meaningless even in the nonnoumenal sense of the word, that is, even as far as man is concerned, because it is not at all certain here that what is necessary and immutable in human experience is the fact of time and space at all (again an appeal back past Kant to Hume)—the outer world is perhaps no more than a dreary addition of zeros, and the supposed progress of time has nothing to sustain it, nothing against which, if measured, it can come to have any meaning. The character in *The Unnamable*, revealed as the inner core about which the other characters revolve, says, ". . . it's every second that is the worst, it's a chronicle, the seconds pass, one after another, jerkily, no flow, they don't pass . . . when you have nothing left to say you talk of time, seconds of time, there are some people add them together to make a life. . . ."

Hume's phenomenalistic conception of reality, where causal relationships are tricks of human tautology and that alone, destroys the metaphysical desire of any ordering of reality, any order in which "reality" might exist apart from the pattern our eyes impose upon us. Since in matter of fact no necessary connection can be perceived within the movement of a cause-and-effect relationship, we can give to this only the name of constant conjunction; we can be certain only of uncertainty, a flux that does not even demand a perceiver to predicate its own existence.

The anarchy of Hume's only halfway serious skepticism can be seen in our time in the rigidly limited rationalism of the logical positivists (who see certainty only in the tautological, probability only in the empirical) and in the temper of modern existentialists—if any general attitude may be hit upon—with their uncertainty about the reality and the significance of anything beyond the existing individual. Beckett's sophisticated variation on the pervading theme of the existential dilemma is to refine man out of his existence in a recognizable world and to inject in this isolated soul the fiction writer's device of memory, a haunted recollection, of a world that may or may not exist. This imposes itself upon the "I" in the dubious forms of "voices" that may be many things—only his own voice, initially manifested in other persons, or messengers who symbolize a remote Kafkan order to which the character subjects himself, messengers who have no messages, and finally the single voice that does not leave him. Since he exists forever as an "I" and presumes to desire only the silencing of this "I"—". . . . All is pretext . . . my doubts which do not interest me, my situation, my possessions, pretext for not coming to the point, the abandoning, the raising of the arms and the going down. . . ." (*Malone Dies*) and in *The Unnamable* a search for the "means to put an end to things, an end to speech"—it is precisely this first state of being that he cannot elude, and that he cannot understand. This is the human condition of finitude that divorces man not only from the ghostly noumenal world of Kant but from the world within, his own soul, which is "buried in the world . . . the old world cloisters [it], victorious." The final character, nameless, is the essence of all the preceding characters, of whom he is aware as though he himself had created them. He contemplates out of his emptied world problems that by their very nature will deny all solutions, or posit antitheses for each solution offered, the nature of life and death, his own identity, and Malone's selfless concern, the "effort to understand, to being to understand, how [men] are possible." The character's monologue—suggestive, of course, of the long monologue of Dostoyevsky's underground creatures—is of that peculiar self-lacerating nature which seesaws from one antipodal thought to another, which negates exactly that which has been said a moment before, and which means to negate itself into a final silence—what Beckett says to be the true prayer, that which asks for nothing.

One moves toward this silence by moving away from the world. The desire is to shake off the incidental, to flee the patterned response to life— ". . . when the icy words hail down upon me, the icy meanings, and the world dies too, foully named. . . . Saying is inventing. Wrong, very rightly wrong. You invent nothing, you think you are inventing, you think you are escaping. . . ." (*Molloy*)— which has its tinge, for all of Beckett's cynicism and, at times, scatological irrelevancies, of an eerie romanticism.

Beckett deals persistently and with a literalism that is unexpected on matters which, surprisingly, do not seem pretentious. What is of primary importance in life? Perhaps it is the experience, taken as a human experience short of its inessential qualities, where "the subject doesn't matter, there is none." What is important, too, may be the condition of relationships, equations in which human identities function as absolute variables; this is enforced by the recurring and very amusing motif of mathematics through the novels, the combinations and permutations of Molloy and his sucking stones, Molloy and his revolving moon, and Moran's remark, "the falsity of the term does not necessarily imply that of the relation." Yet there is always the antithetical enforcement of the wills of these avowedly will-less persons, not so much the Molloy and the Moran of the first novel, steeped in the world as they are even at the conclusion of their journeys, as the dying Malone and the final nameless character. The mathematical allusions are nearly always very funny —if anyone would like an example of Beckett's peculiar humor he need only read the "sucking stones" episode in the first half of *Molloy*. They imply, perhaps, a vision of

91

the immense possibilities of experiences open to man, at least on a quantitative level, which possibilities are destroyed by the committing fact of history, the "nightmare" of history; or perhaps a commentary on the final immutable limit of these possibilities as opposed to the human-supposed infinity of "combinations and permutations" that we study in high school mathematics. But it is most likely that the allusions are parodies of human behavior and pretense as though, in the accidental world, a choice of vanities really mattered.

As the novels progress, the motif of the creative consciousness is emphasized. Malone's stories, or storytelling, are devised to aid him in his understanding of the perplexing creature, man; he deals with his characters as extensions of himself, the recognized inevitable condition of creation—thus in fantasy Lemuel's hatchet reverts back to Malone's pencil—and Malone himself is but another character like his kin Molloy, another "writer," one in a series of disclosed identities that come to light like the parts in the Kierkegaardian Chinese puzzle box. Malone is, then, a character in the dreaming mind of the final narrator who sees his fictional creations as ultimately inadequate, as disguises of himself out of which he must define his own identity. The Unnamable suggests as its central meaning, beyond the persistent metaphysical questioning, the perhaps more interesting of the relationships of the writer to his characters. What is mysterious about the world without is that it is indiscernible from the mysterious world within, and "voices" from a distance may be of one's own creation, an attempt to isolate the condition of finiteness and to understand it in relationship to something beyond it, without which it cannot have even a relative meaning. Thus the Murphys, Molloys, Morans, and Malones are manipulated for a time as surrogate sufferers of one's pain; this pain is projected outward so that it may be witnessed and understood. In the end, however, the dreamer cannot remain content with this. What must concern him is himself alone, and there remains only the blackness of self, "short of all its accidents"; here there is metaphysical chaos, no dimensions, no time, no relatives, no absolutes beyond the fluctuating absolute of the "I" that continues on but that finds no rest because there is no final answer. There are never less than two answers; one must always continue on.

Yet for all of this, Beckett's characters do not despair, and though their world seems illogical and cruel, there is none of the romantic, grim acceptance of "what is" one finds in facets of existentialism, but rather a paradoxical delight in the "black joy" this peculiar world affords. Beckett's situations are so absurd as to beggar parody, and his people realize this and exult in the fact. Thus Molloy, an old, aimless tramp, ends his soliloquy in a ditch wondering how he can traverse a vast moor with the great handicap of his crutches and his shortening legs. He understands somehow that help is coming, but this is not important—"Molloy could stay, where he happened to be." So with the other characters. In the world of the trilogy one always exists positively, in spite of or because of his recognition of the ultimate vanity and endless contradictions of human speculation, and of the fact that nothing can be rejected but that it must be reclaimed, nothing can be claimed but that it must be rejected.

Beckett ends, then, in the anarchy of the soul in juxtaposition to nothing beyond itself. This very eloquent soul is also haunted by voices he can neither believe in nor not believe in; there is no ethics because an ethics without a higher metaphysics is impossible, and there is no metaphysics because one can believe in nothing absolute against which the particular might be measured. Malone says, "I have never seen any signs of [order], inside me or outside me." What remains, in addition to the will to "go on," is the desire to create—in the most immediate case, to create fiction. What gives Beckett's work the quality of art and not the atmosphere of a series of dreary philosophical questions is the poetic presentation of these not very poetic ideas, the series of theses and antitheses that lead to a final balance, a final equilibrium. At the core of Beckett's art is a concern for form—probably beyond the answerless questions that he plies about himself; "for why be discouraged," says Malone, "one of the thieves was saved." The allusion is to St. Augustine's "Do not despair, one of the thieves was saved; do not presume, one of the thieves was damned," a statement that Beckett professes to admire not for its meaning but rather for its form—the beauty that lies in the arrangement of the words themselves—a concern not of the philosopher but of the poet.

Opposed to the created order of art is the metaphor and no doubt the catalyst for the creation of this art, as it is the catalyst for any art: the vision of a physical world "collapsing endlessly." Opposed to the writer's control and omnipotence in his world of literary creation is the outer world where there is, as Molloy says, ". . . [no] possible end to these wastes where true light never was, nor any upright thing, nor any true foundation, but only these leaning things, forever lapsing and crumbling away, beneath a sky without memory of morning or hope of night."

In Beckett, the tragedy of the isolated ego, the creator of

94

all language, is dramatized in a way that cannot be faulted. If one's very existence is the phenomenal stream-of-language, if he cannot pierce through the hypnotic trance of his own self-worship or the worship of his invented language, he is doomed to exist within the confines of his own skull, to babble endlessly about the very process of babbling, to be blown about in purgatory, weightless, soulless, not significant enough to be "evil." It is a fate so terrifying that Beckett, in giving substance to it, should be recognized as a kind of martyr. He shows us the inside of the experience that denies all experience beyond that which can be put into language—the horror of the locked-in self that Lawrence recognized but survived, and came to see as the primary sickness of our civilization.

Our sympathy for Caliban's predicament should not blind us—as it did not blind Shakespeare—to the contradiction embodied in his Beckett-like statement: "You taught me language, and my profit on't is I know how to curse."

4

THE NIGHTMARE
OF NATURALISM:
Harriette Arnow's
"The Dollmaker"

Sunk helplessly in flesh, as in the turbulent uncontrollable mystery of the "economy," the human being with spiritual yearnings becomes tragic when these yearnings are defeated or mocked or, as in *The Dollmaker*, by Harriette Arnow, brutally transformed into a part of the social machine. The visionary quest is thwarted when the individual is violently uprooted from the culture in which he knows enough of himself to be able to "forget" himself —especially when the individual, like Gertie Nevels of *The Dollmaker*, has chosen to be responsible for other people. This predicament is far more significant, more nightmarish, than the self-created predicament of the

99

voice that runs through much of contemporary literature—back through Beckett's nameless self-suffering "I"
to the narrator of *Notes From the Underground*—because
it is one that challenges our right to aspire for a higher
consciousness, indeed, even to create art, while the world
is governed by economic interests that automatically vic-
timize so many. The naturalistic imagination dramatizes
the struggles of those to whom the self-questioning of the
isolated ego is still a future horror: where the dissociated
modern voice seeks to escape the wearisome confines of
its own ego, the economically disenfranchised are seeking
an "ego," a selfhood, a permanent identity that will make
them human. The deliberate juxtaposition of a consideration of Samuel Beckett and Harriette Arnow points up
not simply the tragedy of the victimized Gertie Nevels,
but the wasteful tragedy of the *cogito, ergo cogito* of
Beckett and his followers.

The Dollmaker traces the ways by which the spiritual
must succumb to the material in a society whose basic
principle is competition; the "Christ" in Gertie Nevels
will never be expressed, because she must surrender to the
economic nightmare and prostitute her talent by making
ugly, cheap dolls. The novel is a brutal, beautiful work
that has a permanent effect upon the reader: long after
one has put it aside, he is still in the presence of its people, absorbed in their trivial and tragic dilemma, sorting
out their mistakes, rearranging their possibilities, ponder-
ing upon the fate that makes certain people live certain
lives, suffer certain atrocities, while other people merely
read about them. Because Harriette Arnow's people are
not articulate, we are anxious to give their confusion a
recognizable order, to contribute to their reality, to complete them with language. They are assimilated into us,

and we into them. *The Dollmaker* deals with human beings to whom language is not a means of changing or even expressing reality, but a means of pitifully recording its effect upon the nerves. It is a legitimate tragedy, our most unpretentious American masterpiece.

First published in 1954, *The Dollmaker* tells the story of a dislocated Kentucky family during the closing years of World War II. The Nevels family comes to Detroit so that the father can contribute to the "war effort" by working in a factory. The war is always a reality, though at a distance: real to the Kentucky women who wait anxiously for mail, dreading the arrival of telegrams, real to the workers of Detroit who dread its ending. But the "war" itself becomes abstracted from common experience as the Nevels family gradually is accommodated to Detroit and its culture of machines, the radio being the means by which war news is always heard, and also the primary means of entertainment. In the foreground is a life of distracting, uprooted particulars, everything dependent upon everything else, tied together magically in the complex economic knot of a modern industrial society. How can the human imagination resist a violent assimilation into such a culture? In Kentucky the Nevels are themselves a kind of domestic factory, producing their own food; in Detroit they are the exploited base of a vast capitalistic pyramid, utterly helpless, anonymous cogs in a factory that extends beyond the brutal city of Detroit to take in the entire nation. They are truly American as they become dehumanized—Gertie Nevels is encouraged to make cheap dolls in place of her beautiful hand-carved figures, and her children are enthusiastic about selling themselves in various clever ways, knowing that one must be sold, one must therefore work to *sell oneself*. A pity

101

they can't put up a sign over their door, they say, declaring this three-bedroom apartment to be the "Nevels' Woodworking Plant Number 1"! The enthusiasm of the children's acquiescence to the values of a capitalistic society is one of the most depressing aspects of this novel.

It is a depressing work, like most extraordinary works. Its power lies in its insistence upon the barrenness of life, even a life lived in intimacy with other human beings bound together by ties of real love and suffering. Tragedy does not seem to me to be cathartic, but to deepen our sense of the mystery and sanctity of the human predicament. The beauty of *The Dollmaker* is its author's absolute commitment to a vision of life as cyclical tragedy—as constant struggle. No sooner is one war declared over than the impoverished, overworked citizens of Detroit anticipate the start of another war, the war against "Communists," particularly those in Detroit!—no sooner is one domestic horror concluded, one child mutilated and killed, than another horror begins to take shape. The process of life demands total absorption of one's energies, there is no time to think, no time to arrange fate, no time to express the spiritual life. Life is killing, a killing of other people or of oneself, a killing of one's soul. When the war is over, concluded by the drama of the atomic bombs, "Gertie could hear no rejoicing, no lifting of the heart that all the planned killing and wounding of men was finished. Rather it was as if the people had lived on blood, and now that the bleeding was ended, they were worried about their future food."

It is a fact of life that one must always worry, not about the "planned" killing and wounding of men, but about his own future food.

The Dollmaker begins magnificently on a Kentucky

road, with Gertie in her own world, knowing her strength, having faith in her audacity—a big, ungainly, ugly woman astride a mule, ready to force any car that comes along to stop for her. She is carrying her son Amos, who is dangerously ill, and she must get a ride to town in order to take him to a doctor. Her sheer animal will, her stubbornness, guarantee the survival of her son; she is not afraid to cut into his flesh with a knife in order to release pus. She succeeds in stopping a car with an army officer in it and she succeeds in overwhelming this man by the determination of her will. But it is her last real success: after the novel's beginning, everything goes downhill for Gertie.

Basic to her psychological predicament is a conflict that has been an obsession in the American imagination, particularly the imagination of the nineteenth century—the twin and competitive visions of God, God as love and God as vengeance, a God of music and dollmaking and domestic simplicity, and a God whose hell quivers with murderous heat. The God of hell is the God worshiped by Gertie's mother, who is responsible for the tragedy of the novel. If the God of this hell rules the world also, and it is Gertie's deepest, helpless conviction that He does, then all of life is forecast, determined; and the fires of Detroit's steel mills are accurate symbols for Gertie to mull over. Gertie, like Judas, is foreordained to sin against such a God. The novel resolves itself in a bitter irony as Gertie betrays herself, giving up her unique art in order to make herself over into a kind of free-lance factory worker, turning out dolls or foxes or Christ on order; she is determined to be Judas, to betray the Christly figure in the piece of wood she never has enough time to carve out, and the Christly figure is at once her own and that of the millions of people, Americans like herself, who might have been models for Christ. They do not emerge out of the wood, they do not become incarnated in time, they are not given a face or a voice. They remain mute, unborn. Man is both Christ and Judas, the sacred, divine self and the secular, betraying, human self, the self that must sell itself for "future food" because this is the foreordained lot of man.

"She thought she was going to cry. . . . So many times she's thought of that other woman, and now she was that woman: 'She considereth a field and buyeth it; with the fruit of her own hands she planteth a vineyard.' A whole vineyard she didn't need, only six vines maybe. So much to plant her own vines, set her own trees, and know that come thirty years from now she'd gather fruit from the trees and grapes from the vines. . . .'" Gertie's only ambition is to own a small farm of her own. In order to live she must own land, work the land herself. The owning of property has nothing to do with setting up boundaries [there are no near neighbors]; it is a declaration of personality, an expression of the profound human need for self-sufficiency and permanence. Wendell Berry's *A Place on Earth*, also set during the closing months of World War II but dealing exclusively with those Kentuckians who did not leave home, is a long, slow, ponderous, memorable novel of praise for a life lived close to the earth, to one's own earth, a "place on earth" that is our only hope; the earth and human relationships are our only hope. In the government housing project in Detroit this desire is expressed feebly and pathetically in the tenants' planting of flowers, which are naturally trampled and destroyed, though a few somehow survive—the tragedy is that this desire lies beyond the reach of nearly everyone, and therefore identity, personality, the neces-

104

sary permanence of life itself are denied. To be "saved" in this culture one must remake oneself entirely, one must sell oneself as shrewdly as possible. One's fate depends not upon his sacred relationship with the land, but his secular deceptive relationship with society.

There are great works that deal with the soul in isolation, untouched importantly by history. Sartre's *Nausea,* which concerns the salvation of a historian, is an ahistorical work, a work of allegory; Dostoyevsky's *Notes from the Underground,* neurotic and witty and totally subjective, is nevertheless a historical work. It seems to me that the greatest works of literature deal with the human soul caught in the stampede of time, unable to gauge the profundity of what passes over it, like the characters in certain plays of Yeats who live through terrifying events but who cannot understand them; in this way history passes over most of us. Society is caught in a convulsion, whether of growth or of death, and ordinary people are destroyed. They do not, however, understand that they are "destroyed."

There is a means of salvation: love, particularly of children. But the children of *The Dollmaker* are stunted, doomed adults, destroyed either literally by the admonition "Adjust!" or destroyed emotionally, turned into citizens of a demonic factory-world. There is another means: art. But art is luxury, it has no place in the world of intense, daily, bitter struggle, though this world of struggle is itself the main object of art. Living, one cannot be saved; suffering, one cannot express the phenomenon of "suffering." Gertie Nevels is inarticulate throughout most of this novel, unable to do battle effectively with the immense hallucination of her new life, and her only means of expression—her carving—must finally be sacrificed, so that her family can eat. So the social dislocation of these Kentucky "hillbillies" is an expression of the general doom of most of mankind, and their defeat, the corruption of their personalities, is more basic to our American experience than the failure of those whom James thought of as "freed" from economic necessity, and therefore free to create their own souls. Evil is inherent in the human heart, as good is inherent in it; but the violence of economic suffering stifles the good, stimulates the evil, so that the ceaseless struggle with the fabric of the universe is reduced to a constant, daily heartbreaking struggle over money, waged against every other antlike inhabitant of the city, the stakes indefinable beyond next month's payment of rent or payment on the car.

If the dream of a small farm is Gertie's dream of Eden, the real "Paradise Valley" (a black slum section of Detroit) is an ironic hell, and the "Merry Hill" to which she and her family come to live is, though segregated "by law," no different. Detroit is terrifying as seen through the eyes of this Kentucky farm woman. The machines— the hurrying people—the automobiles—the initial sounding of that ugly word "Hillbilly!"—everything works to establish a demonic world, the antithesis of the Kentucky hills. There, man can have privacy and dignity though he may be poor; in the housing development money appears and is lost, there is no privacy, everyone intrudes upon everyone else, the alley is "one churning, wriggling mass of children." The impact of this dislocation upon children is most terrible: Reuben, the oldest boy, becomes bitter and runs away from home, unable to "adjust"; Cassie, deprived of her invisible playmate Callie Lou, is killed by a train in the trainyards near her home. I can think of no other work except Christina Stead's *The Man Who*

106

Loved Children that deals so brilliantly and movingly with the lives of children, and Mrs. Arnow has chosen not to penetrate the minds of the Nevels children at all but simply to show us their development or deterioration from the outside. It is a fact of slum life that children dominate in sheer numbers. The more impoverished the neighborhood, the more children to run wild in its streets and on its sidewalks, both powerful and helpless. The fear of anarchy, shared by all of us who have been children, materializes in the constant struggle of children to maintain their identities, striking and recoiling from one another; in miniature they live out tragic scenarios, the pressure upon the human soul in our age, the overcrowding of life, the suffocation of the personality under the weight of sheer numbers, noise, confusion. Yet no dream of wealth, no dream of a fine home in Grosse Pointe is too fantastic for these people to have; corrupted by movies, by the radio, by the mystery of the dollar, they succumb happily to their own degradation, alternating between a kind of community and a disorganized, hateful mass that cannot live in peace. Neighbors cannot live in peace with neighbors, nor parents with their own families, nor children with children. The basic split in the American imagination between an honoring of the individual and a vicious demand for "adjustment" and conformity is dramatized by the gradual metamorphosis of the surviving Nevels children. Gertie is still Gertie, though profoundly shaken by the loss of Reuben and Cassie, but her other children have come a long way, by the end of the novel, when they can laugh at a cartoon of a woman with a mule, having learned the proper contempt for a "hillbilly."

Gertie's husband, Clovis, with his liking for machines, adapts himself easily to the new culture. He takes pride in buying his wife an Icy Heart refrigerator (on time) and a car for himself (on time) and in "hunting Christmas" for his family in smelly department-store basements. It is part of the moral confusion of life in Detroit that Clovis, essentially a good, "natural" man, should become a murderer, revenging himself upon a young man hired to beat him up because of his union activities. There is no time to assess properly Clovis' act of murder—Gertie has no time to comprehend it, except to recoil from what she senses has happened. But the struggle continues; nothing is changed by the murder; another thug will be hired to take that man's place, by the mysterious powers with money enough to "hire" other men; at the novel's conclusion Clovis, like millions of other men, is out of work and we can envision his gradual disintegration, forced to look desperately for jobs and to live off his wife and children.

It is part of the industrial society that people of widely varying backgrounds should be thrown together, like animals competing for a small, fixed amount of food, forced to hate one another. Telling an amiable anecdote about factory life, Clovis mentions a Ukrainian: "He hates everything, niggers, hillbillies, Jews, Germans, but worse'n anything he hates Poles an that Polack foreman. An he is a good-hearted guy. . . ." Catholics hate and fear non-Catholics, spurred on by their famous radio priest "Father Moneyhan," but Irish Catholics hate Polish Catholics. However, the hatreds seethe and subside, especially in the face of common human predicaments of drunkenness and trouble; at any rate, they can be easily united into a solid hatred of blacks, should that need arise. Living in fear more or less constantly, being forced to think only of their "future food," these people have no choice but to hate the Other, the constant threat. What a picture of America's promises *The Dollmaker* gives, and how unforgettable this "melting pot" of economic democracy!

Mrs. Arnow writes so well, with so little apparent effort, that critical examination seems almost irrelevant. It is a tribute to her talent that one is convinced, part way through the book, that it is a masterpiece; if everything goes wrong, if an entirely unsuitable ending is tacked on, the book will remain inviolate. The ending of *The Dollmaker* is by no means a disappointment, however. After months of struggle and a near succumbing to madness, Gertie questions the basis of her own existence; inarticulate as she is, given to working with her hands, in silence, she is nevertheless lyrically aware of the horror of the world in which she now lives. Behind her, now unattainable, is the farm in Kentucky her mother talked her out of buying; all around her is the unpredictable confusion of Detroit. What is the point of having children? "What was the good of trying to keep your own [children] if when they grew up their days were like your own—changeovers and ugly painted dolls?" Throughout the novel Gertie has been dreaming of the proper face for the Christ she wants to carve. She never locates the proper face: instead she takes the fine block of wood to be split into smaller pieces, for easily made dolls.

The drama of naturalism has always been the subjecting of ordinary people to the corrosive and killing facts of society, usually an industrial one. *The Grapes of Wrath*, so much more famous than Mrs. Arnow's novel, and yet not superior to it, is more faithful to the naturalistic tradition than is *The Dollmaker*: one learns a great deal about the poetic vulgarities and obscenities of life from Steinbeck, and this aspect of life has its own kind of immortality. *The Dollmaker*, however, is not truly naturalistic; a total world is suggested but not expressed. Mrs. Arnow, like Gertie Nevels, flinches from a confrontation with sexual realities. The frantic naturalism of such a work as the recent *Last Exit to Brooklyn*, superimposed upon this little Detroit epic, would give us, probably, a more truthful vision of Detroit, then and now; but such naturalism, totally absorbed in an analysis of bodily existence, is perhaps equally unfaithful to the spiritual and imaginative demands that some people, at least, still make. So Gertie is an "artist," but a primitive, untheorizing, inarticulate artist; she whittles out figures that are dolls or Christs, figures of human beings not quite human, but expressive of old human dreams. She is both an ordinary human being and an extraordinary human being, a memorable creation, so real that one cannot question her existence, involving us as she does in the solid fact of life's criminal exploitation of those who live it. *The Dollmaker* is one of those excellent American works that have yet to be properly assessed, not only as excellent but as very much *American*.

5

THE
DEATH THROES
OF ROMANTICISM:

The Poetry of
Sylvia Plath

I am not cruel, only truthful—
The eye of a little god. . . .

Plath, *Mirror*

Tragedy is not a woman, however gifted, dragging her shadow around in a circle, or analyzing with dazzling scrupulosity the stale, boring inertia of the circle; tragedy is cultural, mysteriously enlarging the individual so that what he has experienced is both what we have experienced and what we need not experience—because of his, or her, private agony. It is proper to say that Sylvia Plath represents for us a tragic figure involved in a tragic action, and that her tragedy is offered to us as a near-perfect work of art, in her books *The Colossus* (1960), *The Bell Jar* (1963), *Ariel* (1965), and the posthumous volumes published in 1971, *Crossing the Water* and *Winter Trees.*

This essay is an attempt to analyze Plath in terms of her cultural significance, to diagnose, through Plath's poetry, the pathological aspects of our era that make a death of the spirit inevitable—for that era and all who believe in its assumptions. It is also based upon the certainty that Plath's era is concluded and that we may consider it with the sympathetic detachment with which we consider any era that has gone before us and makes our own possible: the cult of Plath insists she is a saintly martyr, but of course she is something less dramatic than this, but more valuable. The "I" of the poems is an artful construction, a tragic figure whose tragedy is classical, the result of a limited vision that believed itself the mirror held up to nature—as in the poem "Mirror," the eye of a little god who imagines itself without preconceptions, "unmisted by love or dislike." This is the audacious hubris of tragedy, the inevitable reality-challenging statement of the participant in a dramatic action he does not know is "tragic." He dies, and only we can see the purpose of his death—to illustrate the error of a personality who believed itself godlike.

The assumptions of the essay are several: that the artist both creates and is created by his art, and that the self—especially the "I" of lyric poetry—is a personality who achieves a kind of autonomy free not only of the personal life of the artist but free, as well, of the part-by-part progression of individual poems; that the autobiographical personality is presented by the artist as a testing of reality, and that its success or failure or bewilderment will ultimately condition the artist's personal life; that the degree to which an audience accepts or rejects or sympathetically detaches itself from a given tragic action will ultimately condition the collective life of an era; and that the function of literary criticism is not simply to dissect either cruelly or reverentially, to attack or to glorify, but to illustrate how the work of a significant artist helps to explain his era and our own. The significance of Plath's art is assumed. Her significance as a cultural phenomenon is assumed. What needs desperately to be seen is how she performed for us, and perhaps in place of some of us, the concluding scenes in the fifth act of a tragedy, the first act of which began centuries ago.

Narcissi

Lawrence said in *Apocalypse* that when he heard people complain of being lonely he knew their affliction: ". . . they have lost the Cosmos." It is easy to agree with Lawrence, but less easy to understand what he means. Yet if there is a way of approaching Plath's tragedy, it is only through an analysis of what Plath lost and what she was half-conscious of having lost:

> I am solitary as grass. What is it I miss?
> Shall I ever find it, whatever it is?
>
> ("Three Women")

We must take this loss as a real one, not a rhetorical echoing of other poets' cries; not a yearning that can be dismissed by the robust and simple-minded among us who like that formidably healthy and impossible Emerson, sought to dismiss the young people of his day "diseased" with problems of original sin, evil, predestination, and the like by contemptuously diagnosing their worries as "the soul's mumps, and measles, and whooping-coughs" ("Spiritual Laws"). Emerson possessed a con-

115

sciousness of such fluidity and explorative intelligence that any loss of the cosmos for him could seem nothing more serious than an adolescent's perverse rebelliousness, at its most profound a doubt to be answered with a few words.

These "few words" in our era are multiplied endlessly —all the books, the tradition at our disposal, the example of a perpetually renewed and self-renewing nature—and yet they are not convincing to the Sylvia Plaths of our time. For those who imagine themselves as filled with emptiness, as wounds "walking out of hospital," as the pronouncements of a practical-minded, combative, "healthy" society of organized individuals, are meaningless. Society, seen from the solitary individual's viewpoint, is simply an organization of the solitary, linked together materially— perhaps, in fact, crowded together but not "together," not vitally related. One of Plath's few observations about larger units of human beings is appropriately cynical:

> And then there were other faces. The faces of nations,
> Governments, parliaments, societies,
> The faceless faces of important men.
>
> It is these men I mind:
> They are so jealous of anything that is not flat! They are
> jealous gods
> That would have the whole world flat because they are.
> ("Three Women")

And, in a rapid associative leap that is typical of her poetry—and typical of a certain type of frightened imagination—Plath expands her sociological observation to include the mythical figures of "Father" and "Son," who conspire together to make a heaven of flatness: "Let us flatten and launder the grossness from these souls"

116

("Three Women"). The symbolic figures of "Father" and "Son" do not belong to a dimension of the mind exclusive, let alone transcendent, of society; and if they embody the jealous assumptions of an imagined family of "parent" and "child," they are more immediate, more terrifyingly present, than either.

"Nations, governments, parliaments, societies" conspire only in lies and cannot be trusted. Moreover, they are male in their aggression and their cynical employment of rhetoric; their counterparts cannot be women like Plath, but the creatures of "Heavy Women," who smile to themselves above their "weighty stomachs" and meditate "devoutly as the Dutch bulb," absolutely mute, "among the archetypes." Between the archetypes of jealous, ruthless power, represented by the Father/Son of religious and social tradition, and the archetypes of moronic fleshly beauty, represented by these smug mothers, there is a very small space for the creative intellect, for the employment and expansion of a consciousness that tries to transcend such limits. Before we reject Plath's definition of the artistic self as unreasonably passive, even as infantile, we should inquire why so intelligent a woman should assume these limitations, why she should not declare war against the holders of power and of the "mysteries" of the flesh—why her poetry approaches but never crosses over the threshold of an active, healthy attack upon obvious evils and injustices. The solitary ego in its prison cell is there by its own desire, its own admission of guilt in the face of even the most crazily ignorant of accusors. Like Eugene O'Neill, who lived into his sixties with this bewildering obsession of the self-annihilated-by-Others, Plath exhibits only the most remote (and rhetorical) sympathy with other people. If she tells us she

117

may be a bit of a "Jew," it is only to define herself, *her*
sorrows, and not to involve our sympathies for the Jews
of recent European history.

Of course, the answer is that Plath did not like other
people; like many who are persecuted, she identified in a
perverse way with her own persecutors, and not with
those who, along with her, were victims. But she did not
"like" other people because she did not essentially believe
that they existed; she knew intellectually that they existed, of course, since they had the power to injure her,
but she did not *believe* they existed in the way she did, as
pulsating, breathing, suffering individuals. Even her own
children are objects of her perception, there for the restless scrutiny of her image-making mind, and not there as
human beings with a potentiality that would someday
take them beyond their immediate dependency upon her,
which she sometimes enjoys and sometimes dreads.

The moral assumptions behind Plath's poetry condemned her to death, just as she, in creating this body of
poems, condemned it to death. But her moral predicament
is not so pathological as one may think, if conformity to an
essentially sick society is taken to be—as many traditional
moralists and psychologists take it—a sign of normality.
Plath speaks very clearly a language we can understand.
She is saying what men have been saying for many centuries, though they have not been so frank as she, and, being
less sensitive as well, they have not sickened upon their
own hatred for humanity: they have thrived upon it, in
fact, "sublimating" it into wondrous achievements of material and mechanical splendor. Let us assume that Sylvia
Plath acted out in her poetry and in her private life the
deathliness of an old consciousness, the old corrupting hell
of the Renaissance ideal and its "I"-ness, separate and

distinct from all other fields of consciousness, which exist only to be conquered or to inflict pain upon the "I." Where at one point in civilization this very masculine, combative ideal of an "I" set against all other "I's"—and against nature as well—was necessary in order to wrench man from the hermetic contemplation of a God-centered universe and get him into action, it is no longer necessary, its health has become a pathology, and whoever clings to its outmoded concepts will die. If romanticism and its gradually accelerating hysteria are taken as the ultimate ends of a once-vital Renaissance ideal of subject/object antagonism, then Plath must be diagnosed as one of the last romantics; and already her poetry seems to us a poetry of the past, swiftly receding into history.

The "I" that is declared an enemy of all others cannot identify with anyone or anything, since even nature—or especially nature—is antagonistic to it. Man is spirit/body but, as in the poem "Last Things," Plath states her distrust of the spirit that "escapes like steam/In dreams, through the mouth-hole or eye-hole. I can't stop it." Spirit is also intellect, but the "intellect" exists uneasily inside a prison house of the flesh; a small, desperate, calculating process (like the ego in Freud's psychology) that achieves only spasmodic powers of identity in the constant struggle between the id and the superego or between the bestial world of fleshly female "archetypes" and hypocritical, deathly male authorities. This intellect does not belong naturally in the universe and feels guilt and apprehension at all times. It does not belong in nature; nature is "outside" man, superior in brute power to man, though admittedly inferior in the possibilities of imagination. When this intellect attempts its own kind of creation, it cannot be judged as transcendent to the

119

biological processes of change and decay, but as somehow conditioned by these processes and, of course, found inferior. Why else would Plath call a poem about her own poetry "Stillborn" and lament the deadness of her poems, forcing them to compete with low but living creatures?— "They are not pigs, they are not even fish. . . ." It is one of the truly pathological habits of this old consciousness that it puts all things into immediate *competition*: erecting Aristotelian categories of *x* and non-*x*, assuming that the distinction between two totally unconnected phases of life demands a kind of war, a superior/inferior grading.

For instance, let us examine one of Plath's lighter and more "positive" poems. This is "Magi," included in the posthumous *Crossing the Water*. It summons up literary affiliations with Eliot and Yeats, but its vision is exclusively Plath's and, in a horrifying way, very female. Here, Plath is contemplating her six-month-old daughter, who smiles "into thin air" and rocks on all fours "like a padded hammock." Imagined as hovering above the child, like "dull angels," are the Magi of abstraction—the intellectual, philosophical concepts of Good, True, Evil, Love, the products of "some lamp-headed Plato." Plath dismisses the Magi by asking "What girl ever flourished in such company?" Her attitude is one of absolute contentment with the physical, charming simplicities of her infant daughter; she seems to want none of that "multiplication table" of the intellect. If this poem had not been written by Sylvia Plath, who drew such attention to her poetry by her suicide, one would read it and immediately agree with its familiar assumptions—how many times we've read this poem, by how many different poets! But Plath's significance now forces us to examine her work very carefully, and in this case the poem reveals itself as a vision as tragic as her more famous, more obviously troubled poems.

It is, in effect, a death sentence passed by Plath on her own use of language, on the "abstractions" of culture or the literary as opposed to the physical immediacy of a baby's existence. The world of language is condemned as only "ethereal" and "blank"—obviously inferior to the world of brute, undeveloped nature. Plath is saying here, in this agreeable-mannered poem, that because "Good" and "Evil" have no meaning to a six-month-old infant beyond the facts of mother's milk and a bellyache, they have no essential meaning at all—to anyone—and the world of all adult values, the world of complex linguistic structures, the world in which Plath herself lives as a normal expression of her superior intellect, is as "loveless" as the multiplication table and therefore must be rejected. It is extraordinary that the original romantic impulse to honor and appreciate nature, especially mute nature, should dwindle in our time to this: a Sylvia Plath willfully admitting to herself and to us that she is inferior to her own infant! The regressive fantasies here are too pathetic to bear examination, but it is worth suggesting that this attitude is not unique. It reveals much that is wrong with contemporary intellectuals' assessment of themselves: a total failure to consider that the undeveloped (whether people or nations) are *not* sacred because they are undeveloped, but sacred because they are part of nature, that and the role of the superior intellect is *not* to honor incompletion, in itself or in anything, but to help bring about the fulfillment of potentialities. Plath tells us that a six-month-old infant shall pass judgment on Plato; and in the poem "Candles" she asks, "How shall I tell anything at all/To this infant still in a birth-drowse?"

121

It is impossible, of course, for her to tell the infant anything, if she assumes that the infant possesses an intuitive knowledge superior to her own. And yet, and yet . . . she does desire to "tell" the infant and us. But her "telling" cannot be anything more than a half-guilty assertion of her own impotence, and she will ultimately condemn it as wasteful. The honoring of mute nature above man's ability to make and use language will naturally result in muteness; this muteness will force the individual into death, for the denial of language is a suicidal one and we pay for it with our lives.

Back from the maternity ward, resting after her painful experience, the most "positive" of Plath's three women is reassured when she looks out her window, at dawn, to see the narcissi opening their white faces in the orchard. And now she feels uncomplex again; she is relieved of the miraculous pain and mystery of childbirth and wants only for herself and for her child "the clear bright colors of the nursery,/The talking ducks, the happy lambs." She meditates:

> I do not will [my baby] to be exceptional.
> It is the exception that interests the devil.
> . . . .
> I will him to be common.

It seems to us pitiful that Plath should desire the "common"—should imagine that her loving words for her infant are anything less than a curse. But her conviction that "the exception interests the devil" is very familiar to us, an expression of our era's basic fear of the intellect; the centuries-old division between "intellect" and "instinct" has resulted in a suicidal refusal to understand that man's intelligence *is* instinctive in his species, simply an instinct for survival and for the creation of civilization. Yet the "loving of muteness" we find in Plath is understandable if it is seen as a sensitive revulsion against the world of strife, the ceaseless battle of the letter "I" to make victories and extend its territory. Even the highest intelligence, linked to an ego that is self-despising, will utter curses in the apparent rhythms of love:

> . . . right now you are dumb.
> And I love your stupidity,
> The blind mirror of it. I look in
> And find no face but my own. . . .
>   ("For a Fatherless Son")

The narcissi of the isolated ego are not really "quick" and "white" as children (see "Among the Narcissi") but victimized, trampled, and bitter unto death. Plath's attitude in these gentler poems about her motherhood is, at best, a temporary denial of her truly savage feelings—we are shocked to discover her celebration of hatred in "Lesbos" and similar poems, where she tells us what she really thinks about the "stink of fat and baby crap" that is forcing her into silence, "hate up to my neck."

The poems of hatred seem to us very contemporary, in their jagged rhythms and surreal yoking together of images, and in their defiant expression of a rejection of love, of motherhood, of men, of the "Good, the True, the Beautiful. . . ." If life really is a struggle for survival, even in a relatively advanced civilization, then very few individuals will win; most will lose (and nearly all women are fated to lose); something is rotten in the very fabric of the universe. All this appears to be contemporary, but Plath's poems are in fact the clearest, most precise (because most private) expression of an old moral predica-

123

ment that has become unbearable now. And its poignant genesis is very old indeed:

And now I was sorry that God had made me a man. The beasts, birds, fishes, etc., I blessed their condition, for they had not a sinful nature; they were not to go to hell after death. . . .

(John Bunyan, *Grace Abounding*)

Male/Female   "I"/"i"
Nature as Object and as Nightmare

All this involves a variety of responses, though behind them is a single metaphysical belief. The passive, paralyzed, continually surfacing and fading consciousness of Plath in her poems is disturbing to us because it seems to summon forth, to articulate with deadly accuracy, the re-regressive fantasies we have rejected—and want to forget. The experience of reading her poems deeply is a frightening one: it is like waking to discover one's adult self, grown to full height, crouched in some long-forgotten childhood hiding place, one's heart pounding senselessly, all the old rejected transparent beasts and monsters crawling out of the wallpaper. So much for Plato! So much for adulthood! Yet I cannot emphasize strongly enough how valuable the experience of reading Plath can be, for it is a kind of elegant "dreaming-back," a cathartic experience that not only cleanses us of our personal and cultural desires for regression, but explains by way of its deadly accuracy what was wrong with such desires.

The same can be said for the reading of much of con-

124

temporary poetry and fiction, fixated as it is upon the childhood fears of annihilation, persecution, the helplessness we have all experienced when we are, for one reason or another, denied an intellectual awareness of what is happening. For instance, the novels of Robbe-Grillet and his imitators emphasize the hypnotized passivity of the "I" in a world of dense and apparently autonomous things; one must never ask "Who manufactured these things? who brought them home? who arranged them?" —for such questions destroy the novels. Similarly, the highly praised works of Pynchon, Barthelme, Purdy, Barth (the Barth of the minimal stories, not the earlier Barth), and countless others are verbalized screams and shudders to express the confusion of the ego that believes—perhaps because it has been told so often—itself somehow out of place in the universe, a mechanized creature if foolish enough to venture into Nature; a too-natural creature for the mechanical urban paradise he has inherited but has had no part in designing. The "I" generated by these writers is typically a transparent, near-nameless personality; in the nightmarish works of William Burroughs, the central consciousness does not explore a world so much as submit pathetically to the exploration of himself by a comically hostile world, all cartoons and surprising metamorphoses. Plath's tentative identity in such poems as "Winter Trees," "Tulips," and even the robustly defiant "Daddy" is essentially a child's consciousness, seizing upon a symbolic particularity (tulips, for instance) and then shrinking from its primary noon, so that the poems —like the fiction we read so often today—demonstrate a dissolution of personality. As Jan B. Gordon has remarked in a review of *Winter Trees* (*Modern Poetry*

Studies, Vol. 2, No. 6, p. 282), Plath's landscapes become pictorial without any intermediate stage, so that we discover ourselves "in *una selva oscura* where associations multiply endlessly, but where each tree looks like every other one. . . ." That is the danger risked by those minimal artists of our time whose subject is solely the agony of the locked-in ego: their agonies, like Plath's landscapes, begin to look alike.

But if we turn from the weak and submissive ego to one more traditionally masculine, activated by the desire to *name* and to *place* and to *conquer*, we discover a consciousness that appears superficially antithetical:

Average reality begins to rot and stink as soon as the act of individual creation ceases to animate a subjectively perceived texture.

(Vladimir Nabokov, from an interview)

The obscure moon lighting an obscure world
Of things that would never be quite expressed,
Where you yourself were never quite yourself
And did not want nor have to be,

Desiring the exhilarations of changes:
The motive for metaphor, shrinking from
The weight of primary noon,
The A B C of being. . . .

(Wallace Stevens, "Motive for Metaphor")

Where in Plath (and in countless of our contemporaries) the ego suffers dissolution in the face of even the most banal of enemies, in such writers as Nabokov and Stevens the ego emerges as confident and victorious. Yet we see that it is the same metaphysics—the same automatic assumption that there is an "average" reality somehow distinct from us, either superior (and therefore terrifying) or inferior (and therefore saved from "rot" and "stink" only by our godly subjective blessing). This is still the old romantic bias, the opposition between self and object, "I" and non-"I," man and nature. Nabokov and Stevens have mastered art forms in which language is arranged and rearranged in such a manner as to give pleasure to the artist and his readers, excluding any referent to an available exterior world. Their work frees the ego to devise and defend a sealed-off universe, inhabited chiefly by the self-as-artist, so that it is quite natural to assume that Nabokov's writing is about the art of writing and Stevens' poems about the art of writing; that the work gives us the *process* of creativity that is its chief interest. Again, as in Plath, the work may approach the threshold of an awareness of other inhabitants of the human universe, but it never crosses over because, basically, it cannot guarantee the existence of other human beings: its own autonomy might be threatened or at least questioned. The mirror and never the window is the stimulus for this art that, far from being overwhelmed by nature, turns from it impatiently, in order to construct the claustrophobic *Ada* or the difficult later poems of Stevens, in which metaphors inhabit metaphors and the "weight of primary noon" is hardly more than a memory. The consciousness discernible behind the works of Nabokov and Stevens is like that totally autonomous ego imagined— but only imagined—by Sartre, which is self-created, self-named, untouched by parental or social or cultural or even biological determinants.

Since so refined an art willfully excludes the emotional context of its own creation, personality is minimal; art is all. It is not surprising that the harsh, hooking images of Plath's poetry should excite more interest, since Plath is always honest, perhaps more honest than we would like, and her awareness of a lost cosmos involves her in a perpetual questioning of what nature is, what the Other is, what does it want to do to her, with her, in spite of her . . . ? Nabokov and Stevens receive only the most incidental stimuli from their "average reality" and "obscure world," but Plath is an identity reduced to desperate statements about her dilemma as a passive witness to a turbulent natural world:

> There is no life higher than the grasstops
> Or the hearts of sheep, and the wind
> Pours by like destiny, bending
> Everything in one direction.
> . . . .
> The sheep know where they are,
> Browsing in their dirty wool-clouds,
> Grey as the weather.
> The black slots of their pupils take me in.
> It is like being mailed into space,
> A thin, silly message.
>   ("Wuthering Heights")

And, in "Two Campers in Cloud Country," the poet and her companion experience a kind of comfort up in Rock Lake, Canada, where they "mean so little" and where they will wake "blank-brained as water in the dawn." If the self is set in opposition to everything that excludes it, then the distant horizons of the wilderness will be as terrible as the kitchen walls and the viciousness of hissing fat. There is never any integrating of the self and its experience, the self and its field of perception. Human consciousness, to Plath, is always an intruder in the natural universe.

This distrust of the intellect in certain poets can result in lyric-meditative poetry of an almost ecstatic beauty, when the poet acknowledges his separateness from nature but seems not to despise or fear it:

> O swallows, swallows, poems are not
> The point. Finding again the world,
> That is the point, where loveliness
> Adorns intelligible things
> Because the mind's eye lit the sun.
> (Howard Nemerov, "The Blue Swallows")

Nemerov shares with Stevens and Plath certain basic assumptions: that poems are "not the point" in the natural universe, and that the poet, therefore, is not in the same field of experience as the swallows. Poetry, coming from the mind of man, not from the objects of mind's perception, is somehow a self-conscious, uneasy activity that must apologize for itself. In this same poem, the title poem of Nemerov's excellent collection *The Blue Swallows*, the poet opposes the "real world" and the "spelling mind" that attempts to impose its "unreal relations on the blue swallows." But despite Nemerov's tone of acquiescence and affirmation, this is a tragic assumption in that it certainly banishes the poet himself from the world: only if he will give up poetry and "find again the world" has he a chance of being saved. It is a paradox that the poet believes he will honor the objects of his perception— whether swallows, trees, sheep, bees, infants—only by withdrawing from them. Why does it never occur to romantic poets that they exist as much by right in the universe as any other creature, and that their function as

poets is a natural function?—that the adult imagination is superior to the imagination of birds and infants?
In art this can lead to silence; in life, to suicide.

The Deadly Mirror: The Risks of Lyric Poetry

Among the lesser-known of Theodore Roethke's poems is "Lines Upon Leaving a Sanitarium," in which the poet makes certain sobering, unambiguous statements:

> Self-contemplation is a curse
> That makes an old confusion worse.
> . . . .
> The mirror tells some truth, but not
> Enough to merit constant thought.

Perhaps it is not just Plath's position at the end of a once-energetic tradition and the circumstances of her own unhappy life that doomed her and her poetry to premature dissolution, but something in the very nature of lyric poetry itself. What of this curious art form that, when not liberated by music, tends to turn inward upon the singer, folding and folding again upon the poet? If he is immature to begin with, of what can he sing except his own self's immaturity, and to what task can his imagination put itself except the selection of ingenious images to illustrate this immaturity? Few lyric poets, beginning as shakily as the young Yeats, will continue to write and rewrite, to imagine and reimagine, in a heroic evolution of the self from one kind of personality to another. The risk of lyric poetry is its availability to the precocious imagination, its immediate rewards in terms of technical skill, which then hypnotize the poet into

130

believing that he has achieved all there is to achieve in
his life as well as in his art. How quickly these six-inch
masterpieces betray their creators! The early successes,
predicated upon ruthless self-examination, demand a
repeating of their skills even when the original psychological dramas have been outgrown or exhausted, since
the lyric poet is instructed to look into his heart and write
and, by tradition, he has only his self to write about. But
poetry—like all art—demands that its subject be made
sacred. Art *is* the sacralizing of its subject. The problem,
then, is a nearly impossible one: How can the poet make
himself sacred? Once he has exposed himself, revealed
himself, dramatized his fantasies and terrors, what can
he do next? Most modern poetry is scornful, cynical,
contemptuous of its subject (whether self or others),
bitter or amused or coldly detached. It shrinks from the
activity of making the world sacred because it can approach the world only *through* the self-as-subject; and the
prospect of glorifying oneself is an impossible one. Therefore, the ironic mode. Therefore, silence. It is rare to
encounter a poet like Robert Lowell, who beginning with
the stunning virtuosity of his early poems, can move
through a period of intense preoccupation with self (*Life
Studies*) into a period of exploratory maneuvers into the
personalities of poets quite unlike him (*Imitations*) and,
though a shy, ungregarious man, write plays and participate in their productions (*The Old Glory*) and move
into a kind of existential political-historical poetry in
which the self is central but unobtrusive (*Notebook*).
Most lyric poets explore themselves endlessly, like pa-
tients involved in a permanent psychoanalysis, reporting
back for each session determined to discover, to drag out
of hiding, the essential problem of their personalities—

when perhaps there is no problem in their personalities at all, except this insane preoccupation with the self and its moods and doubts, while much of the human universe struggles simply for survival.

If the lyric poet believes—as most people do—that the "I" he inhabits is not integrated with the entire stream of life, let alone with other human beings, he is doomed to a solipsistic and ironic and self-pitying art, in which metaphors for his own narcissistic predicament are snatched from newspaper headlines concerning real atrocities. The small enclosed form of the typical lyric poem seems to preclude an active sanctifying of other people; it is much easier, certainly, for a novelist to investigate and rejoice in the foreign/intimate nature of other people, regardless of his maturity or immaturity. When the novel is not addressed to the same self-analysis as the lyric poem, it demands that one look out the window and not into the mirror; it demands an active involvement with time, place, personality, pasts and futures, and a dramatizing of emotions. The novel allows for a sanctification of any number of people, and if the novelist pits his "I" against others, he will have to construct that "I" with care and love; technical virtuosity is so hard to come by—had Dostoyevsky the virtuosity of Nabokov?— that it begins to seem irrelevant. The novelist's obligation is to do no less than attempt the sanctification of the world!—while the lyric poet, if he is stuck in a limited emotional cul-de-sac, will circle endlessly inside the bell jar of his own world, and only by tremendous strength is he able to break free.[1]

The implications of this essay are not that a highly self-conscious art is inferior by nature to a more socially committed art—on the contrary, it is usually the case that the drama of the self is very exciting. What is a risk for the poet is often a delight for his reader; controlled hysteria is more compelling than statements of Spinozan calm. When Thomas Merton cautioned the mystic against writing poems, believing that the "poet" and the "mystic" must never be joined, he knew that the possession of any truth, especially an irrefutable truth, cannot excite drama. It may be a joy to possess wisdom, but how to communicate it? If you see unity beneath the parts, bits, and cogs of the phenomenal world, this does not mean you can make poetry out of it—

> All leaves are this leaf,
> all petals, this flower
> in a lie of abundance.
> All fruit is the same,
> the trees are only one tree
> and one flower sustains all the earth.
>
> ("Unity," from *Manual Metaphysics*
> by Pablo Neruda; trans. by Ben Belitt)

—not Neruda's best poetry.

By contrast, Plath's poems convince us when they are most troubled, most murderous, most unfair—as in "Daddy," where we listen in amazement to a child's voice cursing and rekilling a dead man, in a distorted rhythmic version of what would be, in an easier world, a nursery tune. An unforgettable poem, surely. The "parts, bits, cogs, the shining multiples" ("Three Women") constitute hallucinations that involve us because they stir in us memories of our own infantile pasts and do not provoke us into a contemplation of the difficult and less dramatic

133

future of our adulthood. The intensity of "Lesbos" grows out of an adult woman's denying her adulthood, her motherhood, lashing out spitefully at all objects—babies or husbands or sick kittens—with a strident, self-mocking energy that is quite different from the Plath of the more depressed poems:

> And I, love, am a pathological liar,
> And my child—look at her, face down on the floor,
> Little unstrung puppet, kicking to disappear—
> Why, she is schizophrenic,
> Her face red and white, a panic. . . .
> . . . .
> You say I should drown my girl.
> She'll cut her throat at ten if she's mad at two.
> The baby smiles, fat snail,
> From the polished lozenges of orange linoleum.
> You could eat him. He's a boy. . . .

Though Plath and her friend, another unhappy mother, obviously share the same smoggy hell, they cannot communicate, and Plath ends the poem with her insistence upon their separateness: "Even in your Zen heaven we shan't meet."

A woman who despises herself as a woman obviously cannot feel sympathy with any other woman; her passionate love/hate is for the aggressors, the absent husbands or the dead fathers who have absorbed all evil. But because these male figures are not present, whatever revenge is possible must be exacted upon their offspring. The poem "For a Fatherless Son" is more chilling than the cheerful anger of "Daddy" because it is so relentless a curse. And if it hints of Plath's own impending absence, by way of suicide, it is a remarkably cruel poem indeed.

Here the mother tells her son that he will presently be aware of an absence, growing beside him like "a death tree . . . an illusion,/And a sky like a pig's backside. . . ." The child is temporarily too young to realize that his father has abandoned him, but

> one day you may touch what's wrong
> The small skulls, the smashed blue hills,
>   the godawful hush.

This is one of the few poems of Plath's in which the future is imagined, but it is imagined passively, helplessly; the mother evidently has no intention of rearranging her life and establishing a household free of the father or of his absence. She does not state her hatred for the absent father, but she reveals herself as a victim, bitter and spiteful, and unwilling to spare her son these emotions. Again, mother and child are roughly equivalent; the mother is not an adult, not a participant in the world of "archetypes."

So unquestioningly is the division between selves accepted, and so relentlessly the pursuit of the solitary, isolated self by way of the form of this poetry, that stasis and ultimate silence seem inevitable. Again, lyric poetry is a risk because it rarely seems to open into a future: the time of lyric poetry is usually the present or the past. "This is a disease I carry home, this is a death," Plath says in "Three Women," and, indeed, this characterizes most of her lines. All is brute process, without a future; the past is recalled only with bitterness, a stimulus for present dismay.

When the epic promise of "One's-self I sing" is mistaken as the singing of a separate self, and not the universal self, the results can only be tragic.

Crossing the Water

Plath understood well the hellish fate of being Swift's true counterpart, the woman who agrees that the physical side of life is a horror, an ungainly synthesis of flesh and spirit—the disappointment of all the romantic love poems and the nightmare of the monkish soul. Since one cannot make this existence sacred, one may as well dream of "massacres" or, like the Third Voice in the play "Three Women," express regret that she had not arranged to have an abortion: "I should have murdered this," she says in a Shakespearean echo, "that murders me." "Crossing the water"—crossing over into another dimension of experience—cannot be a liberation, an exploration of another being, but only a quiet movement into death for two "black, cut-paper people":

> Cold worlds shake from the oar.
> The spirit of blackness is in us, it is in the fishes.
> . . . .
> Are you not blinded by such expressionless sirens?
> This is the silence of astounded souls.
>
> ("Crossing the Water")

In most of the poems and very noticeably in *The Bell Jar*, Plath exhibits a recurring tendency to dehumanize people, to flatten everyone into "cut-paper people," most of all herself. She performs a kind of reversed magic, a desacralizing ritual for which psychologists have terms—reification, rubricization. Absolute, dramatic boundaries are set up between the "I" and all others, and there is a

136

peculiar refusal to distinguish between those who mean well, those who mean ill, and those who are neutral. Thus, one is shocked to discover in *The Bell Jar* that Esther, the intelligent young narrator, is as callous toward her mother as the psychiatrist is to her, and that she sets about an awkward seduction with the chilling precision of a machine—hardly aware of the man involved, telling us very little about him as an existing human being. He does not really *exist*, he has no personality worth mentioning. Only Esther exists.

"Lady Lazarus," risen once again from the dead, does not expect a sympathetic response from the mob of spectators that crowd in to view her, a mock-phoenix rising from another failed suicide attempt: to Plath there cannot be any connection between people, between the "I" who performs and the crowd that stares. All deaths are separate, and do not evoke human responses. To be really safe, one must be like the young man of "Gigolo," who has eluded the "bright fish hooks, the smiles of women," and who will never age because—like Plath's ideal self— he is a perfect narcissus, self-gratified. He has successfully dehumanized himself.

The cosmos is indeed lost to Plath and her era, and even a tentative exploration of a possible "God" is viewed in the old terms, in the old images of dread and terror. "Mystic" is an interesting poem, on a subject rare indeed in Plath, and seems to indicate that her uneasiness with the "mill of hooks" of the air—"questions without answer"—had led her briefly to thoughts of God. Yet whoever this "God" is, no comfort is possible because the ego cannot experience any interest or desire without being engulfed:

Once one has seen God, what is the remedy?
Once one has been seized up

Without a part left over,
Not a toe, not a finger, and used,
Used utterly. . . .
What is the remedy?

Used: the mystic will be exploited, victimized, hurt. He can expect no liberation or joy from God, but only another form of dehumanizing brutality. Plath has made beautiful poetry out of the paranoia sometimes expressed by a certain kind of emotionally disturbed person who imagines that any relationship with anyone will overwhelm him, engulf and destroy his soul. (For a brilliant poem about the savagery of erotic love between lovers who cannot quite achieve adult autonomy or the generosity of granting humanity to each other, see Ted Hughes's "Lovesong" in Crow, not inappropriate in this context.)

The dread of being possessed by the Other results in the individual's failure to distinguish between real and illusory enemies. What must be in the human species a talent for discerning legitimate threats to personal survival evidently never developed in Plath—this helps to explain why she could so gracefully fuse the "evil" of her father with the historical outrages of the Nazis, unashamedly declare herself a "Jew" because the memory of her father persecuted her. In other vivid poems, she senses enemies in tulips (oxygen-sucking tulips?—surely they are human!) or sheep (which possess the unsheeplike power of murdering a human being) or in the true blankness of a mirror, which cannot be seen as recording the natural maturation process of a young woman but must be reinterpreted as drawing the woman toward the "terrible fish" of her future self. Plath's inability to grade the possibilities of danger is reflected generally in our society and helps to account for peculiar admissions of helplessness and confusion in adults who should be informing their children: if everything unusual or foreign is an evil, if everything *new* is an evil, then the individual is lost. The political equivalent of childlike paranoia is too obvious to need restating, but we have a cultural equivalent as well that seems to pass unnoticed. Surely the sinister immorality of films like A *Clockwork Orange* (though not the original English version of the Burgess novel) lies in their excited focus upon small, isolated, glamorized acts of violence by nonrepresentative individuals, so that the unfathomable violence of governments is totally ignored or misapprehended. Delmore Schwartz said that even the paranoid has enemies. Indeed he has enemies, but paranoia cannot allow us to distinguish them from friends.

In the summer of 1972 I attended a dramatic reading of Plath's "Three Women," given by three actresses as part of the International Poetry Conference in London. The reading was done in a crowded room, and unfortunately the highly professional performance was repeatedly interrupted by a baby's crying from another part of the building. Here was—quite accidentally—a powerful and perhaps even poetic counterpoint to Plath's moving poem. For there, in the baby's cries from another room, was what Plath had left out: the reason for the maternity ward, the reason for childbirth and suffering and motherhood and poetry itself.

What may come to seem obvious to people in the future—that unique personality does not necessitate isolation, that the "I" of the poet belongs as naturally in the universe as any other aspect of its fluid totality, above all that this "I" exists in a field of living spirit of which it is one aspect—was tragically unknown to Plath, as it has been unknown or denied many. Hopefully, a world of totality awaits us, not a played-out world of fragments; but Sylvia Plath acted out a tragically isolated existence, synthesizing for her survivors so many of the sorrows of that dying age—romanticism in its death throes, the self's ship, *Ariel*, prematurely drowned.

> It is so beautiful, to have no attachments!
> I am solitary as grass. What is it I miss?
> Shall I ever find it, whatever it is?
>
> ("Three Women")

6

THE
VISIONARY ART
OF FLANNERY
O'CONNOR

. . . something is developing in the
world by means of us, perhaps at
our expense.

Teilhard de Chardin

I

The revolt against science and scientism that characterizes much of twentieth-century literature has its origin in nineteenth-century dissatisfaction with the utopian vision of man as essentially rational. Of course, this dissatisfaction was never homogeneous; the concept of man's free will was attacked from a number of directions. Kant, earlier, attempted to show that man's reason is limited and suspect and must be supplemented by intuition; Nietzsche argued, less optimistically, that intuition is really the "irrational" and may indeed endanger man's rational powers. It was the scientifically speculative thinkers, however, who had the greatest impact on our century's attitude toward free will—Darwin, Marx, Frazer, Freud. In the writings of each of these men, freedom of the will and of the mind is severely questioned. It is not generally known that Freud does allow "freedom" for man, but this freedom can only be the result of intensive self-knowledge and analysis, hardly available to the majority of men.

Modern literature, directly influenced by the nineteenth century, attempts to demonstrate the climate of this "new" world. For someone like Thomas Mann's Von Aschenbach in *Death in Venice*, loss of rationality is loss of the social "good" and causes man's death, yet before his fall Aschenbach was not truly alive. Mann demonstrates in *The Magic Mountain* that civilization rests upon barbarism and that this is a fact one must accept. The ethical demands of an earlier, simpler era are baffled here. And when the irrational is not linked to the purely physical but, on the contrary, is linked to the divine, the problem of an ethical determination of good or evil becomes hopelessly complex.

It is this complexity that makes the fiction of Flannery O'Connor so rich and at the same time so perplexing and alienating. She seems unique in her celebration of the necessity of succumbing to the divine through violence that is immediate and irreparable. There is no mysticism in her work that is only spiritual; it is physical as well. She has been accused of being un-Christian or anti-Christian in her insistence upon the limitations of the human will. For, as she says in an introductory note to her first novel, *Wise Blood*, ". . . free will does not mean one will, but many wills conflicting in one man. Freedom cannot be conceived simply. It is a mystery. . . ." Her refusal to account for the mystery leads to the bizarre atmosphere of her world. It is a world of utter mystery whose center is the "bleeding stinking mad shadow of Jesus." Everything is related to the mystery of Christ's Incarnation, Crucifixion, and Resurrection. And, if the promise of the Resurrection seems muted in O'Connor's world, it is because that world has ignored it. O'Connor, who spoke of herself as a born Catholic to whom death "has always been brother to my imagination," can see the "reality" of the contemporary South only in relationship to the higher reality of Christian mystery.

Not meant to be realistic or naturalistic, her fiction should be read as a series of parables. Like the metaphysical poets, especially T. S. Eliot, she yokes together sacred and secular images by violence; it is the artistic arrangement of these images, in themselves grotesque, that leads to the construction of a vision that is not grotesque but harshly and defiantly spiritual. Her death in the summer of 1964 marked not simply the end of the career of a powerful descendant of Faulkner whose individual achievements are at times superior to his, but the end of the career of one of the greatest religious writers of modern times.

Not Faulkner, however, or Nathanael West, but Kafka and Kierkegaard are O'Connor's most important ancestors. Superficially, her work bears strong resemblances to Faulkner's—the exaggeration of physical and psychological horror, the back-country Southern settings—and to West's mainly in surrealistic style; but it is the revelation of a transcendental world of absolute value beyond the cheap, flashy wasteland of modern America that is O'Connor's real concern. She is understandable only in a

145

religious context. If the reality of the transcendental world is denied, as it is in Faulkner and West and other existential writers, her literature becomes vulgar farce and is indecipherable. If there is no central mystery in Christ, then for O'Connor there would be no mystery in life. Everyone in her world is obsessed with the mystery of Christ, not as a curious historical occurrence but as an always-present reality. The Misfit, of the story "A Good Man is Hard to Find," complains that Jesus "thown everything off balance. If He did what He said, then it's nothing for you to do but thow away everything and follow him, and if He didn't, then it's nothing for you to do but enjoy the few minutes you got left the best way you can. . . ." This murderer, whose metaphysical anguish is in direct contrast with his grotesque being, goes on to say that since he was not there with Christ, he cannot know if the story of Christ is true. "It ain't right that I wasn't there because if I had of been there I would of known. . . . I would of known and I wouldn't be like I am now." Hazel Motes of *Wise Blood* tries to escape the "wild ragged figure" of Christ moving from tree to tree in the back of his mind because he cannot reject the evidence of his senses. "Nothing matters but that Jesus don't exist," Motes says; and the violence of his rejection suggests the hopelessness of his commitment. He will cut out the offending eye by blinding himself to the physical world, withdrawing from it into a kind of catatonic state, and finally dying. For O'Connor, his integrity lies in his being unable to rid himself of Jesus—he is not intended, as some readers might think, to be an example of the morbid side effects of religion. Similarly, the hermaphrodite freak of "A Temple of the Holy Ghost" is not introduced to generate irony between the horror of the freak as freak and someone's lofty concept of it as a temple of the Holy Ghost; the freak in all his freakishness *is* a temple of the Holy Ghost, like it or not: "This is the way He wanted me to be and I ain't disputing His way."

Kierkegaard, similarly, calls for a complete commitment to Christ. But this commitment is not to be in terms of a comfortable, joyous communion but in terms of personal anxiety. For to Kierkegaard, man's natural state is one of anxiety. Man is alone, isolated. The world, seemingly created for him, is a dangerous illusion that blinds him to his true home; the world of man, and especially erotic love, blinds man to his real state, which is that of fear and trembling before God. The crowd, Kierkegaard teaches, is untruth. He follows Saint Paul in saying that "only one attains the goal"; he rejects the modern, or pagan, notion that "to be a man is to belong to a race endowed with reason, to belong to it as a specimen, so that the race or species is higher than the individual." The Kierkegaardian Christian, could he exist, would be a misfit in the world of man. Indeed, to be anything else but a misfit and an "individual" would be a betrayal of his destiny.

The anguish of the believer who is not equal to the worship of his God is recorded faithfully by Kafka. In his novels, stories, parables, and diary entries one reads of the plight of the individual for whom the crowd is impossible, and yet the ecstasy of being "one" with God is also impossible. Kafka is not existential in the common sense of the term (believing that existence creates essence or soul) but is rather an essentialist—believing that man does not create his soul through free acts but is instead given a soul with which he must live, however unsuitable

147

it may be. One runs into problems trying to link Kafka's heroes with those of, say, Camus or Sartre. They are of another species altogether, for their anxiety is expressed only in terms of a higher, invisible, possibly malignant Being, while the heroes of the typical existential novel create their own values completely. In Freudian terms, one would say rather clinically that the Kafkan hero represents an ego that is slowly but irresistibly destroyed by a superego. The superiority of the Kafkan "force" (be it a father or an institution) is suggested most horribly at the end of *The Trial*, where Joseph K. understands that he is expected to commit suicide and thereby execute himself—but he cannot perform this final act because he has been created without the strength needed for it. Kafka's men are subjected to ritualistic performances in which they are victims, initiated into the knowledge of their own powerlessness. Eliseo Vivas sees Kafka's art as the expression of the dilemma of empirical method confronted with the world's irrationality:[1] the crisis of the modern age, which is committed to scientific method but can find no ultimate answers by way of this method. Yet there is a deeply religious core to Kafka's art that Vivas does not see.

This is O'Connor's world: Kierkegaardian anguish in the face of man's certitude and Kafkan anguish in the face of man's ignorance, the blending of the two impulses, toward fanatic certainty (her demented preachers) and toward pathetic, groping empiricism in the face of extraordinary events (the "rational" men of *The Violent Bear It Away* and "The Lame Shall Enter First"). Between these two extremes the world is populated by "grotesques." It is the intention of the typical O'Connor story to initiate the unthinking grotesques into a vision of reality. This is accomplished through ceremonial, almost ritualistic devices: the gathering together of the unfaithful in order to witness a "miracle," most likely performed upon them. An analysis of several of her works will bring out the significance of the pattern of violent rituals in O'Connor.

II

O'Connor's two novels deal with essentially the same subject: the romance of the "mad shadow of Jesus" and the soul that demands freedom. As Lewis A. Lawson has noted in his excellent study of *Wise Blood*,[2] she uses the construction of the parable, introducing an abstract idea that will be made concrete, as in the parables of Christ. Hazel Motes, the Christless preacher of *Wise Blood*, represents by his very being the contradictory elements of modern society—pushed, of course, to comic and morbid extremes. It is not necessary to assume, along with Lawson, that O'Connor feels Motes's fundamentalism to be "perverted." In other of her stories ("The River," for one) the vitality and passion of the fundamentalist is contrasted favorably with the skepticism of the "civilized." Motes embodies the soul in rebellion, not simply against Christ but against his own destiny. He is the grandson of a preacher and the son of a woman, both of whom were consumed with religious feeling. "He had gone to a country school where he had learned to read and write but that it was wiser not to; the Bible was the only book he read." In the sterility of a government institution—the army—Motes is told he has no soul, and is anxious to believe this. "He saw the opportunity here to

149

get rid of it without corruption, to be converted to nothing instead of to evil." The choice Motes wants to make, like modern man, is not between good and evil but between the reality of both good and evil, and nothing: for an absolute nothing would seem to insure man's freedom. Clearly, O'Connor is as fascinated by this theme as is Dostoyevsky, and one cannot resist assuming that the battle fought so bravely and hopelessly by her heroes is in part her own battle.

Motes tries to achieve the sterility of absolute freedom by rejecting his destiny. Yet everywhere he goes, people mistake him for a preacher. Even the fake blind man can recognize him: "I can hear the urge for Jesus in his voice." Enoch Emery, a kind of parody of Motes as a searcher for truth, says: "I knew when I first seen you you didn't have nobody nor nothing but Jesus." Mrs. Watts, the prostitute who is "so well-adjusted that she didn't have to think any more," says when she sees Motes: "That Jesus-seeing hat!" When Motes rages to himself, he is actually praying without knowing it. His blasphemous words are punctuated with "Jesus" and "Jesus Christ Crucified." We do not know what O'Connor thought of Freud's vision of man, but apart from its atheistic implications it is quite compatible with her apparent psychology. She sees man as dualistic: torn between the conventional polarities of God and the devil, but further confused because the choice must be made in human terms, and the divine might share superficial similarities with the diabolical. Indeed, it is difficult for the average reader at times to distinguish between the two in her fiction. Freud's anatomy of the mind, involving a dynamic struggle of the conscious ego or self to maintain its individuality against the raging forces of the primitive unconscious and the highly repressive reservoir of civilization is a classic one. It is the struggle of Oedipus with his fate, the struggle of Hamlet with his, and, on a lesser dramatic level, the struggle of O'Connor's perverse saints with the saintly that is in them. It is not the devil they wish to defeat, but grace in them that prevents them from being "free." In all cases it is a struggle toward knowledge—forbidden knowledge. Freud's rationalism has alienated existential writers —Ionesco, for one—because his absolute commitment to a psychology that wants to explain the inexplicable runs counter to the age-old belief in the sanctity of the unconscious or of divine mystery. D. H. Lawrence, no existentialist, hated Freud for these reasons, and we might assume that O'Connor would have shared this reaction. Freud bears too close a resemblance to her intellectual parodies—Rayber of *The Violent Bear It Away* and Joy-Hulga, the Ph.D. with the wooden leg, in "Good Country People." But the constant seesawing between the conscious and the unconscious, the ego-dominated and the repressed, and, above all, the struggle of the ego to main-itself in a dreamlike world of abstractions made concrete (the usual machinery of the dream) is Freudian drama of a unique type.

What is original, at least for our time, is O'Connor's commitment to the divine origin of the unconscious. Despite her elegance as a stylist, she is a primitive; she insists that only through an initiation by violence does man "see." Paradoxically, it is after his blinding that Motes "sees"; he is also a murderer, but is that relevant? If the novel were realistic, yes, for in realistic or naturalistic fiction everything must be tabulated and accounted for. But if his murder of the fake Motes is seen to be a murder of that side of himself, then the purely symbolic nature of the story is made clear. Motes is an allegorical figure, however exaggerated and ridiculous. He represents contemporary man torn between the religion of his past (the Christianity of the modern West) and the religion of the present (the worship of science—the reliance upon sense-data). There can be no reconciliation of the two. If man cannot make a choice between them, as the completely adjusted have—those lucky people who no longer need to think—man must be destroyed. This is man as hero, however, and not as clown. O'Connor dresses her saints in outlandish costumes, gives both Motes and Tarwater absurd black preacher hats that signal their fates, and plays upon the reader's conventional feelings for these signs of oddness. As metaphysical device, the extreme intellectuality of these back-country preachers is not surprising; if they are taken as representatives of the South, they are unbelievable. O'Connor dares to present conventionally absurd figures as heroes and does not sentimentalize their plights. It is no wonder, then, that she is misunderstood. Her fiction seems to make no compromise with tradition, unless one assumes the larger tradition of Christianity. Saint Paul says that what he preaches is "foolishness" to the Greeks, who are rationalists; Tertullian insists upon the absurdity and impossibility and—for these reasons—the inevitability of Christ's death and resurrection; Duns Scotus preaches the primacy of the will over the intellect, contrary to Aquinas. It is necessary to be a misfit, the religious temperament has always told us. Catholicism presents a clear compromise between unbridled religious emotion and an orderly religious system. Had O'Connor not been born a Catholic, this combination of passion and order would surely have appealed to her, for this "rage for order" is evident in each of her works.

The ritualistic formality of *The Violent Bear It Away*
reveals tragic obsessions that are similar to Motes's. Here
the ritual that is demanded of the protagonist is not his
self-blinding, but an act of baptism on an idiot child. For
both Motes and Tarwater the ceremony is inevitable.
Everything in the novels insists upon it—the imagery in
Wise Blood of sight and blindness, and the imagery of
water in *The Violent Bear It Away*. The soul struggles to
assert its freedom, but in the very act of what should be
absolute freedom (the drowning of the child to be baptized) the baptismal ceremony is performed against Tarwater's conscious will. He is initiated into the knowledge
that he does not own his soul. He is not in control of himself, despite the hopeful words of the rationalist and athe-
ist, Rayber. Instead, it is just as he secretly feared all
along, that his hunger for the bread of life is "hidden in
the blood . . . and the bottom of his stomach [split out]
so that nothing would heal or fill it but the bread of life."

The structure of the novel insists upon a classic predestination. Its first paragraph tells us something that
Tarwater will not learn until the conclusion of the novel,
and this knowledge—that his uncle's corpse, which he
tried to burn, has been buried with a cross by the grave—
will destroy Tarwater completely. His mad old uncle
warns him about strangers: "You are the kind of boy,"
the old man says back in Chapter Two, "that the devil is
always going to be offering to assist, to give you a smoke
or a drink or a ride. . . . You had better mind how you
take up with strangers." At the conclusion of the novel he
unwisely accepts a ride with a stranger, who drugs and
rapes him. The novel, which deals with prophecy, has
many small prophecies like these embedded in its early
pages. The sinister stranger is anticipated by Tarwater's

153

"other self," his apparently rational self, which tries to talk him out of burying his uncle and out of his "destiny" of baptism. This stranger's face is "sharp and friendly and wise, shadowed under a stiff broad-brimmed panama hat." When Tarwater repeats his uncle's remark, "Jesus or the devil," the stranger corrects him. "It's Jesus or *you*," he says. Thus the rational side of Tarwater is linked with the devil, and this is supposedly quite a literal devil: he will appear in person in Chapter Eleven, with a "lavender shirt and a thin black suit and a panama hat." Tarwater thinks vaguely that there is "something familiar to him in the look of the stranger." Given liquor to drink by him, Tarwater says recklessly that it is "better than the Bread of Life!" Back in Part I, when he drank some moonshine, he felt as if the "devil were already reaching inside him to finger his soul." He has uncorked the bottle with the corkscrew given him by his Uncle Rayber, saying proudly, "This here thing will open anything." Symbolically, O'Connor is saying here that the gimmicky corkscrew, gift of the would-be skeptic, can open only trouble: it is a product of a technological civilization and, as such, provides a sleazy commentary upon its origin. Faith in rationality leads to a betrayal of the self. Because Tarwater has tried to reject his destiny, he is raped by the devil himself.

The prophecy with which the book ends, "Go warn the children of God of the terrible speed of mercy," has been anticipated back in Chapter Two with the uncle's raging prophecies: "Go warn the children of God . . . of the terrible speed of justice." And when Tarwater is first confronted with the idiot child he must baptize, it is over a telephone (significantly), and though he cannot know who has lifted up the receiver, he hears breathing on the other end of the line, "a kind of bubbling noise, the kind of noise someone would make who was struggling to breathe in water." The fates of Tarwater and Bishop, the idiot child, are certainly predetermined; they can only act out their roles. Hearing the sound, Tarwater "seemed to have been stunned by some deep internal blow that had not yet made its way to the surface of his mind."

O'Connor would need this ceremonial, formal structure even if her temperament did not incline her naturally toward it, for the extremities of behavior in her writing demand a closely knit, even classical confinement. More than this, the religious commitment itself demands a ceremonial approach. As Sister Bernetta comments: ". . . what constitutes a Catholic writer is the realization that for such a person history leads up to and away from what happened on Calvary the first Good Friday."[3] If this is so, then the historical event can only be realized through ritual, for it is no longer available to the Christian in its historical reality. Through the use of ritual, the temporal is united with the eternal, and it is this juxtaposition—so reluctantly approached by O'Connor's saints —that is necessary. She is not a clever satirist of modern society, for clearly she does not care for the temporal except as a contrast to the eternal; Philip Rahv in his introduction to *Wise Blood* in *Eight Great American Short Novels* echoes many New York-oriented critics in saying that she "has created . . . small masterpieces of life in the Southern hinterland,"[4] when it is obvious to anyone who has lived in the South that this is not true at all. The initiation of man into the presence of the divine demands not only a surrealistic style but a surrealistic landscape, for man cannot step out of a familiar environment and into the world of Christ and the prophets. O'Connor did not try, evidently, to subject ordinary, psychologically "real" people to religious violence. "A Temple of the Holy Ghost," perhaps, and "Revelation" deal with recognizable people, but these stories are by no means realistic. The grotesque vision cannot work except in certain selected areas of life: note the sudden jarring incongruity of Rayber's hope to send young Tarwater to college!

The drama of *Wise Blood* is made more complex in *The Violent Bear It Away*. Here the central figure, Tarwater, doomed to baptize and to murder, shares Motes's conflict between the ego and the unconscious, but these two powerful forces are externalized in the novel. The ego, the rational, striving self, is represented by the schoolteacher, Rayber. He is treated in a surprisingly sympathetic way by O'Connor, though we know that behind his skepticism is a hopeless obsession with the very faith he preaches against. A product of a mechanized civilization that has explained everything, Rayber wears glasses and a hearing aid, goes to restaurants, writes up the mad old uncle in a magazine, and presents Tarwater with the symbolic present of the corkscrew that can "open up anything." The offspring of the schoolteacher and the social worker is, significantly, an idiot child. Where most Southern writers use the idiot child to represent the ingrown decadence of the society, O'Connor uses it to represent the ignorance of a society committed to reason: "The Dream of Reason Breeds Monsters."

Opposed to the schoolteacher is the old uncle, a prophet, preacher, and moonshiner. Old Tarwater's domain is the child's unconscious mind, and O'Connor has said that she is on the old man's side because Christ is the center of his life. One might wish, perhaps, that in her zeal to correct misunderstandings she had not so drastically simplified her marvelously complex novel. For Old Tarwater, though a man of God, is at the same time responsible for the child's perversion; unless religious feeling must be absolutely linked with insanity, it is difficult to believe that the old uncle is a positive character. Rather, it would seem that he is responsible as much as Rayber for the violence of Tarwater's initiation into his "destiny." He himself is outraged at the schoolteacher's attempt to psychoanalyze him and thus nullify his alliance with God, but his world is one in which the Atonement does not seem to have worked; it is the atmosphere of the Old Testament, haunted by senseless violence. The child Tarwater feels this:

He knew he was called to be a prophet and that the ways of his prophecy would not be remarkable. . . . The Lord out of dust had created him, had made him blood and nerve and mind, had made him to bleed and weep and think, and set him in a world of loss and fire all to baptize one idiot child that He need not have created in the first place and to cry out a gospel just as foolish.[5]

The characters struggle together, the absence of the old uncle being more powerful, finally, than the presence of the young uncle. Thus Tarwater rows the child out to drown him, but in drowning him he cries out the words of baptism. Here we have the paradox, which Kierkegaard probes, of the sacred operating simultaneously with the ethically evil. Tarwater can rationalize that the murder offsets the baptism, but his doom is complete when he is attacked by the stranger and then returns home to discover his uncle's body miraculously buried beneath a cross. At the end we see him, with fire raging in the background, moving steadily on to the "dark city, where the children of God lay sleeping." An appropriate prophet— a madman and a murderer, as well as a child of God—for the slumbering modern world?

"The River," a comparatively neglected story, also deals with baptism. Two worlds are contrasted: the world of the child's parents, who live in an apartment that smells of stale cigarette butts, where "everything was a joke," and the world of the red muddy river—the domain of the fervent young preacher and the believers who surround him, where nothing said or done is a joke. As soon as the child is taken out of the apartment by the woman in charge of him for the day, he changes his name; he adopts the name of the preacher they are going to hear, "Bevel." When told that the preacher is a healer, he immediately asks, "Will he heal me?" The description of the preacher and the river baptism is magnificent. O'Connor's admiration for the young fundamentalist preacher is obvious; she ascribes to him a rich, melodic talent for preaching, so that the contagious effect of the ceremony is understandable:

"There ain't but one river and that's the River of Life, made out of Jesus' Blood. . . . All the rivers come from that one River and go back to it like it was the ocean sea and if you believe, you can lay your pain in that River and get rid of it because that's the River that was made to carry sin. It's a River full of pain itself, pain itself, moving toward the Kingdom of Christ, to be washed away, slow, you people, slow as this here old red water river round my feet. . . ."[6]

The preacher Bevel and the child Bevel are joined in the ritual of baptism, and the river is more than a metaphorical river for the child's imagination. When the preacher says, "If I baptize you, you'll be able to go to the Kingdom of Christ. You'll be washed in the river of suffering, son, and you'll go by the deep river of life," the child thinks, "I won't go back to the apartment, then, I'll go under the river." The child is baptized into his new life while on the river bank a scoffing old man, Mr. Paradise, watches. "Choose Jesus or the devil!" the preacher demands, suggesting that Mr. Paradise is the devil here. Readers may find alarming the concrete imagination of O'Connor's fiction, where the devil may very well turn up in person to witness a baptism and, later, to tempt the innocent.

When the child is returned to his parents, he is not the same child. He now "counts," where he did not count before. His mother discovers the book he has taken from the woman's home—"The Life of Jesus Christ for Readers Under Twelve"—and reads it mockingly to her guests, who are properly amused by it. The child runs away from home the next morning and returns to the river, where nothing is a joke. Followed by the sinister Mr. Paradise, who carries a peppermint stick with which to tempt the child, he walks into the river: "He intended not to fool with preachers any more but to baptize himself and to keep on going this time until he found the Kingdom of Christ in the river." He turns to see something like a "giant pig bounding after him"—Mr. Paradise, a pig like those shown cast out by Jesus in the child's book—and he plunges into the river and is drawn away by it. O'Connor's deft, blunt strokes suggest here mythical characterizations rather than characters. On one level the story is ironic, but on a higher level it is deadly serious: it is about the capacity for innocence to choose between two worlds without hesitation, rejecting the sensual, materialistic world of Mr. Paradise and the city people, and accepting the world of Christ that is attainable only through death.

III

The greatest of Flannery O'Connor's books is her last, posthumously published collection of stories, *Everything That Rises Must Converge*. Though it is customary to interpret O'Connor's allusion to the philosophy of Teilhard de Chardin as ironic, it seems to me that there is no irony involved. There are many small ironies in these nine stories, certainly, and they are comic-grotesque and flamboyant and heartbreaking—but no ultimate irony is intended and the book is not a tragic one. It is a collection of revelations; like all revelations, it points to a dimension of experiential truth that lies outside the sphere of the questing, speculative mind, but is nevertheless available to all.

The "psychic interpenetrability" of which Teilhard speaks in *The Phenomenon of Man* determines that man, in "rising" to a higher consciousness, will of necessity coalesce into a unity that is basically a phenomenon of mind (hence of man, since only man possesses self-consciousness). It is misleading to emphasize Teilhard's optimism at the expense of his cautious consideration of what he calls the "doctrine by isolation"[7] and the "cynical and brutal theories" of the contemporary world; O'Connor has dramatized the tragic consequences of the locked-in ego in earlier fiction, but in *Everything That Rises Must Converge* nearly every story addresses itself to the problem of bringing to consciousness the latent horror, making manifest the Dream of Reason—which is, of course, a nightmare. It is a measure of her genius that she can so easily and so skillfully evoke the spiritual while dealing in a very concrete, very secular world of fragmentary people.

Despite her rituals of baptism by violence, and her apparently merciless subjecting of ordinary "good" people to extraordinary fates, O'Connor sees the world as an incarnation of spirit; she has stated that the art of fiction itself is "very much an incarnational art."[8] In a way she shares the burdens of her fanatical preachers Motes and Tarwater: she sees herself as writing from a prophetic vision, as a "realist of distances."[9] Her people are not quite whole until violence makes them whole. They must suffer amazing initiations, revelations nearly as physically brutal as those in Kafka—one might explore the similarities between Parker of "Parker's Back" and the heroic, doomed officer of "In the Penal Colony"—because their way into the spiritual is through the physical; the way into O'Connor's dimension of the sacred is through the secular or vulgar. Teilhard's rising of consciousness into a mysterious Super-Life, in which the multiplicity of the world driven to seek unity through love, assumes a mystical "gravity of bodies"[10] that must have appealed to O'Connor's sacramental imagination. Fundamental to the schoolteacher Rayber's insistence upon rationality is his quite justified terror of the unconscious—he must act out of his thinking, calculating, mechanical ego simply in order to resist the gravity that threatens to carry him out of himself; otherwise he will become another "fanatic," another victim of that love that is hidden in the blood—in this specific instance, in terms of Christ. The local, human tragedy is, then, the highly conscious resisting of the Incarnation. As human beings (who are fragments) resist the gravity that should bring them into a unity, they emphasize their isolation, their helplessness, and can be delivered from the trance of self only by violence.

Paradoxically, the way into O'Connor's vision that is least ambiguous is through a story that has not received much attention, "The Lame Shall Enter First." This fifty-seven-page story is a reworking of the nuclear fable of *The Violent Bear It Away*, and since O'Connor explored the tensions between the personalities of the rationalist-liberal and the object of his charity at such length in the novel, she is free to move swiftly and bluntly here. "We are accustomed to consider," says Teilhard in "Beyond the Collective," a discussion of the energies of love, "only the sentimental face of love. . . ."[11] In "The Lame Shall Enter First" it is this sentimental love that brings disaster to the would-be savior, Sheppard. He is a young white-haired City Recreational Director who, on Saturdays, works as a counselor at a boys' reformatory; since his wife's death he has moved out of their bedroom and lives an ascetic, repressed life, refusing even to fully acknowledge his love for his son. Befriending the crippled, exasperating Rufus Johnson, Sheppard further neglects his own son, Norton, and is forced to realize that his entire conception of himself has been hypocritical. O'Connor underscores the religious nature of his experience by calling it a *revelation*: Sheppard hears his own voice "as if it were the voice of his accuser." Though he closes his eyes against the revelation, he cannot elude it:

His heart constricted with a repulsion for himself so clear and intense that he gasped for breath. He had stuffed his own emptiness with good works like a glutton. He had ignored his own child to feed his vision of himself. He saw the clear-eyed Devil, the sounder of hearts, leering at him. . . . His image of himself shrivelled until everything was black before him. He sat there paralyzed, aghast.

Sheppard then wakes from his trance and runs to his son, but even as he hurries to the boy he imagines Norton's face "transformed; the image of his salvation; all light," and the reader sees that even at this dramatic point Sheppard is deluded. It is still *his* salvation he desires, *his* experience of the transformation of his son's misery into joy. Therefore it is poetically just that his change of heart leads to nothing, to no joyous reconciliation. He rushes up to the boy's room and discovers that Norton has hanged himself.

The boy's soul has been "launched . . . into space"; like Bishop of *The Violent Bear It Away*, he is a victim of the tensions between two ways of life, two warring visions. In the image of Christ there is something "mad" and "stinking" and catastrophic, at least in a secularized civilization; in the liberal, manipulative humanitarianism of the modern world there is that "clear-eyed Devil" who cuts through all bonds, all mystery, all "psychical convergence" that cannot be reduced to simplistic sociological formulas. It is innocence that is destroyed. The well-intentioned savior, Sheppard, has acted only to fill his own vacuity; his failure as a true father results in his son's suicide.

He had stuffed his own emptiness with good works like a glutton.

Perhaps this is O'Connor's judgment, blunt and final, upon our civilization. Surely she is sympathetic with Teilhard's rejection of egoism as the last desperate attempt of the world of matter—in its fragmentary forms, "individuals"—to persist in its own limited being. In discussing the evolutionary process of love, the rising-to-consciousness of individuals through love, Teilhard analyzes the motives for "the fervour and impotence" that accompany every egoistic solution of life:

In trying to separate itself as much as possible from others, the element individualizes itself; but in so doing it becomes retrograde and seeks to drag the world backwards toward plurality and into matter. In fact it diminishes itself and loses itself. . . . The peak of ourselves, the acme of our originality, is not our individuality but our person; and according to the evolutionary structure of the world, we can only find our person by uniting together.[12]

What is difficult, perhaps, is to see how the humanitarian impulse—when it is not spiritual—is an egoistic activity. O'Connor's imagination is like Dostoyevsky's: politically reactionary but spiritually fierce, combative, revolutionary. If the liberal, atheistic, man-centered society of modern times is dedicated to manipulating others in order to "save" them, to transform them into flattering images of its own ego, then there is no love involved—there is no true merging of selves but only a manipulative aggression. This kind of love is deadly, because it believes itself to be selfless; it is the sudden joy of the intellectual Julian, in the story "Everything That Rises Must Converge," when he sees that his mother is about to be humiliated by a black woman who is wearing the same outrageously ugly hat his mother has bought—"His grin hardened until it said to her as plainly as if he were saying aloud: Your punishment exactly fits your pettiness. This should teach

164

you a permanent lesson." The lesson his mother gets, however, is fatal: the permanence of death.

"He thinks he's Jesus Christ!" the clubfooted juvenile delinquent, Rufus Johnson, exclaims of Sheppard. He thinks he is divine, when in fact he is empty; he tries to stuff himself with what he believes to be good works in order to disguise the terrifying fact of his own emptiness. For O'Connor *this* is the gravest sin. Her madmen, thieves, misfits, and murderers commit crimes of a secular nature, against other men; they are not so sinful as the criminals who attempt to usurp the role of the divine. In Kafka's words, "They . . . attempted to realize the happiness of mankind without the aid of grace."[13] It is an erecting of the tower of Babel upon the finite, earthly Wall of China: a ludicrous act of folly.

O'Connor's writing is so stark and, for many readers, so difficult to absorb into a recognizable world because it insists upon a brutal distinction between what Augustine would call the City of Man and the City of God. One can reject O'Connor's fierce insistence upon this separation—as I must admit I do—and yet sympathize with the terror that must be experienced when these two "realms" of being are imagined as distinct. For, given the essentially Manichaean dualism of the secular and the sacred, man is forced to choose between them: he cannot comfortably live in both "cities." Yet his body, especially if it is a diseased and obviously, immediately, *perpetually* mortal body, forces him to realize that he is existing in that City of Man, at every instant that he is not so spiritually chaste as to be in the City of God. Therefore life is a struggle; the natural, ordinary world is either sacramental (and ceremonial) or profane (and vulgar). And it follows from this that the diseased body is not only an affirmation, or a symbolic intensification of, the spiritual "disease" that attends physical processes; it becomes a matter of one's personal salvation—Jung would use the term "individuation"—to interpret the accidents of the flesh in terms of the larger, unfathomable, but ultimately *no more abstract* pattern that links the self to the cosmos. This is a way of saying that for Flannery O'Connor (as for Kafka and for D. H. Lawrence) the betrayal of the body, its loss of normal health, must be seen as necessary; it must make sense. *Wise Blood,* ironically begun before O'Connor suffered her first attack of the disease that ultimately killed her, a disease inherited from her father, makes the point dramatically and lyrically that the "blood" is "wise." And rebellion is futile against it. Thus, the undulant fever suffered by the would-be writer, Asbury, is not only directly and medically attributable to *his* rash behavior (drinking unpasteurized milk, against his mother's rules of the dairy), but it becomes the means by which he realizes a revelation he would not otherwise have experienced. Here, O'Connor affirms a far more primitive and far more brutal sense of fate than Teilhard would affirm—at least as I understand Teilhard—for in the physical transformation of man into a higher consciousness and finally into a collective, Godlike "synthesized state,"[14] the transformation is experienced in terms of a space/time series of events, but is in fact (if it could be a demonstrable or measurable "fact") one single event: one phenomenon. Therefore, the "physical" is not really a lower form of the spiritual but is experienced as being lower or earlier in evolution, and the fear of or contempt for the body expressed by Augustine is simply a confusion. The physical *is* also spiritual; the physical only *seems* not to be "spiritual." Though this sounds perplexing, it is really a way of saying that Augustine (and perhaps O'Connor, who was very much influenced by Augustine and other Catholic theologians) prematurely denied the sacredness of the body, as if it were a hindrance and not the only means by which the spirit can attain its "salvation." Useless to rage against his body's deterioration, Lawrence says sadly and nobly, because that body was the only means by which D. H. Lawrence could have appeared in the world. But this is not at all what O'Connor does, for in her necessary and rather defiant acceptance of her inherited disease in terms of its being, perhaps, a kind of original sin and therefore not an accident—somehow obscurely willed either by God or by O'Connor herself (if we read "The Enduring Chill" as a metaphor for O'Connor's predicament)—we are forced to affirm the disease-as-revelation:

The boy [Asbury] fell back on his pillow and stared at the ceiling. His limbs that had been racked for so many weeks by fever and chill were number now. The old life in him was exhausted. He awaited the coming of new. It was then that he felt the beginning of a chill, a chill so peculiar, so light, that it was like a warm ripple across a deeper sea of cold. . . . Asbury blanched and the last film of illusion was torn as if by a whirlwind from his eyes. He saw that for the rest of his days, frail, racked, but enduring, he would live in the face of a purifying terror. A feeble cry, a last impossible protest escaped him. But the Holy Ghost, emblazoned in ice instead of fire, continued, implacable, to descend.

("The Enduring Chill")

This particular story and its epiphany may not have the aesthetic power to move us that belongs to O'Connor's more sharply imagined works, but it is central to an understanding of all of her writing, and like Lawrence's

"Ship of Death," it has a beauty and a terrible dignity that carry it beyond criticism. For while Teilhard's monumental work stresses the uniqueness of the individual through his absorption in a larger, and ultimately divine "ultimate earth," there cannot be in his work the dramatization of the real, living, bleeding, suffering, *existing* individual O'Connor knows so well. She knows this existing individual from the inside and not from the outside; she knows that while the historical and sociological evolution causes one group of people to "rise" (the blacks; the haughty black woman in "Everything That Rises Must Converge"), it is also going to destroy others (both Julian and his mother, who evidently suffers a stroke when the black woman hits her), and she also knows—it is this point, I believe, missed by those critics who are forever stressing her "irony"—that *the entire process is divine.* Hence her superficially reactionary attitude toward the secularized, liberal, godless society, and her affirmation of the spontaneous, the irrational, the wisdom of the blood in which, for her, Christ somehow is revealed. Because she does believe and states clearly[15] that her writing is an expression of her religious commitment, and is itself a kind of divine distortion ("the kind that reveals, or should reveal," as she remarks in the essay "Novelist and Believer"), the immediate problem for most critics is *how* to wrench her work away from her, *how* to show that she didn't at all know herself, but must be subjected to a higher, wiser, more objective consciousness in order to be understood. But the amazing thing about O'Connor is that she seems to have known exactly what she was doing and how she might best accomplish it. There is no ultimate irony in her work, no ultimate despair or pessimism or tragedy, and certainly not a paradoxical sympathy for the devil.[16] It is only when O'Connor is judged from a secular point of view, or from a "rational" point of view, that she seems unreasonable—a little mad—and must be chastely revised by the liberal imagination.

"Everything That Rises Must Converge" is a story in which someone appears to lose, and to lose mightily; but the "loss" is fragmentary, a necessary and minor part of the entire process of "converging" that is the entire universe—or God. The son, Julian, is then released to the same "entry into the world of guilt and sorrow" that is Rayber's and Sheppard's, and his surrender to the emotions he has carefully refined into ironic, cynical, "rational" ideas is at the same time his death (as an enlightened ego) and his birth (as a true adult). So many of the stories in this volume deal literally with the strained relationships between one generation and another, because this is a way of making explicit the psychological problem of ascending to a higher self. In *A Good Man Is Hard to Find,* the tensions were mainly between strangers and in terms of very strange gods. The life you save *may* be your own, and if you cannot bear the realization that a freak is a temple of the Holy Ghost, that is unfortunate for you. As Rufus Johnson says of the Bible, superbly and crazily, *Even if I didn't believe it, it would still be true*—a reply meant to infuriate the rationalist Sheppard, and no doubt most of us. But O'Connor's art is both an existential dramatization of what it means to suffer and a deliberate series of parodies of that subjectivist philosophy loosely called "existentialism"— though it is the solipsistic, human-value-oriented existentialism she obviously despises, Sartrean and not Kierkegaardian. The deist may say "Whatever is, is right," but the deist cannot prove the truth of his statement, for such truths or revelations can only be experienced by an exist-ing, suffering individual whom some violent shock has catapulted into the world of sorrow. When the intellec-tual Julian suffers the real loss of his mother, the real Julian emerges; his self-pitying depression vanishes at once; the faith he had somehow lost "in the midst of his martyrdom" is restored. So complex and so powerful a story cannot be reduced to any single meaning; but it is surely O'Connor's intention to show how the egoistic Julian is a spokesman for an entire civilization, and to demonstrate the way by which this civilization will—in-evitably, horribly—be jolted out of its complacent, worldly cynicism. *By violence.* And by no other way, because the ego cannot be destroyed except violently; it cannot be argued out of its egoism by words, by any logical argu-ment; it cannot be instructed in anything except a phys-ical manner. O'Connor would have felt a kinship with the officer of Kafka's "In the Penal Colony," who yearns for an enlightenment that can come only through his own body, through a sentence tattooed on his body. As Christ suffered with his real, literal body, so O'Connor's people must suffer in order to realize Christ in them.

Yet it is not finally necessary to share O'Connor's specific religious beliefs in order to appreciate her art. Though she would certainly refute me in saying this, the "Christ" experience itself may well be interpreted as a psychological event that is received by the individual according to his private expectations. No writer obses-sively works and reworks a single theme that is without deep personal meaning, so it is quite likely that O'Connor experienced mystical "visions" or insights that she inter-preted according to her Catholicism; her imagination was visual and literal, and she is reported to have said of the

Eucharist that if it were only a symbol, "I'd say to hell with it."[17] This childlike or primitive rejection of a psychic event—*only* a symbol!—as if it were somehow less real than a physical event gives to O'Connor's writing that curious sense of blunt, graphic impatience, the either/or of fanaticism and genius, that makes it difficult for even her most sympathetic critics to relate her to the dimension of psychological realism explored by the traditional novel. Small obscenities or cruelties in the work of John Updike, for instance, have a power to upset us in a way that gross fantastic acts of violence in O'Connor do not, for we read O'Connor as a writer of parables and Updike as an interpreter of the way we actually live. Yet, because she is impatient with the City of Man except as it contrasts with the City of God, she can relate her localized horrors to a larger harmony that makes everything, however exaggerated, somehow contained within a compact vision.

The triumph of "Revelation" is its apparently natural unfolding of a series of quite extraordinary events, so that the impossibly smug, self-righteous Mrs. Turpin not only experiences a visual revelation but is prepared for it, demands it, and is equal to it in spite of her own bigotry. Another extraordinary aspect of the story is the protagonist's assumption—an almost automatic assumption—that the vicious words spoken to her by a deranged girl in a doctor's waiting room ("Go back to hell where you came from, you old wart hog") are in fact the words of Christ, intended for her alone. Not only is the spiritual world a literal, palpable fact, but the physical world—of other people, of objects and events—becomes transparent, only a means by which the "higher" judgment is delivered. It is a world of meanings, naturalistic details

171

crowded one upon another until they converge into a higher significance; an antinaturalistic technique, perhaps, but one that is firmly based in the observed world. O'Connor is always writing about original sin and the ways we may be delivered from it, and therefore she does not—cannot—believe in the random innocence of naturalism, which states that all men are innocent and are victims of inner or outer accidents. The naturalistic novel, which attempts to render the "real" world in terms of its external events, must hypothesize an interior randomness that is a primal innocence, antithetical to the Judaeo-Christian culture. O'Connor uses many of the sharply observed surfaces of the world, but her medieval sense of *correspondentia*, or the ancient "sympathy of all things," forces her to severely restrict her subject matter, compressing it to one or two physical settings and a few hours' duration. Since revelation can occur at any time and sums up, at the same time that it eradicates, all of a person's previous life, there is nothing claustrophobic about the doctor's waiting room, "which was very small," but which becomes a microcosm of an entire godless society.

"Revelation" falls into two sections. The first takes place in the doctor's waiting room; the second takes place in a pig barn. Since so many who live now are diseased, it is significant that O'Connor chooses a doctor's waiting room for the first half of Mrs. Turpin's revelation, and it is significant that Gospel hymns are being played over the radio, almost out of earshot, incorporated into the mechanical vacant listlessness of the situation: "When I looked up and He looked down . . . And wona these days I know I'll we-eara crown." Mrs. Turpin glances over the room, notices white-trashy people who are "worse than niggers any day," and begins a conversation with a well-dressed lady who is accompanying her daughter: the girl, on the verge of a breakdown, is reading a book called *Human Development,* and it is this book that will strike Mrs. Turpin in the forehead. Good Christian as she imagines herself, Mrs. Turpin cannot conceive of human beings except in terms of class, and is obsessed by a need to continually categorize others and speculate upon her position in regard to them. The effort is so exhausting that she often ends up dreaming "they were all crammed in together in a box car, being ridden off to be put in a gas oven." O'Connor's chilling indictment of Mrs. Turpin's kind of Christianity grows out of her conviction that the displacement of Christ will of necessity result in murder, but that the "murder" is a slow steady drifting rather than a conscious act of will.

The ugly girl, blue-faced with acne, explodes with rage at the inane bigotry expressed by Mrs. Turpin and throws the textbook at her. She loses all control and attacks Mrs. Turpin; held down, subdued, her face "churning," she seems to Mrs. Turpin to know her "in some intense and personal way, beyond time and place and condition." And the girl's eyes lighten, as if a door that had been tightly closed was now open "to admit light and air." Mrs. Turpin steels herself, as if awaiting a revelation: and indeed the revelation comes. Mary Grace, used here by O'Connor as the instrument through which Christ speaks, bears some resemblance to other misfits in O'Connor's stories —not the rather stylish, shabby-glamorous men, but the pathetic overeducated, physically unattractive girls like Joy-Hulga of "Good Country People." That O'Connor identifies with these girls is obvious; it is *she,* through

Mary Grace, who throws that textbook on human development at all of us, striking us in the foreheads, hopefully to bring about a change in our lives.

Mrs. Turpin is shocked, but strangely courageous. It is rare in O'Connor that an obtuse, unsympathetic character ascends to a higher level of self-awareness; indeed, she shows more courage than O'Connor's intellectual young men. She has been called a wart hog from hell and her vision comes to her in the pig barn, where she stands above the hogs that appear to "pant with a secret life." It is these hogs, the secret panting mystery of life itself, that finally allow Mrs. Turpin to realize her vision. She seems to absorb from them some "abysmal life-giving knowledge," and at sunset she stares into the sky, where she sees

. . . a vast swinging bridge extending upward from the earth through a field of living fire. Upon it a vast horde of souls were rumbling toward heaven. There were whole companies of white-trash, clean for the first time in their lives, and bands of black niggers in white robes, and battalions of freaks and lunatics shouting and clapping and leaping like frogs. And bringing up the end of the procession was a tribe of people whom she recognized at once as those who, like herself and Claud, had always had a little of everything. . . . They were marching behind the others with great dignity, accountable as they always had been for good order and common sense and respectable behavior. They alone were on key. Yet she could see by their shocked and altered faces that even their virtues were being burned away. . . .

This is the most powerful of O'Connor's revelations, because it questions the very foundations of our assumptions of the ethical life. It is not simply our "virtues" that will be burned away, but our rational faculties as well, and perhaps even the illusion of our separate, isolated egos. There is no way in which the ego can confront Mrs. Turpin's vision except as she does—"her eyes small but fixed unblinkingly on what lay ahead." Like Teilhard, O'Connor is ready to acquiesce in the evolution of a form of higher consciousness that may be forcing itself into the world *at our expense*; as Old Tarwater says, after he is struck and silenced by fire, "even the mercy of the Lord burns." Man cannot remain what he is; he cannot exist without being transformed. We are confronted, says Teilhard, with two directions and only two: one upward and the other downward.

Either nature is closed to our demands for futurity, in which case thought, the fruit of millions of years of effort, is stifled, still-born in a self-abortive and absurd universe. Or else an opening exists—that of the super-soul above our souls; but in that case the way out, if we are to agree to embark upon it, must open out freely onto limitless psychic spaces in a universe to which we can unhesitatingly entrust ourselves.[18]

O'Connor's people are forced into the upward direction, sometimes against their wills, sometimes because their wills have been burned clean and empty. Rayber, who has concentrated his love for mankind into a possessive, exaggerated love for an idiot child, is forced to contemplate a future without the "raging pain, the intolerable hurt that was his due"; he is at the core of O'Connor's vision, a human being who has suffered a transformation but who survives. The wisdom of the body speaks in us, even when it reveals to us a terrifying knowledge of original sin, a perversion of the blood itself.

O'Connor's revelations concern the mystic origin of religious experience absolutely immune to any familiar labels of "good" and "evil." Her perverted saints are Kierkegaardian knights of the "absurd" for whom ordinary human behavior is impossible. Like young Tarwater, horrified at having said an obscenity, they are "too fierce to brook impurities of such a nature." They are, like O'Connor herself, "intolerant of unspiritual evils. . . ." There is no patience in O'Connor for a systematic, refined, rational acceptance of God; and of the gradual transformation of apocalyptic religious experience into dogma, she is strangely silent. Her world is that surreal primitive landscape in which the unconscious is a determining quantity that the conscious cannot defeat, because it cannot recognize. In fact, there is nothing to be recognized—in Kafka's words, there is only an experience to be suffered.[19]

7

THE TELEOLOGY
OF THE
UNCONSCIOUS:

The Art of
Norman Mailer

Here is the real core of the religious problem:
Help! Help!
> William James
> in *Varieties of Religious Experience*

Unloose my stasis.
> Mailer:
> D. J. in *Why Are We in Vietnam?*

Norman Mailer's efforts to dramatize the terror of the disintegrating identity have largely been mistaken as self-display, and his highly stylized, poetic, image-making structures of language have often been mistaken as willful and perverse hallucinations, instead of countermagic. Though I disagree with nearly every one of Mailer's stated or implied ideas, I am always conscious in reading his work that the stasis he dramatizes is a vast, communal tragedy, and that one does not eradicate suffering by declaring that it does not exist or that it fulfills a cosmic design not yet available to us. He is a prophet of what might come to pass but that—perhaps because of the intensity and outrage of his own prophetic voice, among others—might never be a real danger to us, as our civilization moves into a contemplation of its own future, a bypassing of the apocalypse imminent in *An American Dream* in favor of the "ego-less," "atmosphere-less," "spooky" realm of the intellectualized spirit so beautifully described in *Of a Fire on the Moon*. He has never advertised himself as any kind of saint, but he aspires to a kind of native American clownish-savage innocence, the skeptical but horrified sensibility that could "get into" the workings of both Huck Finn as he contemplates the idlers and loafers who sadistically torture animals, and those idlers and loafers themselves; or, indeed, the kind of sensibility that could resurrect for us another Huck, in D.J. of *Why Are We in Vietnam?*—a boy who somehow embodies the blackness of Jim in himself, or the nervous white "experience" of blackness, and who, teamed with another version of Tom Sawyer, is leaving in the morning for Vietnam. Yet, saintliness, apart, Mailer still shares with another "prophet" of our time, Allen Ginsberg, the obsession of needing to dramatize the *self* in order to make the self truly public, communal, as well-trampled as a public park, and as democratic:

> I am the defense early warning radar system
> History will make this poem prophetic and its awful
>   silliness a hideous spiritual music.

> (Ginsberg)

Like Ginsberg, Mailer is obsessed with the need to trust his own deepest instincts, all the "omens," "hallucinations," "dreams," "visions," "breakthroughs," and varieties of magic translatable into language; he has said that the "unconscious . . . has an enormous teleological sense"

(*Advertisements for Myself*, p. 328), and all of his serious writing is an attempt to locate suitable images for the expression of an incandescent vision, which at times seems too white-hot, too brutal, for him to force into an aesthetic structure. He would therefore, and not immodestly, classify himself with those to whom the "selfness" of the "self" is no longer very significant—the "mystics, psychopaths, existentialists, saints, lovers, bullfighters" who are not made impotent but rather inspired by the possibilities of imminent death.[1]

I would like to examine Mailer's faith in the "teleological unconscious" as a revolt against what he sees to be the cancerous magic of the totalitarian mass-democracy and as an expression of his own intellectual stasis, which is symptomatic of a far-reaching malaise of the spirit: as passionate now as when Donne feared the "New Science," but no longer as necessary. Mailer's most important work is *Why Are We in Vietnam?*—an outrageous little masterpiece—and his most poetic, prophetic work is *Of a Fire on the Moon*, so a concentration on these books should help to illuminate Mailer's enormous autobiographical venture, a "self" in search of an author.

The Time of His Time

An evil time: "syphilization" (D.J.'s term, Huck Finn by way of James Joyce and Burroughs) has somehow come between us and the instinctive tenderness that should be ours, making fathers and sons small concentrations of murder, murderers united in order to sublimate the domestic murders they truly desire, and making men "killer brothers" instead of lovers. This time of dark, cancerous, wasteful magic is characterized by enormous "democracies" in which the mass media, mass morality, mass consciousness itself exist somehow outside of the individual, yet with the power to control him. Such a totalitarianism is, then, not political so much as spiritual. The air is filled with bland shouts, a mixture of radio and television voices, anonymous slogans and whisperings of commercialized love, commercialized hate, which the boy D.J., "Disc Jockey to America," imitates in this record of his own disintegration.

He is eighteen at the time of this "broadcast"— ". . . America, this is your own wandering troubadour brought right up to date, here to sell America its new handbook on how to live, how to live in this Electrox Edison world, all programmed out, Prononzo! . . ." (p. 8)—but the crucial event of his life occurred two years before, during an Alaskan safari when he experienced a Godly visitation. Mailer's belief in the possibilities of visions, and the need for us to face them—horrific as they may be—makes of *Why Are We in Vietnam?* an aesthetic equivalent of those clever plastic advertisements that seem to say one thing when viewed from a certain position and quite another when we walk a few feet farther. Thus, the novel is darkly comic and "obscene" the first time it is read, but every subsequent reading reinforces its tragic message.[2] Mailer must have considered alternate endings for the work, possibly a flash into the future that would reveal D.J., Ranald Jethrow Jellicoe Jethroe, a victim of the same killer instinct that seems to have electrified him into a new life—in other words, a corpse being shipped back to Dallas. But I think his decision to limit the work in this way makes it more deadly, for the reader is forced to interpret "D.J." as a voice at loose in the world, not a historical event; for me, at least, the destruction of D.J. is a foregone conclusion, since he is already destroyed as a human being.

In *City of Words: American Fiction, 1950–1970* (New York, 1971), the English critic Tony Tanner theorizes that there has been in American literature, along with its establishment of a realistic and at times "documentary" literary tradition, an "intermittent sense of the futility of pretending that the putative exactitude of words can ever measure up to the exact mystery of things" (p. 27). One could direct Tanner to the absolute confidence of an Emerson, a Thoreau, or a Whitman, but the tradition he is most concerned with is a darker one: how Melville drifts into silence, how Faulkner assigns heroism to those who merely "endure" (but assuredly do not write novels), how two decades of American novelists express doubts concerning the very existence of the world, let alone their value in it. Because an intelligent, abstract vision of the whole seems no longer possible, or not aesthetically imaginable, we are left with fragments—particles—books that are self-conscious "cities of words" and that ricochet off one another more often than they do off reality: ". . . forgive D.J. for acting like Dr. James Joyce, all junkies are the same, you know. Follow the hunt" (p. 126).

Mailer seems to me by far the best of the novelists who have constructed "language-systems," because he does so without the coyness, the small-boy innocence and cunning we flinch at in other, less disturbed novelists who are largely American sons of Nabokov, Borges, and Beckett; his maniac broadcast by way of D.J. (or D.J.'s alter ego somewhere in Harlem) is meant to be a real broadcast, a real communication to the public, and its hysterical scatology and obscenity are probably its most important

183

message. Later I will discuss Mailer's intellectual Manichaeanism, and his habit of erecting Aristotelian First Principles from which he descends to syllogistically logical but empirically illogical (in fact outrageous: see *The Prisoner of Sex*) deductions; here, I want to concentrate on the hypothetical existence of the "totalitarian" system, and what it demands of its sensitive victims.

It has always been characteristic of utopias or dystopias (in life as in literature) that they attempt to control history through a rewriting of the past, into book-packaged *trompe l'œil* forms of the type Winston Smith, in Orwell's 1984, was creating, or in fantastic poetic myths of the type Plato suggests in *The Republic*: a totalitarian poetry that would banish all other poetry. What is even more deathly for the individual is the System's control of his brain through the control of language, for if Benjamin Whorf and other linguists are correct,[3] one cannot have a thought without an adequate word or group of words to express it. Reality exists; death exists; injustice exists; I exist; and yet, without language, such forms of existence are totally inaccessible. (It might be parenthetically stated—and in an essay on Norman Mailer this is hardly a distraction—that the word *emasculate* has no corresponding "female" term; to realize this is to realize the ubiquitousness of forms of totalitarian thought-control.) Through the systematic control of language, the tyrannical powers at the center of the modern anonymous state seek to enclose the individual, to make him (in Marcuse's eerie metaphor) one-dimensional, like a playing card seen from the side. Mailer believes, and has believed for many years, that our civilization was founded on the "Faustian urge to dominate nature by mastering time, mastering the links of social cause and effect," and it is appropriate that his Texans, yearning for a return to a near-primitive state of hunting and risking death, are well equipped with powerful weapons and helicopters: the means by which the human being becomes a murdering machine in the very process of seeking his own salvation.

To assert himself against the oppressive language-system, then, the individual must be a kind of artist; he must attempt the creation of his own special language. To create a mythology in order to escape being enslaved by someone else's has been, perhaps, the dynamic urge behind much art, at least art created in a time of social confusion. Yet the irony is that D.J. can draw his language only out of the excremental flow all around him, and approximate its deadly desacralizing of the world in his own head (the entire novel is told as he and his friend Tex are enduring a "going-away" dinner in Dallas): exactly the opposite in effect, but similar in strategy, to D.J.'s counterparts who chant mantras several thousand times a day to purify themselves of the soiled world, their heads shaven, their faces beatific; the Hare Krishna devotees who alarm and mystify shoppers in large Western cities.

Mailer stated in *The Armies of the Night* that he felt most like an American when he was "naturally obscene," and so, after years of keeping obscene language out of his work, he decided to return again to a use of obscenity: "so discovering everything he knew about the American language," but also asserting Mailer as Mailer, a defiant American son setting himself against his bland elders. Here, it seems to me, Mailer characteristically underestimates himself,[4] inviting us to take D.J.'s language as "very literary in the best way" (Mailer's words) when, in fact, the dynamic core of *Why Are We in Vietnam?*

is a plea for help, for a real language, for an adult sensibility that will save D.J. from the hell inside his head. For the real message of the novel is that a belief in a tyrannical System forces an intelligent person to regress to personal and racial aggressions of the most infantile sort, through which glimmerings of a vital intelligence may be seen (as if the wasted genius of Swift, "dying from the top down," occasionally expressed itself in the old Swiftian language)—the obscenity without this intelligence being simply tiresome, dead.

To be a mature adult in our society, one usually surrenders the privileges and limitations of adolescence; but to get back into a more vital self, as Twain and Salinger (in all his works) have shown, one must sometimes go back into adolescence, though with a conscious adult sensitivity. It must always be the adolescent as Antiadult, not the adolescent as Preadult, who has the power to analyze, to judge the adult world. It is true, obviously, that adolescents do express judgments, many of them negative, on the adult world, but they do so without having been adults; Huckleberry Finn, Holden Caulfield, Alex (of A *Clockwork Orange*—another "city of words"), and Mailer's boy are adults-as-adolescents, vehicles for adult writers who feel, for reasons that may be psychological as well as literary, that they *must* go back in order to possess the freedom to tell what they see of the truth. The childhood and early adolescence of boys is characterized by a fascination with obscenity and other taboos, as if the expression of such things were a magical shortcut into adulthood, as well as a way of defining their powers and setting them apart from girls. (When the "girls" appropriate this language, the "boys" are demoralized and frightened—as Mailer is shocked by the militant women and their exuberant use of obscenity; see *The Prisoner of Sex.*) In our culture this behavior is probably normal, or at least it is commonplace; only when it persists into adulthood does it become peculiar, and of course one symptom of a disturbed mind is an obsession with filth. Mailer seems to be suggesting that the "poetry" of our troubled, self-despising time is D.J.'s medley of voices, and that the regression of the adult into the adolescent is a doomed defiance. Certainly, in *The Armies of the Night,* he is very honest about his own aesthetic disdain for the "drug-vitiated jargon-mired children" all about him—involved in a mass protest movement that, like the Space Program and its egoless components of men and machines, somehow excludes Mailer and the entire Romantic tradition of the inventive imagination. In *Cannibals and Christians* Mailer remarks: ". . . the obsession of many of us with scatology is attached to a disrupted communication within us, within our bodies" (New York, 1966; p. 320), and—though we should guess it from his work—he believes that sex would be "meaningless" if it were divorced from "guilt" (*The Armies of the Night,* New York, 1968; pp. 34-35). All this is to suggest that Mailer's being is totally divided, that he is fighting a heroic war with himself, living out the metaphor-into-mythical-role of the artist as creator/destroyer: for he tries to interpret his own inclination for destruction in terms of a general dying of culture, saying that, "it becomes more excruciating each year for [artists] to perform the civilized act of contributing to a collective meaning. The impulse to destroy moves like new air into a vacuum. . . ." (*The Presidential Papers,* p. 228). What is destroyed is not the culture, of course, or the invisible totalitarian system, but the artist himself.

E. M. Forster said of *Ulysses* that it covered the universe with mud—an unfair judgment, surely; but *Why Are We in Vietnam?* covers the universe with excrement, that is, the universe of the imagination. And then? Then? The act of adolescent defiance only turns back upon itself, for like the black rioters in our American cities some years back, the adolescent must then live in the universe he has tried to destroy; magic fails, D.J. goes to Vietnam because that is the next (metaphorical) stop, and he must shiver with the knowledge that "no man cell in him can now forget that if the center of things is insane, it is insane with force . . ." (p. 143). Mailer's pessimism is deeper than that of William Burroughs, whom he admires, and his writing is far more significant, for it is connected to a vital daylight present that only fades away, at its extremes, into the underground.

Mailer's "Paradise Lost"

Our time may induce symptoms of paranoia in highly energetic men, for millions of years of evolution have provided them (I use this pronoun quite deliberately—not "us") with instincts meant to preserve and swell the species, to dominate highly visible earthly creatures, including women; to fulfill themselves *through* conquest. And now the animal enemies are largely vanished, some of them extinct forever; the most dangerous are now microscopic, and it takes not only technological equipment but years of training to slay them . . . and women, the mystical "Other," the *tabula rasa* upon which ascetic or lover or madman may flash his own poetic vision, are

188

now challenging the basic fabric of the dominant/domi-
nated society . . . and the real enemies are abstract, mere
"ideas" involving the economics of poverty, the mathematical hieroglyphics of the stars, an entire scholarship
of nature that the romantic artist—trusting to "instinct,"
abhorring "reason"—cannot share. *Why Are We in Vietnam?* and James Dickey's *Deliverance* (novels so similar
that their titles might be exchanged, to the honor of
both) are extremely poignant expressions of a vanishing
sensibility, which attempts a restatement of manhood in
ritualistic acts, far from a civilized urban existence that
has made so difficult the isolation and slaughter of
enemies. Both novels deal with the fear of man's possible
tenderness for other men, the denial of the male as possible lover (Dickey has set up this denial in such terms as
to render it irresistible, and his homosexual villains seem
to deserve the savagery they receive—in fact, *Deliverance*
should be required reading for anyone who thinks the
sexual revolution is going to be an easy one) and his
apotheosis as killer. Dickey's male ideal is so brutal that
one half wonders if Dickey might not be Mailer's model
for D.J.'s friend Tex ("full of daddy-love, Tex got that
mean glint in the eye for which Texans are justly proud
and famous"), while D.J. himself is the more Mailerian,
possessing a sweet meanness ("D.J. has got the sweet
smile of my-momma-loved-me-and-I'm-sweet-as-a-birth-
day-cake kind of mean look")—the two of them a "natural hunting couple." In one of Dickey's most powerful
poems, "The Eye-Beaters," the poet-narrator experiences
a vision similar to the "vision" D.J. and Tex have of the
Beast God:

>   . . . Beast, get in
> My way. Your body opens onto the plain. Deer, take me

into your life-
lined form. I merge, I pass beyond in secret in perversity and the sheer
Despair of invention my double-clear bifocals off my
reason gone
Like eyes. Therapist, farewell at the living end. Give
me my spear.[5]

Give me my spear! The poet surrenders to an ancient, archaic shape of himself, in "despair of invention" to show him a way forward into his own adult future.

Mailer has written movingly of Beckett's *Waiting for Godot* that it brought despair to the surface, the despair of the twentieth century over man's "impotence" when he attempts to alter history; this essay of 1956 assumes an additional meaning when it is juxtaposed with *Of a Fire on the Moon* of fifteen years later, when Mailer is forced to realize—and with characteristic honesty pursues his realization to its furthest implications—that not everyone felt the despair of impotence, not everyone was paralyzed like Beckett, not every expression of the imagination had to be couched in dark, passive, deathly terms. Mailer stands in the "first cathedral of the age of technology," brooding over the Space Program, and he is forced to admit that he must recognize that the world was changing,

that [it] *had* changed, even as he had thought to be pushing and shoving on it with *his* mighty ego. And it had changed in ways he did not recognize, had never anticipated, and could possibly not comprehend now. . . . Yes, this emergence of a ship to travel the ether was no event he could measure by any philosophy he had been able to put together in his brain.

(*Of a Fire on the Moon,* Boston, 1969; pp. 57–58)

The revealing phrase here is *any philosophy he had been able to put together in his brain*: for it tells us how strongly Mailer is committed to a pastoral past, a magical realm in which one has not the need to learn, to study, to train oneself in the complexities of his civilization. The romantic believes that visions will sustain him, that great works of art will spring spontaneously out of his unconscious; he hates and fears "reason" because that seems to him Faustian and evil.

The paralysis of the imagination suffered by contemporary romantic writers grows immediately out of the accelerated pace of the world and their own diminishing capacity to register it; but more importantly, it is a natural result of a faith in themselves as isolated "egos" burdened, if male, with the need to conquer, and if female—like Sylvia Plath—terrified of the prospect, seen as inevitable, of being conquered. In Mailer's case he has constructed an entire body of work around a Manichaean existentialism, a combination of two deathly pseudo-philosophical propositions. He asserts a belief in a limited God, a God Who is a "warring element" in a divided universe and Who may somehow be using man in His struggle to impose upon the universe His conception of being against other conceptions. When God finally appears, as He does at the climax of *Why Are We in Vietnam?*, this God cannot surprise us, as He does Mailer, when He turns out to be a prehistoric version of "God." Men create God in their own images, do they not? And Mailer has surrendered entirely the uses of the imaginative intelligence, mistaking a faith in the conscious for a denial of the unconscious.

His desire to awaken a sense of "dread" in man has its roots in a firm belief in the absolute existence of Evil, as

191

a process of waste or "cancer" in the universe, and from this belief it is a logical step to balanced oppositions of God/Devil, Imagination/Technology, Male/Female, and the other strenuous substitutions of metaphor for unclassifiable processes of reality that may be as simple as "body *vs.* mind" and "romantic *vs.* classic," or as bewildering as "sex *vs.* religion" or "murder or homosexuality *vs.* cancer" (four of sixty-five paired items in "The Hip and the Square" of many years ago). He seems to understand fully the self-destructive nature of his predicament, though not the means to transcend it:

. . . his genius brain can grope ultimates and that's not for every short-hair butterball in town, no, figure this, the electricity and magnetism of the dream fief is reversed—God or the Devil takes over in sleep—what simpler explanation you got, M.A. expert type? nothing better to do than put down Mani the Manichee, well, shit on that, D.J. is here to resurrect him. . . .

(p. 172)

But the effort to resurrect the dead Manichaean gods or to reaffirm the romanticism Hemingway seemed to represent (see the "Aquarius" section of *Of a Fire on the Moon*) involves so willful a distortion of one's adulthood as to make the surrender to primitive impulses inevitable.

But even if Mailer could put aside his belief in God and devil, the terrorization of man by the forces of evil "waste," he has other severe intellectual doubts. For at the very heart of *Why Are We in Vietnam?* is this memory, which springs out of D.J.'s unconscious mind during the Alaskan hunt, when he and his father are together:

192

. . . D.J. is shivering on the death in this hot-ass vale of breath, cause each near-silent step of his toe on the tail sounds a note, chimes of memory, angel's harp of ten little toes picking out the blows of Rusty's belt on his back, he five years old and shrieking off the fuck of his head, cause the face of his father is a madman ass, a power which wishes to beat him to death—for what no longer known—a child's screaming in the middle of, and so interrupting, a Hallelujah Sir Jet Throne fuck? nobody know now, D.J. just remembers the beating, screaming, pleading. . . .

(p. 137)

In this passage Mailer comes very close to assigning D.J.'s fate to a witnessing of the classical Primal Scene, when D.J. was a child of five; he has suppressed his terror and hatred of his father, Rusty, and a decade later the "collective father and son" are able to spare each other only by concentrating their savagery on a nine-hundred-pound grizzly bear. Surely this is a miniature society—a "syphilization" of two:

Whoo! Death is on him, memory of a father near to murdering the son, breath of his own murder still running in the blood of his fingers, his hands, all murder held back, and then on the trail came a presence, no longer the fear of death but concentration, murder between the two men now came to rest, for murder was outside them now, same murder which had been beaming in to D.J. while he thinking of murdering his father, the two men turned to contemplate the beast.

(p. 138)

This is a demonic voice of Freud, telling us that all of culture grows out of the Oedipus complex; that civilization *is* its own discontent, and man can never be saved. In "Why War?" and other essays, Freud brings to this subject a gravity and wonder Mailer does not achieve,

193

trying as he is for rapid, manic flashes of insight. Is man absolutely determined by his earliest experiences, and is man as a species "determined" by what his earliest ancestors underwent? Freud's deterministic psychology, based largely upon a pathological model, has evolved by way of European existentialist philosophy and American "humanistic" psychology to the point at which it is possible for the late Abraham Maslow to suggest, quite seriously, that a "transhuman psychology" must be begun—and by that Maslow meant a psychology for the next phase of human evolution. Mailer and other contemporary writers have cheated themselves cruelly of intellectual growth by their romantic assumption that "truth" will come to them out of the air or will float up to them out of the deepest parts of their own brains: no wonder Mailer as Aquarius is ill at ease in the Apollonian cathedral.

Ultimately, there may be no psychological truths— only philosophical propositions. And one of these is the proposition *Passion is superior to Intellect*. That is, and always has been, a philosophical proposition. Passion has no language.

But if one accepts, as Mailer does, the dead weight of psychological determinism that renders a healthy boy like D.J. nearly without volition, there is nothing to do but follow the symbolic hunt through to its predestined conclusion. D.J., fearing he will "somnambulate long enough to beat in Rusty's head" because his father has selfishly taken credit for killing the bear, wakes his friend Tex and the two of them escape from the adults' camp. He is relieved forever of the burden of love for Rusty, the father who is more juvenile than his son: "Whew. Final end of love of one son for one father." And now they head for the "icy vise of the magnetic north," going back to "Aurora Borealis cause it is the only mountain of heavenly light."

This section of the novel contains some of Mailer's finest writing, and hints at the kind of work he may do someday in a long, leisurely, complex novel in which the warring parts of his personality are wedded, a poetry of wholeness and unities: the projected long novel "in the style of Melville," perhaps. It is a very self-conscious and literary purification ceremony that the boys perform, but beautifully rendered, in such clean prose that we may believe we are reading about this for the first time. Indeed, most of the self-mocking literary allusions fade away; as we get deeper into the symbolic core of the novel, which is reminiscent of *Moby Dick* and Faulkner's *The Bear* and innumerable aspects of D. H. Lawrence, we seem to be approaching a transcendent, holy place where obscenities are forgotten in the presence of twelve Dall rams on an outcropping of snow, and wolves, squirrels, Arctic flowers, berries, sunlight, mice, sparrows, hares, caribou that are "a convention of antlers . . . fine and unbelievable as a forest on the march."

Weaponless, the boys pitch a tent and try to sleep. But J. D. is "afraid of sleep, afraid of wolves, full of beauty, afraid of sleep, full of beauty . . ." and he senses a secret near to him, some mystery, knowing "the meaning of trees and forest all in dominion to one another and messages across the continent . . . the great sorrow up here brought by leaves and wind some speechless electric gathering of woe. . . ." A King Moose approaches. But the boys are remote, very separate from nature and from each other, like "two rods getting charged with magnetism in electric coils." In referring to Lawrence's *Women in Love*, especially Chapter Twenty and the conclusion, I

195

am not suggesting that Mailer is sub-Lawrentian, but that he is very much like D.J.—a medium, a medley of voices —and that the fear of Gerald Crich for his friend Birkin's proffered love comes back to us again in D.J. and Tex, who cannot even touch each other. And, certainly, Gerald's icy death in the Arctic of his own soul, the death of the mechanical ego whom even—even!—a woman will despise, must be in Mailer's consciousness throughout.

The boys cannot surrender their opposition to each other, they are not to be joined in any mystical union— D.J., at least, has been ruined for this by his earlier disgust for his father—and so their vision of God is no more than the "wild wicked . . . intelligence" D.J. has already seen in the dying bear's eyes, the promise of *Baby, you haven't begun:*

. . . God was here, and He was real and no man was He, but a beast . . . and secret call: come to me. . . . For God was a beast, not a man, and God said, "Go out and kill—fulfill my will, go and kill," and they hung there each of them on the knife of the divide in all conflict of lust to own the other yet in fear of being killed by the other . . . and the lights shifted, something in the radiance of the North went into them, and owned their fear, some communion of telepathies and new powers, and they were twins, never to be near as lovers again, but killer brothers. . . .

(pp. 202–4)

So the Alaskan hunt ends and the boys are united with the men, all of them flown back to Fairbanks in planes that "led the way into the new life smack right up here two years later in my consciousness," as D.J. sits at his farewell dinner. Tomorrow, "Tex and me, we're off to see the wizard in Vietnam. . . . This is D.J., Disc Jockey to America turning off. Vietnam, hot damn." So the novel

196

ends; but the novel does not answer the question, "Why are we in Vietnam?"

The problem is that Mailer substitutes metaphors for reality, but he does so in such a quick, deft, passionate manner that we cannot always see how he has blurred his central issue. The sheer momentum of his inspired writing carries us onward, and D.J.'s self-mockery seems too contemporary to be a vehicle, ultimately, for Spenglerian despair: the novel is more archaic, in fact, than Mann's *Magic Mountain*, which also ends with a representative young man passing into the anonymity of war. But Mann offers a variety of interpretations that assure us of some measure of freedom of choice, a hope that we are superior to Hans Castorp if for no other reason than the fact that we have read about him, and he has only experienced his fate. In Mailer's novel, however, we are led to suspect that D.J.'s consciousness is also Mailer's, and that the vision of God in the Arctic is Mailer's unquestioning metaphor for the ultimate God of mankind—not just the God one might conceivably expect, given the circumstances of a hunting expedition and a mindless and passive acquiescence to "nature." It might seem paradoxical that Mailer, whose novels are so lively, is in fact a writer of static conditions; the issue is not sheer muscular response to stimulus, which is not even a measure, always, of life, but a human and intelligent and *willful* method of perception, which accepts or rejects sensual stimuli and makes of them an arrangement not dissimilar to a work of art. Yet Mailer has prescribed for himself so limited an omniscience (I use this phrase deliberately) that if, on page 15 of *An American Dream*, Rojack-Mailer believes the roots of motivation to be "magic, dread, and the perception of death," we know there cannot be a transcen-

197

dence of this existential vision but only an affirmation of it; just as, realizing the grave human limitations of all the Dallas adults, and assuming a Newtonian determinism in the universe, it is necessary that D.J. be "up tight with the essential animal insanity of things" (p. 70). Only when the "animal insanity" passes into him and a kind of cold magnetic "telepathy" of the Arctic night electrifies his soul is he integrated, given a power more deadly (because far less human) than Rojack's. Richard Poirier, in a thoughtful study of Mailer, believes that it might be necessary for Mailer to "remain the embattled embodiment of . . . two worlds" in order to continue writing, and he assigns to Mailer a position higher than that of, say, Bellow, because of Mailer's "partiality for those moments where more is happening than one can very easily assimilate."[6]

However, a recent book, *Existential Errands*, suggests that the intoxication with sheer unassimilated reality may bring permanent harm to an ego ever sensitive to new, distending shapes of reality, believing itself to be most "human" when involved in making movies "without retakes," where improvisation is an attempt to match the unrehearsed drift and flow of ordinary life. In the end the teleological force of the unconscious will bring us only to . . . ordinary life. Mailer's romantic existentialism may account for some of the most exciting moments in his writing, but it is an excitement that does not last, for his positing of himself in a universe that is a mere cascade of matter is a self-hypnotizing curse; this accounts for his interest in Burroughs' fiction, which deals with all kinds of addictions, and in which the "addict" is the archetype for human behavior. Yet in Burroughs' omniscient mind, casual relationships are easily obliterated and a random "flow" or "field of consciousness" appears to us in a vacuum, timeless, extrapolated from an elemental universe but receiving its meaning when applied, like any fable or fairy tale, to the immediate world of newspapers and headlines. Mailer is trying for more than this, much more. There is no other way to account for D.J.'s nervous apologies to the counterconsciousness that may be operating its own disc jockey program out of Harlem: Mailer knows, and wants to state clearly, that he has not the proper claim to a truly devastated, magical "perception of death"—not so long as one black man exists in America. Any effort to resurrect dying or dead Manichaean gods can be, from Mailer's point of view, a feat of imagination he somehow has not earned. The "genius brain" of Mailer and D.J. crams itself with phenomena that appear to have the spontaneity of a consciousness-in-the-making, believing that an awareness of extremes, a submergence in the chaos of impenetrable mystery, is a necessary initiation into Time, a cosmic Time that has nothing to do with ordinary time. Yet the fallacy is—and I say this with utter admiration for the way Mailer *uses* it—that he has forced into his imagination an "other" style of life, one he has not experienced but believes he should, one he *cannot* imagine, and he assigns to this counterconsciousness the power to defeat the white, Faustian, "committee" civilization that is his own—the civilization that has made Mailer possible, especially the "Faustian" Mailer of all the books published under that name. For, considering again his definition of our culture—that it is founded upon the Faustian urge to "dominate nature by mastering time, mastering the links of social cause and effect"—we see that this is a precise definition of the truly serious novelist. Mailer believes there is something evil about the urge in men to subject time to their will; yet this "evil" is at the very basis of great art. Existential art, in which the protagonist achieves his identity only through enduring the phenomenal flow and resisting any intellectual relatedness to the objects of his perceptions, is quite another thing: and Mailer, with typical American ambition, is not content with this. Yet his energetic Manichaeanism forbids a higher art.

Initiation, then, brings the protagonist not to newer visions, more complex and future-oriented images of his own power, but to a dead end, a full stop. The territory one lights out for is not Rojack's unexplored West or even the Byronic wilds of the Yucatan (one is reminded of Byron's temporary indecision over whether to go to a pastoral "South America" where the peasants were all noble and gentle or to go to Greece), but Vietnam: a full stop. When Rojack muses that the "arid empty wild blind deserts" of the West are producing a new breed of man, he is taking up again the passionate certainty Lawrence expressed so beautifully in *Women in Love*—that the life force is inexhaustible, though man as a species may die out.

But D.J. remains "marooned on the balmy tropical isle of Anal Referent Metaphor," and Mailer, who survives him, carries on the romantic tradition he has, himself, rejected by telling us that Muhammed Ali is "the very spirit of the twentieth century."

Therefore, stasis. Therefore, the celebration with increasingly defensive and feverish language-structures of archaic rites, events in the history of man that were once deeply meaningful initiations *into a future*—but are now pseudoreligious reminders of something dimly felt, because never experienced. Mailer, in dramatizing this predicament, is speaking for a multitude of voices—or perhaps the voices are speaking through him? A casual reading of *Why Are We in Vietnam?* reveals the presence of T. S. Eliot, James Joyce, Robert Lowell, William Burroughs, Hemingway, Faulkner, Melville, Twain, Sterne, Swift, Beckett, Céline, Kafka, Pynchon, Hawkes, Gass, Barth, Proust, Burgess, Freud, Roth, Selby, Genet, Bellow, Lenny Bruce, Borges, and Lawrence, and of course Mailer of the self-interviews and *Advertisements*, Mailer-as-Juvenile voicing his disgust at Mailer-as-Adult. None of these voices are disguised, the novel is an intentional literary *event* of magical telepathies (what Mailer is picking out of the air waves that swirl so violently around him), and it is a healthy acknowledgment on his part that he is not and has never been an original writer, but only deluded by the contemporary prejudice for Originality. Great art is communal, and "originality" is a term applied only to the uses which superior personalities make of all that is rich and unsynthesized in their culture.

Yet, one of the few writers whom Mailer doesn't echo seems to me a true brother of his: John Milton. For with Milton we have the feat of genius forcing into an outmoded cosmology his own creative energies, his "vision" of magical powers and minimally intelligent human creatures, everything structured, a hodgepodge of Mailerian "freak activities," the politics of power contracted to an essentially domestic tension and then maniacally expanded to include, and to explain, the entire pre-Copernican universe. But Milton, of course, transformed his own need for a totalitarian wholeness into great art, and Mailer, resisting the artist's need to transcend his material, to *be* finally and unashamedly totalitarian (if no other gentler, Jamesian term can be found), approaches the threshold of greatness but does not cross over.[7]

Mailer's fears in *Of a Fire on the Moon* that the humanistic, liberal tradition of the imagination that he represents, or believes he represents, do not prevent him from entering into a kind of mystical union with the very "root-destroying" people who are his subject. The book has many beautiful, extremely moving passages, moments of sheer psychic tension in which one participates, almost breathlessly, sensing how Mailer's mind is about to move in one direction or in another—or in another—and who can say but that the NASA expenditure did not justify itself when Mailer gazes at photographs of the moon and theorizes about Cézanne? Whether Cézanne "is" the father of modern art hardly matters, but that the un-Cézannelike Mailer can come to this vision of man's need for a "search into the logic of the abstract"—and that, so poetically, Mailer can record a possible answer to the question of why we are in Vietnam or anywhere, without seeming to realize it:

". . . we're going to the moon [Neil Armstrong, one of the astronauts, answers in reply to a question] because it's in the nature of the human being to face challenges." He looked a little defiant, as if probably they might not know, some critical number of them might never know what he was talking about, "It's by the nature of his *deep inner soul.*" The last three words came out as if they had seared his throat by their extortion. . . . "Yes," he nodded, as if noting what he had had to give up to writers, "we're required to do these things just as salmon swim upstream."

(pp. 46–47)

Armstrong, who seems superficially to be one of the "ego-less" components of a vast machine, but who is in fact as individual and as unique as Mailer himself, is speaking through Mailer to us: and he is giving voice to a newer consciousness, one which accepts for better or worse the fact that, in evolution, the old unconscious is now being taken up consciously, deliberately, in a Faustian manner if no other word will serve—that, even at its worst (Vietnam), it is an expression of a teleological striving, half-unconscious, half-conscious, that can account for its disasters as for its victories without recourse to archaic, fixed, prehistoric assignments of Good and Evil. If one must be romantic, then he may speculate upon the psychology of machines—or he may "behold the world again as savages who knew that if the universe was a lock, its key was metaphor rather than measure" (p. 415).

Given such a vision, Mailer surely has his finest work ahead of him; it will be interesting to see if he can put aside his nihilistic bifurcation of human nature, which he has quite needlessly projected outward onto civilization, and come to see how he might share his desire to "effect a revolution in the consciousness of our time" with a multitude of others, not competitors, or "killer brothers," but awakened adults involved in a common search for the "logic of the abstract."

8

OUT OF STONE, INTO FLESH:

The Imagination of James Dickey

Despair and exultation
Lie down together and thrash
In the hot grass, no blade moving. . . .

Dickey, "Turning Away"

A man cannot pay as much attention to
himself as I do without living in Hell
all the time.

Dickey, "Sorties"

The remarkable poetic achievement of James Dickey is characterized by a restless concern with the poet's "personality" in its relationships to the worlds of nature and of experience. His work is rarely confessional in the sense of the term as we have come to know it, yet it is always personal—at times contemplative, at times dramatic. Because Dickey has become so controversial in recent years, his incredible lyric and dramatic talent has not been adequately recognized, and his ceaseless, often monomaniacal questioning of identity, of the self, of that mysterious and elusive concept we call the personality, has not been investigated.

207

Yet this is only natural: it is always the fate of individuals who give voice to an era's hidden, atavistic desires, its "taboos," to be controversial and therefore misunderstood. Dickey's poetry is important not only because it is so skillful, but because it expresses, at times unintentionally, a great deal about the American imagination in its response to an increasingly complex and "unnatural" phase of civilization. (To Dickey mental processes have come to seem "unnatural" in contrast to physical acts: hence the "Hell" of the quote from his journal, *Sorties*.) He has said, quite seriously, that "the world, the human mind, is dying of subtlety. What it needs is force" (*Sorties*, Garden City, New York, 1971; p. 85). His imagination requires the heroic. But the world cannot and will not always accommodate the hero, no matter how passionately he believes he has identified himself with the fundamental, secret rhythms of nature itself. One comes to loathe the very self that voices its hopeless demands, the "I" that will not be satisfied and will never be silent. *I myself am hell* is a philosophical statement, though it is expressed in the poetic language of personal emotion.

The volumes of poetry Dickey has published so far— *Into the Stone* (1960), *Drowning with Others* (1962), *Helmets* (1964), *Buckdancer's Choice* (1965), *The Eye-Beaters, Blood, Victory, Madness, Buckhead and Mercy* (1970)—present a number of hypothetical or experimental personae, each a kind of reincarnation of an earlier consciousness through which the "self" of the poet endures. He moves, he grows, he suffers, he changes, yet he is still the same—the voice is a singular one, unmistakable. It asks why, knowing the soul heroic, the man himself is so trapped, so helpless? Dickey's central theme is the frustration that characterizes modern man, confronted with an increasingly depersonalized and intellectualized society—the frustration and its necessary corollary, murderous rage. Dickey is not popular with liberals. Yet one can learn from him, as from no other serious writer, what it is like to have been born into one world and to have survived into another. It might be argued that Dickey is our era's Whitman, but a Whitman subdued, no longer innocent, baptized by American violence into the role of a "killer/victim" who cannot locate within his society any standards by which his actions may be judged. A personality eager to identify itself with the collective, whether nature or other men, can survive only when the exterior world supports that mystical union of subject and object. Dickey speaks from the inside of our fallen, contaminated, guilt-obsessed era, and he speaks its language.

This was not always so: his earliest poems are lyric and meditative. They present a near-anonymous sensitivity, one hypnotized by forms, by Being in which dramatic and ostensibly intolerable truths are resolved by a formal, ritualistic—essentially magical—imagination into coherent and well-defined unities; his later poems submit this sensitivity to a broken, overheated, emotionally and intellectually turbulent world. The "stoneness" of the first volume undergoes an astonishing variety of metamorphoses until, in "The Eye-Beaters" and "Turning Away: Variations on Estrangement," it emerges as stark, isolated, combative self-consciousness, in which "A deadly, dramatic compression/Is made of the normal brow. . . ." The poet begins as Prospero, knowing all and forgiving all, and, through a series of sharply tested modes of perception, comes to seem like Hamlet of the great, tragic soliloquies.

Who can tell us more about ourselves?—about our

"American," "masculine," most dangerous selves? Even
more than Whitman, Dickey contains multitudes; he
cannot be reproached for the fact that some of these
aspects of a vast, complex self are at war with the others.
He experiments with the art of poetry and with the external world and the relationships it offers him (will he
be lover?—murderer?—observer?), but what is most moving about his work is his relentless honesty in regard to
his own evolving perception of himself, the mystery of
his "personality." He refuses to remain in any explored
or conquered territory, either in his art or in his personality. Obsessed with the need to seek and to define, he
speaks for those who know that the universe is rich with
meaning but are not always able to relate the intellectual,
conscious aspect of their natures to it. Thus, the need to
reject the "conscious" mind and its public expression,
civilization itself, which is so disturbing in Dickey. Indeed, *Sorties* is very nearly a confession of despair—the
poet seems unable to integrate the various aspects of his
nature, conceiving of the world of the intellect and art as
"Hell." "Believe me, it is better to be stupid and ordinary," Dickey tells us early in the book. What such a
temperament requires, however, is not less intelligence,
but more.

Dickey has not always expressed himself in such extreme terms, and he has been, all along, a careful craftsman, knowing that meaning in poetry must be expressed
through language, through a system of mental constructs.
In fact, it must be invented anew with each poem; it
must be rigorously contracted, abbreviated, made less
explosive and less primitive. In an excellent essay in *The
Suspect in Poetry* he cautions young poets against aban-

doning themselves to their unconscious "song," which he defines as "only a kind of monstrousness that has to be understood and ordered according to some principle to be meaningful."[1] The unrestrained and unimagined self must be related syntactically to the external world in order to achieve meaning.

Yet the phenomenal world changes; language shifts, evolves, breaks free of its referents; and the human ego, mysteriously linked to both, is forced to undergo continuous alterations in order simply to survive. In the poem "Snakebite" (1967) the "stage of pine logs" and the "role/I have been cast in" give way suddenly and horribly to the dramatic transition from the pronoun "it" to the pronoun "me" as the poet realizes he is confined in his living, breathing, existential body: he is not playing a role after all. If he wants to survive he will have to drain that poison out of his blood stream. Therefore, one of the burdens of the poet's higher awareness is to discover if there is any metamorphosis, any possible reincarnation, that is ultimately more than a mode of perception, *a way of arranging words.* Otherwise we begin to imagine ourselves as totally "estranged." To deny that estrangement we must deny our very framework of perception—language and sanity and logic—as if, by annihilating the mental construct of incarnation, we might somehow experience it on a level far below consciousness. Certainly Dickey has emphasized the poem as physical experience; he has set up opposing pseudocategories of the poetry of "participation" and the poetry of "reflection" (*Sorties,* p. 59). Such an estrangement rests, however, upon the metaphysical assumption that man's intellect is an intruder in the universe and that the language systems he has devised are not utterly natural, natural to his species. Surely the human invention or creation of language is our species' highest achievement; some psycholinguists speculate that human beings are born with a genetic endowment for recognizing and formulating language, that they "possess genes for all kinds of information, with strands of special, peculiarly human DNA for the discernment of meaning in syntax."[2] Failing to accept the intellect as triumphantly human, rather than somehow unnatural, the poet is doomed to endless struggles with the self. The "variations on estrangement" at the end of *The Eye-Beaters* deal with countless battles and meadows strewn "with inner lives," concluding with the hope that the poet's life may be seen "as a thing/That can be learned,/As those earnest young heroes learned theirs,/Later, much later on."

An objective assessment of one's situation must be experienced apart from life itself, then. And only "much later on." To use a critical term Dickey appropriated from Wordsworth, he is a poet of the "Second Birth," not one who, like Rimbaud or Dylan Thomas, possessed a natural instrument for poetry but one who eventually reduces the distinction between "born" and "made" poets only by hard work, by the "ultimate moral habit of trying each poem, each line, each word, against the shifting but finally constant standards of inner necessity" (*The Suspect in Poetry*, pp. 55-57). Contrary to his instinct for direct, undiluted self-expression, the poet has tried to define and develop his own personality as a "writing instrument"; he has pared back, reduced, restrained the chaotic "monstrousness" of raw emotion in order to relate his unique experience to common experience. He contradicts Eliot's ideal of an impersonal poetry, yet paradoxically refuses to endorse what he would call the monstrousness of confessional verse: "The belief in the value of one's personality has all but disappeared. . . ."

But what is personality, that a belief in it might save us?

Not a multileveled phenomenon, Dickey's sense of "personality," but rather a series of imagined dramas, sometimes no more than flashes of rapport, kinships with beasts or ancient ancestors—as in the apocalyptic "The Eye-Beaters," in which personality is gained only when "Reason" is rejected in favor of primitive action. The process of increasing self-consciousness, as image after image is explored, held up like a mask to the poet's face,[3] absorbed, and finally discarded, comes to seem a tragic movement, as every existential role in the universe must ultimately be abandoned.

"Intact and Incredible Love"

Dickey has said that the century's greatest phrase is Albert Schweitzer's "reverence for life." This conviction runs through his work but is strongest in the earliest volumes. *Into the Stone* consists of contemplative, almost dreamlike poems that investigate the poet's many forms of love: beginning with the mythical, incantatory dissolution of the individual personality into both "dark" and "light" and concluding with the book's title poem, which emphasizes the poet's confident "knowing" and his being "known" through his relationship with a woman.

"Sleeping Out at Easter" is terse, restrained, as the "Word rising out of darkness" seems to act without the deliberate involvement of the poet. As dawn arrives in the forest, the "Presences" of night turn into trees and "One eye opens slowly without me." Everything moves in its own placid, nonpersonalized pattern, out of darkness and into the sunlight, and the world is "made good" by the springing together of wood and sun. The metamorphosis of Presences into daytime trees is one that could occur without the poet's song, yet the poet voices a total acceptance, as if he knew himself uniquely absorbed in the cycle of night/day, his "magical shepherd's cloak . . . not yet alive on [his] flesh." In other, similarly incantatory poems, the poet lies at the edge of a well, contemplating himself and his smile and the "grave face" of his dead brother, or lies "in ritual down" in a small unconsecrated grove of suburban pines—trying to get back, to get down, beneath both gods and animals, to "being part of the acclaimed rebirth" of spring ("The Vegetable King"). (Years later, when his poetry has undergone tremendous changes, Dickey will deal again with the transformation of a human being into a tree, in "The Fiend," one of his most eccentric poems).

Into the Stone contains a number of war poems, but in spite of their subject they absorb the poet's personality much as the nature poems do, locating in confusion and panic certain centers of imagination, of decision, that the poet is able to recall years later, when "at peace." "The Enclosure" is the first of Dickey's many poems that "enclose" and idealize women: a group of war nurses on a Philippine island are protected by a compound with a wire fence, but the poet imagines them whispering to the soldiers outside "to deliver them out/Of the circle of impotence. . . ." In lines of curious, ceremonial calm the poet declares how, after the war, this vision led him to "fall/On the enemy's women/With intact and incredible love." Of the war poems, the most vivid is "The Performance," which celebrates the paradox of pain and triumph in the memory of David Armstrong, executed by the Japanese; Dickey remembers Armstrong doing a handstand against the sun, and his death by decapitation is seen as another kind of "performance." Even here there is a sense of acquiescence, finality, as if the cycle of nature could absorb this violent death as easily as it could absorb the shapes of trees back into primordial Presences.

The reverential awe of "Trees and Cattle" places the poet's consciousness in a "holy alliance" with trees, cattle, and sunlight, making his mind a "red beast"—his head gifted with ghostly bull's horns by the same magic that allowed Lawrence to imagine his head "hard-balanced, antlered" in "A Doe at Evening"; the sun itself burns more deeply because trees and cattle exist. A miracle of some kind has occurred, though it cannot be explained, and the poet half believes he may be saved from death; as, in a later poem, "Fog Envelops the Animals," the poet-hunter is somehow transformed into the "long-sought invisibility" of pure things or events or processes: "Silence. Whiteness. Hunting." But *Into the Stone* is characterized by passivity and no hint of the guilty, pleasurable agitation of physical life, whether hunting or love; the title poem describes the poet "on the way to a woman," preoccupied with a mystical absorption into the "stone" of the moon. The woman is outside the concern of the poem, undefined, not even mythologized; the poet is not vividly portrayed, as in "Cherrylog Road"; he could be any man, any lover, believing that "the dead have their chance in my body." All is still, mysterious, calm. The

215

poet "knows" his place and his love, quite unlike the moon-drawn men of a later poem, "Apollo," who are seen as floating "on nothing/But procedure alone" and who symbolize "all humanity in the name/Of a new life. . . . " This later poem makes the "stone" of the moon into "stones," breaks up a seamless cosmology into a universe of "craters" and "mountains the animal/Eye has not seen since the earth split" (the earth-moon split an ancient and honored moon theory, of obvious symbolic, if not scientific, value)—not the Platonic oneness of stone, but stones:

> . . . We stare into the moon
> dust, the earth-blazing ground. We laugh, with the beautiful
> craze
> Of Static. We bend, we pick up stones.
>
> ("Apollo")

A more dramatic sense of self is evident in Dickey's second book, *Drowning with Others*. Here he imagines the torturous memories of a lifeguard who failed to save a drowning child; he imagines himself inside the hunting dream of a dog sleeping on his feet; he contemplates fish in "The Movement of Fish" with the alert, awed scrutiny of Lawrence himself, making a judgment, like Lawrence's, that arises from the distant Otherness of the fish's world, where its sudden movement has the power to "convulse the whole ocean" and teach man the Kierkegaardian terror of the leap, the "fear and trembling" of great depths that are totally still, far beneath the superficial agitation that men see or float upon in their boats.

Yet the hunted/hunting animals of "The Heaven of Animals" are poetic constructions, Platonic essences of

216

beasts wholly absorbed in a mythical cycle of life-death-rebirth: at the very center of nature these beasts "tremble," "fall," "are torn," "rise," and "walk again," like Emerson's red slayer and his perpetual victim. "The Heaven of Animals" is all but unique in Dickey's poetry because the poet himself has no clear position in it, as if its unity of Being somehow excluded an active intellectual consciousness; if we look back at the poem from "Fog Envelops the Animals" and other hunting poems and from Dickey's statements in *Self-Interviews* (Garden City, New York, 1970) about the mysterious "renewal" he experiences when hunting, we can assume that his deepest sympathies are with the predators, but this is not evident from the poem itself, which is one of his finest, most delicate achievements. The owl of "The Owl King" is another poetic (and not naturalistic) creature, a form of the poet himself who sits "in my shape/With my claws growing deep into wood/And my sight going slowly out,/Inch by inch. . . ." Superior forces belong to those who, like the owl, can see in the dark; or to those who, like Dickey himself, possess extraordinary powers of vision[4] that set them apart from other, average men. But the forces are benevolent, godly, and restrained—the owl king participates in a mysterious ceremony with the blind child "as beasts at their own wedding, dance" and is not the symbol of cold, savage violence of the owl perched upon the tent in *Deliverance*, just as the poet-narrator of the volume *Drowning with Others* is not the helplessly eager murderer of *Deliverance*. Here, in the owl king's Roethkian kingdom, all nature is transformed by mind, its brutal contingencies and dreams suppressed, the possible "monstrousness" of its song made into a childlike lyric. Its final stanzas link it to earlier poems of Dickey's in which tension has been resolved by an act of impersonal, godly will:

> Far off, the owl king
> Sings like my father, growing
> In power. Father, I touch
> Your face. I have not seen
> My own, but it is yours.
> I come, I advance,
> I believe everything, I am here.

Through the child's (blind) acceptance, Dickey accepts the world; just as, in the anguished "The Eye-Beaters," he rejects the world of normal, rational vision, having been shaken by the experience of seeing blind children beat at their eyes in order to "see." In "The Owl King" the transcendent, paternal bird withdraws into the darkness of his own vision, while the lost child's father emerges, "In love with the sound of my voice," to claim his child; both aspects of the poetic consciousness are required if the child is to be saved, cherished, and yet both are dependent upon the child's acquiescence. (Just as, for the hunter, the imagined "acquiescence" of the hunted—the slain— is a ritualistic necessity; see Dickey's attempted justification of his love of hunting in *Self-Interviews*). This poem is a "song of innocence" whose unearthly simplicity—the child moves from tree to tree as if blessing them—will be transformed, years later, into the nightmarish "song of experience" of the crazed blind children in "The Eye-Beaters." Then, the objects of the poet's pity being, in themselves, hopeless, not even human children, beyond all love or language, the poet himself will narrowly escape madness. But this is years later, years deeper into flesh.

Entering History

In his third book, *Helmets,* Dickey begins to move out of the perfected world of eternal recurrence, no longer the awed, alert, but essentially passive observer, now ready to experience history. It is clear that Dickey desires to take on "his" own personal history as an analogue to or a microcosmic exploration of twentieth-century American history, which is one of the reasons he is so important a poet. In his inspired, witty, and ingeniously balanced essay on Randall Jarrell in *The Suspect in Poetry,* Dickey says he can discover in Jarrell's poetry very little excellence of technique, but he insists that Jarrell's contribution—"that of writing about real things, rather than playing games with words"—is a valuable one. Dickey indicates implicitly that *he* will take on both the challenge of being an artist and a historian of our era, which he has, applying a superior poetic talent to Jarrell's "realm . . . of pity and terror . . . a kind of non-understanding understanding, and above all of helplessness."[5]

Once he is released from the sacred but bloodless cycle of nature, Dickey is concerned with giving life to this "non-understanding understanding" of creatures simpler than himself, or of an earlier form of himself, as in the beautiful, perfect poem, "Drinking from a Helmet." In "The Dusk of Horses" the emphasis has shifted from acceptance to a sharper awareness of distinctions be-

tween self and object, the need for the human participant
in an action to judge it:

> No beast ever lived who understood

> What happened among the sun's fields,
> Or cared why the color of grass
> Fled over the hill while he stumbled,

> Led by the halter to sleep
> On his four taxed, worthy legs. . . .
> ("The Dusk of Horses")

In this and similar poems in *Helmets* the graceful fluidity
of the lines is like the fluidity of the earlier poems: the
god's-eye vision set to music. As the the. ~ of "helplessness" grows, however, Dickey loses interest in well-made
and sweetly sounding poetry and pours his remarkable
energies into such extravaganzas of shouts and shrieks as
"May Day Sermon." And where death might once have
been resolved by a mystical affirmation of unity, in the
recent poem "Diabetes" it is resolved by a surreptitious
drink of beer; in "The Cancer Match," by whiskey.

Throughout *Helmets* there is an increasing growth, as
if the subjects long loved by the poet are now shifting out
of the hypnosis of love itself, beginning to elude his incantatory powers: coming alive and separate. In a poem
reminiscent of Wallace Stevens' "Anecdote of the Jar,"
Dickey stands by a fence with his palm on the top wire
and experiences a vision or a nervous hallucination of the
disorder that would result if the tension of the wire were
broken:

> If the wire were cut anywhere
> All his blood would fall to the ground

> And leave him standing and staring
> With a face as white as a Hereford's. . . .
> ("Fence Wire")

The "top tense strand" is like a guitar string "tuned to an E," whose humming sound arranges the acres of the farm and holds them "highstrung and enthralled." Suddenly the poet in his human role must accept a position in nature which is superior to that of trees and cattle, an intellectual responsibility that will involve both exultation and the risk of despair. But because of Dickey's hand on this fence wire,

> The dead corn is more
> Balanced in death than it was,
> The animals more aware

> Within the huge human embrace
> Held up and borne out of sight
> Upon short, unbreakable poles
> Where through the ruled land intones
> Like a psalm. . . .

Because of the sensational aspects of some of his later poems, Dickey is not usually known to have concerned himself so seriously, and so perceptively, with the metaphysics behind aesthetic action; it is characteristic of his energy and his pursuit of new challenges that a very few poems about "poetry" are enough for him. If read in its proper chronological place in Dickey's work, "Fence Wire" is a moving as well as a significant poem; it is the first clear statement of the poet's sense of himself as involved responsibly in history. In his most powerful poems the tension between that "top thread tuned to an E" and the abandonment to one's own possible, probable "monstrousness" provides a dramatic excitement generally

221

lacking in these early, though entirely admirable poems, and less content with lyric verse itself, Dickey will experiment with wildly imaginative monologues in which words float and leap all over the page.

In *Helmets* there is also a new sense of exploration into an "Otherness," not a declaring of unities, analogues, "correspondences" between all phenomena in nature: Dickey stands "At Darien Bridge" and muses upon the chain-gang workers who built the bridge many years ago, when he was a child; he hopes to see a bird, the one bird "no one has looked for," and the scratched wedding band on his finger recalls the convicts' chains—like them, he longs for freedom, or even death, or at least the ability to believe again in "the unchanging, hopeless look/Out of which all miracles leap." (In contrast to the miraculous vision of "Trees and Cattle.") In "Chenille" he encounters another kind of poet, an old woman who darns quilts endlessly, not ordinary bedspreads of the kind made by machine and sold in the normal world but quilts decorated with red whales, unicorns, winged elephants, crowned ants—"Beasts that cannot be thought of/By the wholly sane." Increasingly, the surreal intrudes into what should be the real, or sane; in "On the Coosawattee" Dickey and his companion on a canoeing trip are shocked to see how the water has been defiled by a poultry-processing plant upstream:

> All morning we floated on feathers
> Among the drawn heads which appeared
> Everywhere, from under the logs
>
> Of feathers, from upstream behind us,
> Lounging back to us from ahead,

Until we believed ourselves doomed
And the planet corrupted forever. . . .

Though the two men shoot the rapids and finally escape this horror, the canoeists of *Deliverance* return to experience the river's mysterious dangers and the unhuman ground-bass of sound that becomes "deeper and more massively frantic and authoritative" as they continue—and this time not all will survive, and none will get back to civilization with anything like this poem's triumphant declaration of the human ability to escape other human defilement. In the blaze of noon the canoeists on the Coosawattee River feel

The quickening pulse of the rapids
And entered upon it like men
Who sense that the world can be cleansed

Among rocks pallid only with water,
And plunged there like the unborn
Who see earthly streams without taint
Flow beneath them. . . .

"Cherrylog Road" is the first of the unmistakably Dickeyesque poems: nostalgic and comic simultaneously, demystifying the love so laborously mystified elsewhere, even naming names ("Doris Holbrook") and giving directions:

Off Highway 106
At Cherrylog Road I entered
The '34 Ford without wheels,
Smothered in kudzu,
With a seat pulled out to run
Corn whiskey down from the hills. . . .

And in this automobile graveyard the boy moves from car to car, delighted to be naming, placing, experiencing, without the need to make anything sacred or even essentially important: from the Ford to an Essex to a blue Chevrolet to a Pierce-Arrow, "as in a wild stock-car race/In the parking lot of the dead. . . ." He hopes his girl friend will come to him from her father's farm "And . . . get back there/With no trace of me on her face"; when she does arrive and they embrace, their love-making takes place in the same "stalled, dreaming traffic" as the hunting of mice by blacksnakes, and beetles soon reclaim the field of the car's seat springs. The narrator leaves on his motorcycle, which is unglamorized, "Like the soul of the junkyard/Restored, a bicycle fleshed/With power"—an earlier, more convincing version of the spectacular "May Day Sermon."

"The Poisoned Man" deals with the same situation explored in a later poem, "Snakebite" (from FALLING, in Poems 1957–1967) in which the victim of a poisonous snake is forced to cut himself with a knife in order to drain out the poison. In the earlier poem a formal, almost allegorical meaning evolves from the terrifying experience; the poet has a kind of vision, feeling that his heart's blood could flow "Unendingly out of the mountain. . . ." "Snakebite" reduces this visionary abstraction to "I have a problem with/My right foot and my life." Aging, the poet is urgently concerned with survival itself; he has called himself a poet of "survival." In another poem about snakes, "Goodbye to Serpents," Dickey and his son observe snakes in a Parisian zoo, and Dickey tries to concentrate on them as he never has in the past. His meditation is so complete that he seems to pass into them, seeing the human world of towers and churches and streets "All old, all cold with my gaze. . . ." and he longs to believe that he has somehow retained, at the same time, his own human presence, the human miracles of "self" and "love." But it is a failure:

> And I know I have not been moved
> Enough by the things I have moved through,
> And I have seen what I have seen
>
> Unchanged, hypnotized, and perceptive. . . .

Unchanged, hypnotized, and perceptive: a strange combination of words. But in the first of Dickey's "reincarnation" poems in a later volume, *Buckdancer's Choice,* he becomes a snake with head "poisonous and poised." Perhaps he is suggesting that the very awe of nature that mesmerized him has prevented his being "moved" humanly by the things he has experienced. The mystic's world of total acceptance has always contrasted sharply with the world of human suffering.

Helmets concludes with one of Dickey's most remarkable poems, the little-discussed "Drinking from a Helmet." The young narrator, in wartime, drinks from a helmet he picked up near his foxhole and sways "as if kissed in the brain," standing

> . . . as though I possessed
> A cool, trembling man
> Exactly my size, swallowed whole.

He throws down his own helmet and puts on the one he has found, an inheritance from the dead. Then he seems to "see" in his own brain the dying man's last thought— a memory of two boys, the soldier and his older brother in a setting of tremendous trees "That would grow on the sun if they could. . . ." Where "Approaching Prayer" traced what seemed to be the poet's conscious effort to imagine a dying hog's experience, "Drinking from a Helmet" seems sheer unwilled vision:

> I saw a fence
> And two boys facing each other,
> Quietly talking,
> Looking in at the gigantic redwoods,
> The rings in the trunks turning slowly
> To raise up stupendous green.
> . . . .
> I would survive and go there,
> Stepping off the train in a helmet
> That held a man's last thought,
> Which showed him his older brother
> Showing him trees.
> I would ride through all
> California upon two wheels
> Until I came to the white
> Dirt road where they had been,
> Hoping to meet his blond brother,
> And to walk with him into the wood
> Until we were lost,
> Then take off the helmet
> And tell him where I had stood,
> What poured, what spilled, what swallowed:
>
> And tell him I was the man.

The relationship between the two brothers is interesting, because it reverses the relationship of Dickey and his own older brother, who evidently died before Dickey was born. (See "The Underground Stream," "The String," and other poems, in which the "tall cadaver" of the brother is summoned up by the poet, who believes himself conceived by his parents "out of grief" and brought to life

226

"To replace the incredible child" who had died. The psychologically disastrous results of such a belief, if sincere, hardly need to be examined; one is always a "survivor," always "guilty," and always conscious of being an inferior substitute for some superior being.) Here, the younger brother has died and Dickey himself will go to visit the surviving older brother, as if, somehow, both he and his older brother were living and able to speak to each other; a life-affirming magic, in spite of a young soldier's death.

Monsters

After *Helmets* Dickey's poetry changes considerably. The colloquial tone and unserious rhythms of "Cherrylog Road" are used for deadly serious purposes as Dickey explores hypothetical selves and the possibility of values outside the human sphere. Where in an early poem like "The Performance" a mystical placidity rendered even a brutal execution into something observed, now most actions, most states of being, are examined bluntly, brutally, emotionally, as the poet subjects himself to raw life without the sustaining rituals of Being.

Dickey has many extraordinary poems, fusions of "genius" and "art," but the central poem of his work seems to be "The Firebombing," from *Buckdancer's Choice*. No reader, adjusted to the high, measured art of Dickey's first three volumes, can be ready for this particular poem; it is unforgettable, and seems to me an important achievement in our contemporary literature, a masterpiece that could only have been written by an American, and only by Dickey.

"The Firebombing" is an eight-page poem of irregular
lines, abrupt transitions and leaps, stanzas of varying
length, connected by suburban-surreal images, a terrifying
visionary experience endured in a "well-stocked pantry."
Its effort is to realize, to *feel*, what the poet did twenty
years before as a participant in an "anti-morale raid" over
Japan during the closing months of World War II. Its
larger effort is to feel guilt and finally to feel anything.
One of the epigraphs to the poem is from the Book of
Job: "Or hast thou an arm like God?" This is Dickey's
ironic self-directed question, for it is he, Dickey, the
homeowner/killer, the Job/God, who has tried on the
strength of vast powers and has not been able to survive
them. Irony is something altogether new in Dickey:

Homeowners unite.

All families lie together, though some are burned alive.
The others try to feel
For them. Some can, it is often said.

The detachment is not godly, but despairing. Though he
is now Job, he was at one time the "arm of God," and
being both man and God is an impossibility. Dickey's
earlier war poems always show him a survivor, grateful
to survive, rather boyish and stunned by the mystery of a
strange rightness beneath disorder; it seems to have taken
him many years to get to this particular poem, though its
meaning in his life must have been central. Now the survivor is also a killer. What of this, what of killing?—What
is a release from the sin of killing? Confession, but, most
of all, guilt; if the poet cannot make himself feel guilt
even for the deaths of children, how will it be possible for
him to feel anything human at all?—

228

> . . . some technical-minded stranger with my hands
> Is sitting in a glass treasure-hole of blue light,
> Having potential fire under the undeodorized arms
> Of his wings, on thin bomb-shackles,
> The "tear-drop-shaped" 300-gallon drop-tanks
> Filled with napalm and gasoline.

This stranger is, or was, Dickey himself, who flew one hundred combat missions through the South Pacific, the Philippines, and Okinawa and participated in B-29 raids over Japan; but he is only a memory now, an eerily aesthetic memory. He exists in the mind of a suburban husband and father, worrying about his weight and the half-paid-for pantry that is part of his homeowning and his present "treasure-hole":

> Where the lawn mower rests on its laurels
> Where the diet exists
> For my own good   where I try to drop
> Twenty years. . . .

So many years after the event, what remains? He is now a civilian, a citizen, an American who understands himself in ironic, secret charge of all the necessary trivia of unaesthetic life—the purchasing of golf carts and tennis shoes, new automobiles, Christmas decorations—that he knows as the "glue inspired/By love of country," the means by which the possibly atomistic or death-bound ego is held fast in its identity. Though the wonder remains, he is far from the moon-hypnotized, somnambulistic rhythms of the past; "The Firebombing" is what Dickey would call an "open poem," one in which a certain compulsiveness in the presentation of the subject matter precludes or makes peripheral an aesthetic response,[6] and the poet's own recollection of his action is mocked, if it must be assessed in stylized terms:

As I sail artistically over
The resort town followed by farms,
Singing and twisting
All the handles in heaven   kicking
The small cattle off their feet
In a red costly blast
Flinging jelly over the walls
As in a chemical war-
fare field demonstration.

Remembering this, he knows that "my hat should crawl on my head" and "the fat on my body should pale"—but one of the horrors of this bombing raid is that it has somehow destroyed a normal human response, as if the "arm of God" the pilot had assumed had also annihilated him. Having shown us so convincingly in his poetry how natural, how inevitable, is man's love for all things, Dickey now shows us what happens when man is forced to destroy, forced to step down into history and be an American ("and proud of it"). In so doing he enters a tragic dimension in which few poets indeed have operated. Could Whitman's affirmation hold out if he were forced to affirm not just the violence of others, but his own? If war is necessary, warriors are necessary; someone must sacrifice his cosmic love; and not only is the traditional life-praising song of the poet savagely mocked by his performance as a patriot in wartime, but the poet cannot even experience his own deeds, for he has acted as a machine inside a machine. In "The Firebombing" everything must remain remote and abstract, not experienced in any vital way. The Machine Age splits man irreparably from his instinctive need to see, to feel, to *know* through the senses. The Whitmanesque affirmation of man is difficult to sustain if the poet can see the objects of his love only from a great height, through an intellectual telescope. When Whitman feels he is "on the verge of a usual mistake" ("Song of Myself," stanza 38), it is only an emotional mistake; he could never have considered the nihilism of a self without emotions, in which his inventiveness could really attach itself to nothing because it could experience nothing.

After this dreamlike unleashing of "all American fire," the poet states flatly that *death will not be what it should* —a counterstatement, perhaps, to Schweitzer's *reverence for life*. This is the poet's unique vision:

> Ah, under one's dark arms
> Something strange-scented falls—when those on earth
> Die, there is not even sound;
> One is cool and enthralled in the cockpit,
> Turned blue by the power of beauty,
> In a pale treasure-hole of soft light
> Deep in aesthetic contemplation,
> Seeing the ponds catch fire
> And cast it through ring after ring
> Of land. . . .
>
> . . . .
> It is this detachment,
> The honored aesthetic evil,
> The greatest sense of power in one's life,
> That must be shed in bars, or by whatever
> Means, by starvation
> Visions in well-stocked pantries. . . .

These "visions" will inspire in the poet wilder and wilder imaginings in his own creative life and an abandonment of the ego as "homeowner" in favor of the ego as "hunter" or "primitive." The mechanized State tempts one to an aesthetic evil, and so perhaps salvation may be found in a pre-aesthetic, prehistorical animality that will seize upon possible rites (the structural basis of *Deliverance*) in order to exorcise the despairing and suicidal violence of the animal self. Whether Dickey's themes are explorative rather than absolute, whether his work traces an autobiographical query or a record, the function of his poetry seems to be the demonstration of the failure of such a vision. And yet it is certainly tempting to take on the viciousness—and the innocence—of the animal, to take for our totems owls, snakes, foxes, wolverines, and to reject forever the possibilities of detachment and evil that are inherent in civilization.

Like Dostoyevsky, Dickey considers the helplessness of the *killer*. But, unlike Dostoyevsky, he cannot imagine a transformation of the killer into a higher form of himself: the mysterious process by which Raskolnikov grows and by which Smerdyakov can be seen as a rudimentary form of Father Zossima. But Dickey cannot operate through metaphor, as Dostoyevsky did, for he was the man, he did these things, *he* and no one else. Though his poetry charts a process of wonders, a changing of selves, finally he is only himself, a particular man, trapped in a finite and aging body with memories that belong to him and not to the rest of us, not to any liberalized concept of the guilt we all "share." (Like Marcuse, Dickey could probably feel no more than scorn for the "repressive tolerance" of some aspects of liberalism.) If made general and universal, in order to be shared, is guilt itself not made an aesthetic event?—a luxury?—a perversion?

But the narrator of the poem cannot concern himself with such abstractions:

> All this, and I am still hungry,
> Still twenty years overweight, still unable
> To get down there or see

What really happened.

. . . .

       . . . It is that I can imagine
At the threshold nothing
With its ears crackling off
Like powdery leaves,
Nothing with children of ashes, nothing not
Amiable, gentle, well-meaning. . . .

A poetry of Being can move to perfect resolutions, but this poetry of anguished Becoming cannot. ("Some can, it is often said," Dickey has remarked, ironically and sadly.) The narrative and confessional elements of "The Firebombing" demand a totally different aesthetic: the aesthetic-denying open form. No reconciliation of opposites is possible here because the poet cannot reconcile himself to his earlier self. And so what of "Absolution? Sentence?" These do not matter for "The thing itself is in that."

"The Firebombing" is central to an understanding of Dickey's work. It could not have been prophesied on the basis of the earlier, Roethke-inspired poems; but once it appears, unsuppressed, it is so powerful an illumination that it helps to explain a great deal that might remain mysterious and puzzling. *Buckdancer's Choice*, "Falling," and, above all, *The Eye-Beaters* deal with mortality, decay, disease, perhaps attributable in part to the poet's actual aging, but only in part, for the descent into a physically combative and increasingly unaesthetic world is not the usual pattern our finest poets follow, as both Roethke and Yeats, and other poets of the "Second Birth," suggest. Yet the emphasis Dickey places upon mortality, his self-consciousness about it, is a motif that begins to appear even in his literary criticism. How is it

233

possible that the man who believes in nature—in natural processes—should feel uneasy about the natural process of aging? It is a paradox in Hemingway also, but perhaps it is to be understood in Rilke's terms: our fear is not of death, but of life unlived. In an introduction to Paul Carroll's *The Young American Poets* (Chicago, 1968), Dickey makes a statement that totally contradicts the contemplative, balanced criticism of *The Suspect in Poetry* of only four years previous:

The aging process almost always brings to the poet the secret conviction that he has settled for far too little. . . . The nearer he gets to his end the more he yearns for the cave: for a wild, shaggy, all-out, all-involving way of speaking where language and he (or, now, someone: some new poet) engage each other at primitive levels, on ground where the issues are not those of literary fashion but are quite literally those of life and death. All his lifelong struggle with "craft" seems a tragic and ludicrous waste of time. . . .

(p. 7)

One would imagine, from such remarks, that the speaker is far older than forty-five; "the nearer he gets to his end . . ." is a visionary statement that might be comprehensible in the Yeats of *Last Poems*, but astonishing in a poet who is the same age as the Yeats of *The Green Helmet*. But if a denial of "craft" (or civilization) is needed in order to release spontaneous energy, then one can see why, for Dickey, it must be attempted.

Entropy

Buckdancer's Choice received the National Book Award in 1965, and in 1967 Dickey put together his *Poems 1957–*

1967 for Wesleyan University Press. The *Poems* do not observe strict chronological order, however, beginning with the demonic "May Day Sermon to the Women of Gilmer County, Georgia, by a Woman Preacher Leaving the Baptist Church," one of Dickey's most flamboyant poems. Clearly, Dickey does not want the reader to enter the world of *Into the Stone* with the innocence he himself had entered it; that celebration of forms is all but outshouted by the eleven-page sermon, which is about violence done to and by a young girl in Georgia, and about her escape with her motorcycle-riding lover, "stoned out of their minds on the white/Lightning of fog"—

> singing   the saddlebags full of her clothes
> Flying   snagging   shoes hurling away   stockings grabbed-off
> Unwinding and furling on twigs: all we know   all we could
>   follow
> Them by was her underwear   was stocking after stocking
>   where it tore
> Away, and a long slip stretched on a thorn   all these few gave
> Out. Children, you know it: that place was where they took
> Off into the air   died   disappeared   entered my mouth
>   your mind

It is an incredible achievement, with the intonations of a mad, inspired sermon, the flesh elevated beyond the spirit, but both elevated into myth. It is a myth that transforms everything into it: everything turns into everything else, through passion. The intellect exercises very little control in this "wild, shaggy, all-out, all-involving" work, and though Dickey has expressed doubt over the value of Allen Ginsberg's poetry,[7] one is forced to think of certain works of Ginsberg's and of how, under ether sniffing or morphine injection, Ginsberg wrote all of *Ankor Wat*

and that extravaganza "Aether," in which a preaching
voice proclaims certain truths to us: "we are the sweep-
ings of the moon/we're what's *left over* from perfection"
—"(my) Madness is intelligible reactions to/Unintelli-
gible phenomena"—

And—

> What *can* be possible
> in a minor universe
> in which you can see
> God by sniffing the
> gas in a cotton?
>
> ("Aether," in *Reality Sandwiches*)

Dickey is much more violent, more heartless than Ginsberg, of course, since he is driven by energies more archaic
than is Ginsberg, who is a philosopher with a respect
for the syntax of the imagination if not of superficial
grammar; the "May Day Sermon" is at once revenge for
and repetition of the helplessness of the bomber pilot, a
mythic annihilation of a punishing, near-invisible father,
and an escape off into space, the girl's clothing cast off
behind her like the airline stewardess' clothing in "Falling." In all the exuberant spurts of language there is violence, but especially here:

> And she comes down   putting her back into
> The hatchet   often   often   he is brought down   laid out
> Lashing   smoking   sucking wind: Children, each year at this
>   time
> A girl will tend to take an ice pick in both hands   a lone pine
> Needle   will hover   hover: Children, each year at this time
> Things happen quickly   and it is easy for a needle to pass
> Through the eye of a man bound for Heaven   she leaves it
>   naked goes
> Without further sin through the house

236

After countless readings, "May Day Sermon" still has the power to shock: consider the "needle-eye-Heaven" joke. The maniacal repetitions make one wince ("get up . . . up in your socks and rise"), and the Dylan Thomas-surreal touches sometimes seem forced ("Dancing with God in a mule's eye"), but the poem's shrieking transmutation of murder, nakedness, eroticism, fertility, and poetry into a single event has an irresistible strength: "everything is more   *more*   MORE." Nature itself becomes active in the process of transmutation as even "peanuts and beans exchange/Shells in joy," and in a poetic sleight of hand reminiscent of Thomas' *Ballad of the Long-Legged Bait* at its apocalyptic conclusion, "the barn falls in/Like Jericho." The countryside itself is speaking through the woman preacher "as beasts speak to themselves/Of holiness learned in the barn." It is mysticism, but existential and ribald, noisy, filled with the humming of gnats and strange prophecies:

> Each May you will crouch like a sawhorse to make yourself
> More here   you will be cow chips   chickens croaking. . . .
> . . . .
>   and every last one of you will groan
> Like nails barely holding   and your hair be full of the gray
> Glints of stump chains.   Children, each year at this time you will have
> Back-pain, but also heaven

In "May Day Sermon" Dickey creates a patchwork of images that go beyond the "not wholly sane" images of "Chenille."

However, *Buckdancer's Choice* contains several very personal and moving poems dealing with mortality, the title poem and "Angina" (which deal with Dickey's mother, an invalid "dying of breathless angina"), "Them, Crying," "The Escape," and one that reasserts the mystical possibility of transcending death, its certainties expressed in a steady three-beat line:

> All ages of mankind unite
> Where it is dark enough.
> . . . .
> All creatures tumbled together
> Get back in their wildest arms
> No single thing but each other. . . .
>
> ("The Common Grave")

But the most passionate poems are counterstatements concerned with developing images adequate to express horror; in "Pursuit from Under" the poet summons up a terrifying image that does not have its place in his own experience, or even in his probable experience, but is a conscious re-creation of a memory. He is standing in a meadow, in August, and imagines he hears the "bark of seals" and feels "the cold of a personal ice age. . . ." Then he recalls having once read an account of Arctic explorers who died of starvation and whose journal contained a single entry of unforgettable horror:

> . . . under the ice,
>
> The killer whale darts and distorts,
> Cut down by the flawing glass
>
> To a weasel's shadow,
> And when, through his ceiling, he sees
> Anything darker than snow
> He falls away

238

To gather more and more force

· · · · · · · ·

        . . . then charges
Straight up, looms up at the ice and smashes
Into it with his forehead. . . .

And so the killer whale pursues the poet, even in this
familiar meadow in the South, and he thinks of "how the
downed dead pursue us"—"not only in the snow/But in
the family field." It is interesting to note that Norman
Mailer's nihilistic and very deliberately "literary" novel
Why Are We in Vietnam? also transports its protago-
nist/victim to the Arctic in order to allow him a vision
of God-as-beast; this "vision" is then imposed upon all
of American (universal?) experience and can allow for no
possibilities of transcendence. If God is a beast (as Dickey
concludes in "The Eye-Beaters"), then the beast is God,
and one must either acquiesce to Him and experience the
helplessness of terror in an ordinary southern meadow,
or imitate Him, taking on some of His powers. But, increasingly, the poet reaches out beyond his own geo-
graphical and historical territory to appropriate this vision.
It demands a distortion or a rejection of naturalistic life;
at times, as he admits, a kind of necessary theatricality, as
he explains in *Self-Interviews* why hunting is so important to him: ". . . the main thing is to re-enter the cycle
of the man who hunts for his food. Now this may be play-
acting at being a primitive man, but it's better than not
having any rapport with the animal at all . . . I have a
great sense of renewal when I am able to go into the
woods and hunt with a bow and arrow, to enter into the
animal's world in this way." And, in *Deliverance*, the
experience of "renewal" or deliverance itself is stimulated
by a hunt for other men; simple animals are no longer

239

enough, and the whole of the novel is constructed around those several intensely dramatic moments in which the narrator sights his target—a human and usually forbidden target—and kills him with an arrow from his powerful bow. The arrow is at least real; the napalm and gasoline bomb are not, since they are dropped upon abstractions. And, too, the necessary intimacy of the besieged men in *Deliverance* approximates a primitive brotherliness, excluding the confusion that women bring to a world of simple, clear, direct actions. For women, while mysterious and unfathomable, are also "civilization."

But if women are objects, goddess objects, they too can be assimilated into the mystique of primitive power-worship. One of the most striking poems in all of Dickey's work is "The Fiend," which magically transforms a voyeur/lover into a tree, into an omnipotent observer, back into a voyeur again, while throughout he is the poet who loves and desires and despairs of truly knowing his subject; the poem is a long, hushed, reverential overture to murder. Yet the equation of the voyeur with the poet is obvious, and the poem concludes ominously by remarking how "the light/Of a hundred favored windows" has "gone wrong somewhere in his glasses. . . ." Dickey is remarkably honest in acknowledging the value he puts upon his own fantasies, in contrast to the less interesting world of reality. What is important is *his* imaginative creation, *his* powers of seeing. In praise of what a Jungian would call the "anima," Dickey has said in *Sorties* that "poor mortal perishable women are as dust before these powerful and sensual creatures of the depths of one's being" (p. 4). A dangerous overestimation of the individual's self-sufficiency, one might think, especially since there is always the possibility of that interior light going "wrong somewhere in his glasses."

In fact, in Dickey's later poems eyesight becomes crucial, aligned with the mysterious grace of masculinity itself. When one's vision begins to weaken, there is an immediate danger of loss of control; conversely, "sight" itself can be rejected, denied, as a prelude to glorious savagery. Or the denial of vision can facilitate a more formal, sinister betrayal, as Dickey imagines himself as, simultaneously, a slave owner on a southern plantation and the white father of an illegitimate black son and the father-who-denies-his-son, a master driven to madness by his role as an owner, in the poem "Slave Quarters." Dickey's question concerns itself with many forms of paternal betrayal, a betrayal of the eyes of others:

> What it is to look once a day
> Into an only
> Son's brown, waiting, wholly possessed
> Amazing eye, and not
> Acknowledge, but own. . . .

How take on the guilt . . . ? is the poem's central question.

In the section FALLING in *Poems 1957–1967*, Dickey explores further extensions of life, beginning with "Reincarnation (II)," in which the poet has taken on the form of a bird. His first reincarnation was into a snake, which we leave waiting in an old wheel not for food but for the first man to walk by—minute by minute the head of the snake becoming "more poisonous and poised." But as a bird the poet undergoes a long, eerie, metaphysical flight that takes him out of mortality altogether—

to be dead
In one life is to enter
Another   to break out   to rise above   the clouds

But "Reincarnation (II)" is extremely abstract and does not seem to have engaged the poet's imaginative energies as deeply as "Reincarnation (I)" of *Buckdancer's Choice*. It is balanced by the long "Falling," an astonishing poetic feat that dramatizes the accidental fall of an airline stewardess from a plane to her death in a corn field. "The greatest thing that ever came to Kansas" undergoes a number of swift metamorphoses—owl, hawk, goddess—stripping herself naked as she falls. She imagines the possibility of falling into water, turning her fall into a dive so that she can "come out healthily dripping/And be handed a Coca-Cola," but ultimately she is helpless to save herself; she is a human being, not a bird like the spiritual power of "Reincarnation (II)," and she comes to know how "the body will assume without effort any position/Except the one that will sustain it   enable it to rise live/Not die." She dies, "driven well into the image of her body," inexplicable and unquestionable, and her clothes begin to come down all over Kansas; a kind of mortal goddess, given as much immortality by this strange poem as poetry is capable of giving its subjects.

The starkly confessional poem "Adultery" tells of the poet's need for life-affirming moments, though they are furtive and evidently depend upon a belief that the guilt caused by an act of adultery is magical—"We have done it again   we are/Still living." The poem's subject is really not adultery or any exploration of the connections between people; it is about the desperate need to prove that life is still possible. *We are still living*: that guilty, triumphant cry. In this poem and several others, Dickey

242

seems to share Norman Mailer's sentiment that sex would be meaningless if divorced from "guilt." What role does the woman play in this male scenario? She is evidently real enough, since she is driven to tears by the impossibility of the adulterous situation; but in a more important sense she does not really exist, for she is one of those "poor mortal perishable women" temporarily illuminated by the man's anima-projection, and she is "as dust" compared to the fantasy that arises from the depths of the lover's being. Descartes' *I doubt, hence I think; I think, hence I am* has become, for those who despair of the Cartesian logic of salvation, *I love, hence I exist; I am loved, hence I must exist. . . .*

With Dickey this fear is closely related to the fundamental helplessness he feels as a man trapped in a puzzling technological civilization he cannot totally comprehend. Even the passionate love of women and the guilt of adultery will not be sufficient, ultimately, to convince the poet that he will continue to exist. He identifies with the wolverine, that "small, filthy, unwinged" creature whose species is in danger of extinction, in the poem "For the Last Wolverine." The wolverine is an animal capable of "mindless rage," enslaved by the "glutton's internal fire," but Dickey recognizes a kinship with it in the creature's hopeless desire to "eat/The world. . . ."

Yet, for all its bloodthirsty frenzy, the wolverine is in danger of dying out. It is a "nonsurvivor" after all. The poet's mystical identification with this beast is, paradoxically, an identification with death, and death driven, indeed, is the impulse behind his musing: "How much the timid poem needs/The mindless explosion of your rage. . . ." Like Sylvia Plath and innumerable others, the poet imagines a division between himself as a human being

243

and the rest of the world—the universe itself—symbolized by the fact that his consciousness allows him to see and to judge his position, while the rest of nature is more or less mute. It is doubtful, incidentally, that nature is really so mute, so unintelligent, as alienated personalities seem to think; it is certainly doubtful that the human ego, the "I," is in any significant way isolated from the vast, living totality of which it is a part. However, granted for the moment that the poet is "timid" when he compares himself to the most vicious of animals, it is still questionable whether such viciousness, such "mindless explosion" of rage, is superior to the poem, to the human activity of creating and organizing language in a coherent, original structure. The prayer of the poem is very moving, but it is not the wolverine's consciousness that is speaking to us: "Lord, let me die   but not die/Out."

Dickey has dramatized from the inside the terrors of the personality that fears it may not be immortal after all; its control of itself and of other people and of the environment seems to be more and more illusory, fading, failing. "Entropy"—a much-used and misused term—refers to the phenomenon of energy loss and increasing disorder as a system begins to falter, and is always a threat, a terror, to those who assume that the system to which they belong or which they have themselves organized was meant to be infinite. There is no space here to consider the psychological reasons for the shift from man's assumption of immortality as an abstraction (the "immortal" soul was expected to survive, but not the "mortal" man—the personality or ego) to his frantic and futile hope for immortality in the flesh. There are cultural, political, economic reasons, certainly, but they cannot entirely account for the naïveté of the wish: *I want to live forever.* Because this wish is so extraordinarily naïve, even childish, it is never allowed in that form into the consciousness of most intelligent people. When it emerges, it is always disguised. It sometimes takes the form of a vague, disappointed despair; or rage without any appropriate object; or a hopeless and even sentimental envy of those human beings (or animals) who strike the despairing one as too stupid to know how unhappy they should be. The excessive admiration of animals and birds and other manifestations of "unconscious" nature is, in some people, a screen for their own self-loathing. They are in "hell" because the activity of their consciousness is mainly self-concerned, self-questioning, self-doubting. The rest of the world, however, seems quite content. As entropy is irrationally feared by some, it is as irrationally welcomed by others. Disorganization—chaos—the "mindless explosion" of repressed rage: all are welcomed, mistaken for a liberating of the deepest soul.

Mysticism: Evolution, Dissolution

Mysticism is generally considered in the light of its highest religious and spiritual achievements. Most literature on the subject deals exclusively with saintly human beings, some of whom have experienced not only a powerful emotional enlightenment but an intellectual enlightenment as well. These mystics are the ones who have, in a sense, created our world: it is unnecessary to mention their names, since in a way those of us who live now have always lived, unconsciously, involuntarily, within the scope of their imaginations—as a writer lives, when he is writing, within the vast but finite universe of his language. There is an existence beyond that, surely; but he cannot quite imagine it. That I exist at this moment— that I am a writer, a woman, a surviving human being— has very little to do with accident, but is a direct, though remote, consequence of someone's thinking: *Let us value life. Let us enhance life. Let us imagine a New World, a democracy.* . . . It is not true, as Auden so famously stated, that poetry makes nothing happen. On the contrary, poetry, or the poetic imagination, has made everything happen.

Yet "mysticism" can swing in other directions. Essentially, it is a loss of "ego," but it may result in a loss of "ego control" as well. A mysterious, unfathomable revolution seems to be taking place in our civilization, and like all upheavals in history it is neither knowable nor governable; like inexplicable branchings in the flow of life, in evolution, it goes its way quite apart from the wishes of entire species, let alone individuals. However, it seems to be characterized by loss of ego, by experiences of transcendence among more and more people, especially younger people. Yet one brings to that other world of mysticism only the equipment, the conscious moral intelligence, that one has developed through the activities of the ego: the experience of oneness with the divine, the knowledge of *That Art Thou*, gives us in its benevolent expression Jesus Christ, Gautama Buddha, and other founders of great religions, and in its malignant and grotesque expression a Hitler, a Stalin, a Charles Manson. The most important study of this subject still remains William James's *Varieties of Religious Experience*, since it was written by a man who did experience a sense of his ego's dissolution but who had not a ready-made religious structure into which he might leap. The mystic breaks free of human codes of morality, of all restraints, of "civilization," of normality itself. Useless to argue with him, for he *knows*. When D. H. Lawrence declares that he is allied with the sun and not with men, he is speaking out of the certainty of his religious knowledge that he *is* a form of energy and derives his finite being only from a higher, external form of energy. Literary critics may concern themselves with metaphors, symbols, and allusions, but most writers are writing out of their deepest experience; the playful organization of words into structures, the aesthetic impulse, is always a secondary activity. And so is social action. And so is that social being, the "ego."

But when the conscious ego has despaired of discovering values in the social world or in the world of spirit, the dissolution of that ego will probably not result in a higher wisdom, in an elevation of the moral sense so passionately required for survival. Instead, the mystic may plunge into his own ancestral past, into his own "animal" nature. This is especially tempting in an era characterized by superficiality, bad thinking, and outright inhumanity, for these abnormalities are considered "normal" and therefore "human." Something must be valued—some god must be worshiped. Where is he? Where is it? *Who has experienced him?*

So it is not surprising that many people value the "animal" over the "human," as if animals were not extraordinarily intelligent in their own contexts. In any case animals are not valued for what they are, but for their evidently uncivilized qualities; perhaps even for their cunning and savagery, their "innocence." Should it be argued that animals live and die within strict codes of behavior (which in our species is "morality"), the romantic will

247

not listen; he is certain that *his* animals are free, wild, even immortal in their own way. They always do all the things he has wished to do, but has not dared. They are not so obviously and embarrassingly his own creation as a cartoonist's animals are his, but they share, often with the female sex, that special numinous grace of being the image bearers of men. If it is a question of mere survival, the ideal will be a predator who cannot not survive, because he demands so little of his environment. Ted Hughes's *Crow* poems, for instance, are concerned with a minimal consciousness that is always human, though reduced to beak and claws and uncanny keenness of vision. But the poems are, upon examination, oddly abstract, even rhetorical and argumentative; they have very little of the slashing emotional immediacy of Dickey's best poems. What to Ted Hughes is an allegorical possibility is for Dickey an existential fact.

As the poet wakes from his dream of "stone," enters the turbulent contests of "flesh," he will no longer be able, even, to "sail artistically over" the wars of his civilization. He must participate in them as a man; if they will not come to him, he must seek them out.

The horror of Dickey's novel *Deliverance* grows out of its ordinary, suburban framework, the assimilation of brutal events by ordinary men; not near-Biblical figures like Crow, or men trapped in a distant and hostile world, but four middle-aged, middle-class men who want to canoe along a dangerous but attractive river not far from their homes. The novel is about our deep, instinctive needs to get back to nature, to establish some kind of rapport with primitive energies, but it is also about the need of some men to do violence, to be delivered out of their banal lives by a violence so irreparable that it can never be confessed. It is a fantasy of a highly civilized and affluent society, which imagines physical violence to be transforming in a mystical—and therefore permanent—sense, a society in which rites of initiation no longer exist. This society asks its men: *How do you know you are men?* But there is no answer except in terms of an earlier society, where the male is distinguished from the female, so far as behavior is concerned, by his physical strength and his willingness to risk life. But killing other men can be made into a ritual, a proof of one's manhood; *Deliverance* is about this ritual. It is like Mailer's short novel *Why Are We in Vietnam?* in its consideration of homosexuality, though for Mailer homosexuality evokes terror and for Dickey it evokes loathing. The boys in the Mailer novel tremble on the verge of becoming lovers in their Arctic camp, but they draw back from each other, terrified, and are then given tremendous energies as "killer brothers" now united to go fight the war in Vietnam. Both novels demonstrate not any extraordinary fear of homosexuality but, what is more disturbing, a fear of affection. Dickey has so created his backwoods degenerates as to be beyond all human sympathy, so that most readers are compelled to become "killers" along with the narrator. The murder of the homosexual threat, whether an exterior force or an inner impulse, results in an apparent increase in animal spirits and appetite, and the narrator is able to return to civilization and to his wife, a man with a profound secret, in touch with an illicit, demonic mystery, delivered. Violence has been his salvation—his deliverance from ordinary life.

The Eye-Beaters, Blood, Victory, Madness, Buckhead

and Mercy is as crammed and various as its title suggests. A few poems are bluntly confessional, the "Apollo" poem is linked to a historic event, and all are in the same tone of musing, sometimes cynical, sometimes tender contemplation. The volume ends with "Turning Away: Variations on Estrangement," a complex, abstract work of philosophical inquiry; but most of its poems are linked firmly to domestic things, and even the difficult subjects of disease and death are made "livable," in Dickey's words.

The book is disturbing because it asks so many questions but refuses to answer them. It is filled with questions: *What did I say? Or do? Am I still drunk? Who is this woman? Where? Can you see me? Can the five fingers/Of the hand still show against/anything? Have they come for us?* It is also disturbing because of its attitude toward certain subjects: men suffering from diabetes and cancer are not treated solemnly, and in Dickey's fantasy of dying from a heart attack (or love) he and the nurse/prostitute flicker downward together "Like television like Arthur Godfrey's face/Coming on huge happy." The book's seventeen poems are of widely varying length and seem to make up a dialogue or combat among their various themes, as if the poet were entering into a battle with aspects of his soul—the word "battle" used deliberately here, because Dickey declares in "Turning Away" how it is necessary to turn "From an old peaceful love/To a helmet of silent war/Against the universe."

Many of the poems are about diseased emotions or diseased forms of hope, such as the futility of seeking out one's youth by "going home" decades later; but several deal with specific disorders—"Diabetes," "The Cancer Match," "Madness," and "The Eye-Beaters" (which is

250

about both blindness and insanity). "Diabetes" is a brutally frank, sardonic confessional poem in two parts, which begins with the poet's gigantic thirst: "One night I thirsted like a prince/Then like a king/Then like an empire like a world/On fire." But the thirst is not a thirst for life, it is not a metaphor; it is clinically real. After the illness is diagnosed, the poet sees sugar as "gangrene in white," and his routine of exercise is attended by an ironic counting, a parody of his earlier poetic themes:

> Each time the barbell
> Rose each time a foot fell
> Jogging, it counted itself
> One death two death three death and resurrection
> For a little while. Not bad! . . .

He will endure a "livable death," scaled down and presided over by a nice young physician. The second half of the poem, "Under Buzzards," has Dickey imagining in heavy summer the "birds of death" attracted by the "rotten, nervous sweetness" of his blood, the "city sugar" of his life. In a final, defiant gesture, the poet deliberately summons the birds of death, but he does it in a curiously unheroic way, by taking a forbidden drink of beer:

> Red sugar of my eyeballs
> Feels them [the buzzards] turn blindly
> In the fire rising turning turning
> Back to Hogback Ridge, and it is all
> Delicious, brother: my body is turning is flashing
> unbalanced
> Sweetness everywhere, and I am calling my birds.

Characteristic of this volume is a repeated use of terms to link the reader with the poet: "my friend," "brother," "companion," "my son," "you." The whole of "Venom"

251

is a kind of prayer, the poet and his listener joined as brothers who must "turn the poison/Round," back on itself, the venom that comes "from the head" of man and corrupts his life blood. "Madness" is about a domestic dog that contracts rabies and must be killed, but it is also a call for "Help help madness help."

Balancing the poems of disease are several about Dickey's sons and the *Life*-commissioned double poem, "Apollo," placed near the physical center of the magazine and divided by a black page—a symbol of the black featureless depths of space in which our planet, "the blue planet steeped in its dream," has a minute existence. The poems to or about Dickey's sons are all excellent, though there is an air of sorrow about them. "The Lord in the Air" is prefaced by a quotation from Blake: ". . . If the spectator could . . . make a friend & companion of one of these Images of wonder . . . then would he meet the Lord in the air & . . . be happy." Dickey seems to be re-imagining an earlier role of his own as he describes a son's performance with a crow whistle, so deceiving the crows that they come to him from miles away, "meeting the Lord/Of their stolen voice in the air." The crows have but one word, a syllable that means everything to them, and in gaining control of it the boy becomes a kind of poet. A "new/Power over birds and beasts" has been achieved by man, but "not for betrayal, or to call/Up death or desire, but only to give" a unique tone "never struck in the egg." *O Chris come in, drop off now* is the language Dickey allots to himself; magic has become the property of his boy.

"Messages" deals with images of life—(butterflies with "ragged, brave wings") and death (a cow's skeleton), and matches the father's protectiveness with his wisdom, which his sleeping son cannot yet be told: that life is a gamble, a play "in bones and in wings and in light." The poem is also about the necessity of a father's surrendering his son to life—"to the sea"—with the reminder that human love exists in its own world, unchallenged by the nihilistic depths of the ocean or the speechless primitive world. The love evident in the "message" poems is totally lacking in the disease poems, as if the speakers were angrily fighting self-pity; "The Cancer Match" imagines cancer and whiskey fighting together, in the drunken mind of a dying man who has "cancer and whiskey/In a lovely relation": "I watch them struggle/All around the room, inside and out/Of the house, as they battle/Near the mailbox. . . ." No dignity here, even in dying; the poem refuses to mourn the body's decay.

Addressing himself to the Apollo moon shot, Dickey synthesizes the diverse emotions of awe, suspicion, cynicism, and acquiescence; like Mailer in *Of a Fire on the Moon*, he cannot help but wonder if some catastrophe will be unleashed ("Will the moon-plague kill our children . . . ?"), and just as Mailer contemplated photographs of the moon's surface and thought of Cézanne, Dickey, in the imagined consciousness of one of the moon explorers, hears lines from Gray's Elegy "helplessly coming/From my heart. . . ." A triumph of technology is seen in terms of aesthetic triumphs of the past. Both men express doubt about the future, but both accept its inevitable direction, though Dickey is characteristically more emotionally involved:

> My eyes blind
> With unreachable tears   my breath goes all over
> Me and cannot escape. . . .

Our clothes embrace we cannot touch we cannot
Kneel. We stare into the moon
dust, the earth-blazing ground. We laugh, with the beautiful
craze
Of static. We bend, we pick up stones.

The future is explorable, however, only through one's imaginative identification with other men. The most powerful poems in *The Eye-Beaters* are those that refuse to deal with the future at all and explore old obsessions with the past. The pathetic double poem "Going Home" takes the poet ("the Keeper") back to his own lost childhood, where he encounters his Old Self like a "younger brother, like a son," in a confusion of homes, times, places, rooms that live "only/In my head." His childhood is distant from the adulthood he now inhabits, in which he is a Keeper of rooms "growing intolerable," through which he walks like a stranger, "as though I belonged there." The riddle of *Identities! Identities!* the younger Dickey puzzled over (in the poem "Mangham" of *Buckdancer's Choice*) still taunts him, as past and present contend, and the Keeper fears he will go mad with his questions:

> And tell me for the Lord God
> 's sake, where are all our old
> Dogs?
>   Home?
>   Which way is that?
> Is it this vacant lot? . . .

In a final admission of defeat, the "mad, weeping Keeper" realizes that he cannot keep anything alive: none of his rooms, his people, his past, his youth, himself. Yet he cannot let them die either, and he will call them "for a little while, sons." In "Looking for the Buckhead Boys," a poem on the verge of turning into a short story, the futile search for one's youth in the past is given a specific location, and the poet returns to his home town to look for his old friends; if he can find one of them, just one, he believes his youth will once again "walk/Inside me like a king." But his friends are gone, or changed, or paralyzed or, like Charlie Gates at the filling station, not really the person for whom the poet has a secret "that has to be put in code." The poem ends with a flat anticlimactic imperative: "Fill 'er up, Charlie." Encountering one's past, in the form of an old friend, underscores the impossibility of "keeping" the past.

"The Eye-Beaters" is an extravagant, curious fantasy, supposedly set in a home for children in Indiana. In this home some children have gone blind, evidently since admission; not just blind, but mad, so that their arms must be tied at their sides to prevent their beating their eyeballs in order to stimulate the optic nerves. By no naturalistic set of facts can one determine how this "home" can be real, and so the reader concludes that the entire poem is an explorative fantasy, like "The Owl King," which dealt with a child's blindness. The blindness of the children and their pathetic response to it is so distressing that the Visitor must create a fiction in order to save himself from madness. He tries to imagine what they see:

> Lord, when they slug
> Their blue cheeks blacker, can it be that they do not see the wings
> And green of insects   or the therapist suffering kindly but
>   a tribal light old
> Enough to be seen without sight?

255

The vision he imagines for them is prehistoric; a cave-man artist, "Bestial, working like God," is drawing beasts on a cave wall: deer, antelope, elk, ibex, quagga, rhinoceros of wool-gathering smoke, cave bear, mammoth, "beings that appear/Only in the memory of caves." The niches of the children's middle brain, "where the race is young," are filled not with images of the Virgin but with squat shapes of the Mother or with the bloody hand print on the stone "where God gropes like a man" and where the artist "hunts and slashes" his wounded game. Then the Visitor's rational, skeptical nature argues with him, addressing him as "Stranger"; perhaps the children want to smash their eyes in order to see nothing, and the Visitor's invention of the cave-man artist is an expression of his own blindness, his hope for magic that might "reinvent the vision of the race." He admits his desire to believe that the world calls out for art, for the magical life-renewal of art, and not for the blankness of nothing save physical pain. Otherwise it is possible that he will go mad. Otherwise what can he value in his own poetry? The artist must be a therapist to the race, and not simply to himself; but Dickey concludes this complex poem by acquiescing to his own self-defined "fiction," a kind of lie that enables him to identify himself with the cave-man artist and to escape the deadening truths of his Reason by choosing "madness,/Perversity." He projects himself back into a dim racial memory, a hideous vision that excludes history. No salvation, except by way of a total surrender to the irrational and uninventive:

> Beast, get in
> My way. Your body opens onto the plain. Deer, take me
> into your life-

lined form. I merge, I pass beyond in secret   in perver-
                                            sity and the sheer
Despair of invention   my double-clear bifocals off   my
                                            reason gone
Like eyes. Therapist, farewell at the living end. Give me
                                            my spear.

The prayer, addressed to a "Beast," necessarily involves
the poet in a transformation downward, into a kind of
human beast whose "despair of invention" forces him to
inarticulate, violent action. It is possible that the conclusion is an ambiguous one—the artist denying his art
through a self-conscious work of art—or, as Raymond
Smith has seen it, in an essay called "The Poetic Faith of
James Dickey,"[8] the poet rejecting any art-for-art's-sake
aesthetic. However, the final words of the poem seem
the expression of a suicidal loss of faith in anything but
action, and that action primitive and bloody.

Dickey has diagnosed this action as "Perversity," and
the poem has a passionate, religious feel about it, the
testament of a loss of faith in one religion (Art) and the
tentative commitment to another (the "Beast"). This is
the mystical leap that Dickey's imagination has yearned
for, the defiance of his higher, artistic, moral self, experienced in middle age as a banality from which he must—
somehow—be delivered.

The forms of Dickey's "heroism" are anachronistic,
perhaps, but his despair may be prophetic.

In these later poems, the poems of "flesh," there is a
dramatic ferocity that goes beyond even the shimmering
walls of words he created for "Falling" and "May Day
Sermon." Dickey is there, inside the poem; reading it,
we are inside his head. He is willing to tell everything,
anything; he is willing to become transparent, in war now

257

against his own exquisite sensibility. *Help help mad-ness help:* the book's shameless cry.

Society did not always shy away from the self-expression of its most sensitive and eccentric members. Much has been written about the relationship of so-called primitive people with their priests and shamans: these societies benefited from their leaders' ecstasies and bizarre revelations and did not destroy them as heretics or castrate them by interpreting their visions as "only poetry." What value can the visionary give to his own experience if, returning to the world with it, he is at the very most congratulated for having invented some fascinating, original metaphors? Dickey, so disturbing to many of us, must be seen in a larger context, as a kind of "shaman," a man necessarily at war with his civilization because that civilization will not, cannot, understand what he is saying. Mircea Eliade defines the shaman as a "specialist in ecstasy": traditionally, he excites himself into a frenzy, enters a trancelike state, and receives the power of understanding and imitating the language of birds and animals. He is not a "normal" personality, at least in these times. He participates in what is believed to be divine.

If the shaman, or the man with similar magical powers, has no social structure in which to interpret himself, and if he is obviously not normal in the restrictive sense of that word, his instincts will lead him into a rebellion against that world; at his most serene, he can manage a cynical compromise with it. Irony can be a genteel form of savagery, no less savage than physical brutality. In some intellectuals, irony is the expression of disappointed hopes; in others, it is a substitute for violence. It *is* violent. If the release offered by words no longer satisfies the intense need of the sufferer, he will certainly fall into despair, estrangement. Hence a preoccupation, in Dickey, with physical risk, a courting of the primitive in art and in life (in carefully restricted areas, of course), and a frantic, even masochistic need to continually test and "prove" himself.[9] The ritual of hunting cannot ultimately work, because it is so obviously a "ritual"—a game—and bears no relationship at all to what hunting was, and is, to people who must hunt for their food. It is just another organized adventure, another "timid poem." Consciousness is split on a number of levels: the sensual keenness inspired by adultery and guilt, the excitement inspired by near death, the mindless rage of the beast who fears extinction, the plight of the overweight suburban homeowner, the husband, the father, the poet . . . and yet the truest self seems somehow detached, uninvolved. "Turning Away," the last poem in *The Eye-Beaters*, deals with aspects of estrangement not simply in terms of marriage but in terms of the self, which hopes to see "Later, much later on" how it may make sense—perhaps as a fictional creation, in a book.

If regression cannot be justified by calling it "ritual"—hunting, fighting, excessively brutal sports—it must be abandoned. If the poet can no longer evoke the "primitive," since his body cannot keep pace with the demands of his imagination, the primitive ideal must be abandoned. Physical prowess—extraordinary keenness of eyesight—can be undermined by that baffling human problem, mortality and disease. Death awaits. Yet one is not always prepared for it. If it is seen as an embarrassment, another obscure defeat, it will never be accepted at all; better to pray for the Apocalypse, so that everyone can die at once, with no one left to think about it afterward. The stasis celebrated in much of contemporary literature,

259

the erecting of gigantic paranoid-delusion systems that are self-enclosed and self-destructing, argues for a simple failure of reasoning: the human ego has too long imagined itself the supreme form of consciousness in the universe. When that delusion is taken from it, it suffers. Suffering, it projects its emotions outward onto everything, everyone, into the universe itself. Our imaginative literature has largely refused to integrate ever-increasing subtleties of intuitive experience with those of intellectual experience; it will not acknowledge the fact that the dynamism of our species has become largely a dynamism of the brain, not the body. Old loves die slowly. But they die.

The concluding poem in *The Eye-Beaters* differs from the rest in many ways. It is primarily a meditation. It is almost entirely speculative, an abstract seventeen-stanza work dealing with the mystery of the soul. The familiar theme of battle and certain specific images involved (helmets, meadows of "intensified grass") are used in a way new to Dickey; its tone of hard, impassive detachment contrasts with the despairing ferocity of "The Eye-Beaters" and the poems of disease.

The immediate occasion for the poem is evidently dissatisfaction with an "old peaceful love." Another person, nearby, is "suddenly/Also free . . . weeping her body away." But the confessional quality of the poem is not very important; the poet's detachment approaches that of Eliot's in "Four Quartets." Dickey could very well be writing about himself—his relationship with his "soul" (which in mystical literature is usually identified with the feminine, though that interpretation is probably not necessary). The poet's problem is how, as a "normal" man, to relate his predicament with the human condition generally. As in "Reincarnation (II)," the poet discovers himself released from one life and projected into another, where he feels himself "Like a king starting out on a journey/Away from all things that he knows." Outside the "simple-minded window" is a world of ordinary sights, from which one may take his face; yet this world is one of danger and "iron-masked silence." In utter stillness the poet stands with his palm on the window sill (as he once stood with his palm on the fence wire) and feels the "secret passivity" and "unquestionable Silence" of existence: man wears the reason for his own existence as he stands and, in such a confrontation, the "tongue grows solid also."

Imagined then as a kind of Caesar (Dickey would like to "see with/the eyes of a very great general," here as elsewhere), he realizes he has nothing to do in his own life with his military yearnings and his hope for himself to be utterly free of any finite time or place, an omnipotent life force released from identity to "breed/With the farthest women/And the farthest also in time: breed/ Through bees, like flowers and bushes:/Breed Greeks, Egyptians and Romans   hoplites/Peasants   caged kings clairvoyant bastards. . . ." His desire is so vast as to exclude the personal entirely; he must turn away, at least in imagination, from the domesticity of his life, so that his soul can achieve the release it demands. It is nothing less than the wide universe that is the object of its desire; like the wolverine, the poet's soul hungers to "eat the world." This desire is in itself a kind of miracle or reincaration:

> Turning away, seeing fearful
> Ordinary ground, boys' eyes manlike go,
> The middle-aged man's like a desperate
> Boy's, the old man's like a new angel's. . . .

261

Dreaming, the poet sees horses, a "cloud/That is their oversoul," and armed men who may spring from his teeth. He must speak of battles that do not stain the meadow with blood but release "inner lives"—as if through a pure concentration of will, of artistic creation, the poet realizes:

> So many things stand wide
> Open!   Distance is helplessly deep
> On all sides   and you can enter, alone,
> Anything   anything can go
> On wherever it wishes   anywhere in the world or in time
> But here and now.

What must be resisted is the "alien sobbing" nearby; the poet's attachment to a finite self, a domestic existence, must be overcome, as if he were a guard on duty to prevent the desertion of the higher yearnings of his soul. The most abstract charge of all is his sense that he might be, even, a hero in a book—his life might be "a thing/That can be learned,/As those earnest young heroes learned theirs,/Later, much later on."

"Turning Away" is a tentative reply to the despairing vision of "The Eye-Beaters," and it concludes a collection of widely varying poems with a statement about the need to transcend the physical life by an identification with the timeless, "physical life" having been examined frankly and unsparingly and found to be generally diseased. The poem's immediate occasion is marital discord, but Dickey's imagery of battle is a very generalized one—"So many battles/Fought in cow pastures fought back/And forth over anybody's farm/With men or only/With wounded eyes—" Dickey's most inclusive metaphor for life is life-as-battle; for man, man-as-combatant.

The emphasis Dickey places in his later poems upon decay, disease, regression, and estrangement suggests that they may constitute a terminal group of poems: terminal in the sense that the poet may be about to take on newer challenges. Having developed from the mysticism of Stone into and through the mysticism of Flesh, having explored variations on unity and variations on dissolution, he seems suspended—between the formal abstractions of "Turning Away" and the jagged primitive-heroic music of "The Eye-Beaters," perhaps still seeking what Blake calls the "Image of wonder" that allows man to "meet the Lord in the Air & . . . be happy."

In any case, Dickey's work is significant in its expression of the savagery that always threatens to become an ideal, when faith in human values is difficult to come by —or when a culture cannot accommodate man's most basic instincts, forcing them backward, downward, away from the conscious imagination and back into the body as if into the body of an ancient ancestor: into the past, that is, forbidding intelligent entry into the future.

9

KAFKA'S
PARADISE

There is no need for you to leave the house. Stay at your table and listen. Don't even listen, just wait. Don't even wait, be completely quiet and alone. The world will offer itself to you to be unmasked; it can't do otherwise; in raptures it will writhe before you.

. . . not only [might we] remain in Paradise permanently, but . . . [we may] in fact be there permanently, no matter whether we know it here or not.

Kafka, *Reflections on Sin, Suffering, Hope, and the True Way*[1]

Kafka is not only one of the finest writers of this century, now legendary and saintly, and bearing, as Auden remarked in 1941, the same sort of relation to the age that Dante, Shakespeare, and Goethe bore to theirs, but he has become for many of his readers a kind of perpetual riddle, a Zen koan—the ultimate, interior, soul-transforming experience, to "solve" which would be to "solve" the problem of existence itself. How to interpret Kafka, how to transcend the position of a typical Kafka hero, and to realize the secrets of the Castle itself!—it seems an incredible task, and yet Kafka seems almost to be addressing us in this enigmatic exchange:

267

. . . a man once said: Why such reluctance? If you only followed the parables you yourself would become parables and with that rid of all your daily cares.

Another said: I bet that is also a parable.

The first said: You have won.

The second said: But unfortunately only in parable.

The first said: No, in reality: in parable you have lost.[2]

Can Kafka mean this, and the despairing problems of life are finally tricks of language, the ceaseless self-torment of hell merely that—a self-torment that willfully constructs parables? Unlike Beckett, whose poetic despair may grow out of a conviction that beyond poetry there is nothing, beyond the human invention of language there *is* nothing at all, not even humanity, Kafka asserts boldly that in "reality" we always win. Our victories are assured. Only in parable, or in the self-conscious speculations of the mind, can failure be a possibility: the word *failure* is a word that must be believed in before the condition of failure can become real. The more Kafka's heroes strive for victory, the more violently their intellects demand explanations, the more inevitable their doom. All these men are given hints of this truth, but they are so infatuated with their eloquence that they become helplessly trapped in their own casuistry or in the depths of their own egos; and it appears that they have lost. But only in parable, as Kafka says. In reality—in nature—they have won.

It appears that there is no solution, no way out, but it is this conception of life-as-paradox that cripples the human spirit. To break through the paradox is to transcend the self; as in Zen Buddhism, the realization of the koan or riddle must be experienced as an event, and not as a puzzle—by a sudden obliteration of the ego, a realization

268

of the identity of the finite self with the infinite, a vision of paradise that is at the same time the "profane" world. Kafka's visionary art is certainly religious, though not in any conventional Western sense, for so terrifying is his investigation of paradise/hell that usually perceptive critics like Eliseo Vivas,[3] distinguishing between Kierkegaard and Kafka, mistake Kafka's dramatization of anguish for his ultimate vision, when it is, in fact, the record of the ego's crisis as it approaches its own transcendence—the necessary anguish that precedes that "radiance" mentioned so often in his work. As long as the reader identifies with Kafka's antiheroes, investing emotional and intellectual energy in the heroic but doomed struggle of the self to retain its selfness, Kafka is one of the darkest of writers. But there is another, higher Kafka, the creator of Joseph K. of *The Trial* and K. of *The Castle,* the visionary who cannot be contained within any single identity in his work. While Joseph K. and K. struggle to achieve an impossible goal—the self-defined autonomy of the self —Kafka directs us toward the realization that their struggles are pointless, for the salvation they crave is already in their possession "no matter whether [they] know it here or not."

Life is a paradox only when it is defined as such. In the brief "An Imperial Message," Kafka speaks directly of the possibility of experiencing enlightenment through an interior vision (a dream) when the external world of history and of other men fails us. "An Imperial Message" is central to Kafka's work, and since it suggests his interest in Oriental philosophy and psychology as well, it is helpful to summarize it:

The emperor . . . has sent a message to you, the humble subject, the insignificant shadow cowering in the remotest

269

distance before the imperial sun. . . . The messenger immediately sets out on his journey; a powerful, an indefatigable man; now pushing with his right arm, now with his left, he cleaves a way for himself through the throng. . . . But the multitudes are so vast; their numbers have no end. If he could reach the open fields how fast he would fly, and soon doubtless you would hear the welcome hammering of his fists on your door. But instead how vainly does he wear out his strength. . . . if at last he should burst through the outermost gate—but never, never can that happen—the imperial capital would lie before him, the center of the world, crammed to bursting with its own refuse. Nobody could fight his way through here, least of all one with a message from a dead man. But you sit at your window when evening falls and dream it to yourself.

The relationship between Emperor, messenger, and "humble subject" is one that fascinated Kafka and lies at the core of most of his works. Does the Emperor exist?—Is he always dead?—Who is the messenger, and what vast distances must he cross, how many thousands of years must he endure, simply to bring to the subject a "message from a dead man"? He wears out his earthly strength in vain, and if he is a projection of the subject's willful mind, he is doomed to failure; like the doorkeeper in the parable "Before the Law" (from *The Trial*) and like the despairing, suicidal officer of "In the Penal Colony," he is more deluded than the subject himself, who waits passively for enlightenment. This would be tragic, but Kafka does not really believe in tragedy. Dissimilar though they may be on the surface, he shares with D. H. Lawrence a fundamental detestation of the conscious, private, grasping self, and a belief that tragedy is an art form which expresses this overestimation of the self to the exclusion of

270

other realms of being. Therefore the attempt to achieve victory of any kind—even victory over one's own impulses —even victory over the flow of time—is the tragic revision of paradise into hell, a misreading of the "parable" for the "reality." The complicated questions with which the narrator of "Josephine the Singer, or the Mouse Folk" concludes his reminiscence ("Was her actual piping notably louder and more alive than the memory of it will be? Was it even in her lifetime more than a simple memory? Was it not rather because Josephine's singing was already past losing in this way that our people in their wisdom prized it so highly . . . ?") are in obvious, ironic contrast to the beauty and simplicity of Josephine's mysterious singing, which is wordless. The ordinary mouse folk, who are redeemed by this music without understanding it, are devoted to her though they are "people who love slyness beyond everything, without any malice . . . and childish whispering and chatter, innocent, superficial chatter . . . people of a kind [who] cannot go in for unconditional devotion," and it is such ordinary childish people who continually fashion a parable out of reality and imagine this parable as a necessary means by which the hellish, fallen world can be understood, as if it were not paradise all along. Gregor Samsa of "The Metamorphosis," lured out of the stale confines of his room and out of his past life by the beauty of his sister's violin playing, feels "as if the way were opening before him to the unknown nourishment he craved." He too seeks redemption through an art beyond words.

But Gregor Samsa is also a form of the hero, the questing self; ironically, he is a version of Nietzsche's *Übermensch*, the tightrope between man and the abyss of an overintellectualized world. In Kafka's mythology, how-

271

ever, the hero must die, must be swept out with the trash, in order that a transcendence may take place that is somehow exterior to him—in nature itself, perhaps, represented by his sister's increasing vivacity, "in spite of all the sorrow of recent times. . . ." After Gregor's death, his parents and sister take a journey into the countryside; in the warm sunshine new dreams arise, a totally new assessment of the family's fortunes is made, and the girl, stretching her young body, is that final, wordless affirmation of life that Gregor—or that aspect of Kafka—could not make: the "metamorphosis" is complete. In tragedy this metamorphosis is similarly accomplished after the fifth act, after the tragic hero has been sacrificed, but tragedy does affirm the violently individualistic, idiosyncratic hero who is clearly a superior human being; Kafka does not. What is "heroic" in Kafka is the entire process, of which the realization of radiance is the highest achievement, but it does not and cannot matter who, specifically, experiences it.

The grotesque comedy of Kafka's work may have influenced contemporary "black humorists," but it is based upon assumptions that are shared by very few of our contemporaries. Kafka's antiheroes evolve, or degenerate, into the anonymous mechanical men of Beckett and Ionesco, who are sometimes even further reduced to parts of bodies; but the vast, incomprehensible, and essentially divine world of Being in which these antiheroes perform their ludicrous battles against themselves has vanished. The heroic is a mode of action, not contemplation; if it is related to language, this language is one of strife, logic, analysis, ceaseless classifications, and exhaustive, hubristic attempts to dissect reality and conquer it. Kafka goes against the entire Western concept of the hero: the brave, isolated, not-to-be-daunted self against all other selves and, of course, against nature, which exists merely to be conquered or at least classified and dissected. To be a hero one must assume that there is a struggle of some kind; if one aspires to the heroic and there seems to be no struggle available, the hero must then create it for himself. It is ironic that, in our time, Kafka's most fervent admirers have been men who have demonstrated, through their critical analyses of Kafka, an amazing *identification* with Kafka's deluded heroes and not with the vision that Kafka sets over and against these heroes!—as if the struggle is not clearly shown to be attributable to an attitude, a cultural or psychological expectation, of which nature knows nothing; which nature, being wordless, will simply annihilate. It is not tragic that the hunger artist, so spiteful and self-concerned, should waste away in a corner of his cage, unobserved, while a splendid young panther draws everyone's attention—and should he not draw our attention as well?—for the hunger artist admits that his fasting is based upon a lie, and the panther, like Gregor's sister, possesses the "joy of life" that lies outside the ego's torturous dominion; in fact, it knows nothing of the ego's struggles to assert a special, proud destiny, because it "knows" nothing at all. Tragedy demands an emotional investment in the ego, in the particular fate of a Hamlet or an Oedipus, who dramatize for us—and sometimes with embarrassing transparency—the pale cast of thought that will eventually be destroyed because it has simply evolved too far in one direction. The intellect, a technique of perception and an aid for survival, can evolve too far, can become confused by its own inventions (Kafka's background in law surely aided him in this realization—though Kafka's "law" stories are much simpler than their analogues in real life), and must perish, must die out, just as certain animals with extraordinarily developed characteristics of specialization (enormous antlers, enormous size) must give way to those more suited for adaptation to the environment. As Dostoyevsky's Underground Man says contemptuously, the intellect knows only what it has been told; and trapped in history, are we not trapped by the limited development of science, by the limited accumulation of facts, if we place our absolute faith in the intellect? For the intellectual quests of Kafka's heroes are quests against nature, in fact "unnatural"—in the sense that nature knows nothing of hierarchies of being, only of survival in a harmonious field of relationships that can appear unharmonious or cruel only to a limited point of view. "The Metamorphosis" is not concerned solely with Gregor Samsa, but with a metamorphosis that includes and transcends him.

"The Hunter Gracchus" is an unusual work for Kafka, in that one can perhaps discern the origin of the hunter's guilt: the hunting of a chamois in the Black Forest, when his calling was evidently as a hunter of wolves. "I lay in ambush, shot, hit my mark, flayed the skins from my victims," he says. "Was there any sin in that?" He denies the possibility of his own sin and can only blame the boatman for the fact that his death ship never ascends to a higher world. If one interprets the hunter's sin as a sin against nature—the hunting of the chamois—the story makes a kind of sense; if one assumes that the Hunter Gracchus did only what his role demanded of him, fulfilled him as a hunter whose attitude toward his "victims" is not meant to repel, it is more in line with the mysterious, visionary expressions Kafka has made of the guiltless guilt, the sinless sin, the "Guilt that is never to be

doubted" of "In the Penal Colony." But the hunter will
not acknowledge any possibility of his sinfulness. Therefore he is "always in motion" and can never come to rest;
his death ship approaches the other world, but

"I am forever . . . on the great stair that leads up to it. On
that infinitely wide and spacious stair I clamber about, sometimes up, sometimes down, sometimes on the right, sometimes on the left, always in motion. . . . Do not laugh."

This terrible, ceaseless movement is the resistance of the
individual to his fate, and reminds us movingly of Kafka's
exhaustive introspective entries in his diaries and journals.
Like the Hunter Gracchus, Kafka perhaps could not overcome the perpetual motion of his own intellect, which he
saw as necessary before one might ascend to a higher existence. Refusing to accept his own sin or even the likeli-
hood of his having sinned, the hunter say bravely, "I am
here, more than that I do not know, further than that I
cannot go. My ship has no rudder, and it is driven by the
wind that blows in the undermost regions of death."
How does one finally make the ascent? How does one
finally construct the perfect self-protecting burrow, the
most eloquent and devastating of courtroom arguments;
how does one outwit his senile father, make contact with
the Castle though the Castle does not wish this contact;
how does one absorb the threat of the leopards in the temple by "calculating" it into the ceremony?—How does one
finally and ultimately, for all time, conquer all possible
opponents, perhaps even humiliate them, crush them utterly? The hero is a man of action, and the perfect man
of action—as William Carlos Williams said—is the suicide. All these struggles of the self to conquer itself are
suicidal, a hopeless elbowing through the throng that sur-

rounds the Emperor's palace. The message, the vision, the experience of enlightenment, comes only to the subject who remains at home at his window when evening falls: it comes to him in a dream, it is given to him in a dream. He does not create the dream; he does not control it. It is given. It is a gift.

Enlightenment is possible in Kafka—indeed, it is not to be doubted. It is always available. But it is available only to the imagination that lets mind and body fall away. It cannot be delivered to the individual by messenger, or by the external apparatus of the Church (the ingenious torture instrument of "In the Penal Colony"), not by any authority outside the individual. Kafka allows the priest at the conclusion of *The Trial* a concern for Joseph K. that is more loving, more charitable, than anyone else's concern for him, but still this is not sufficient to save him, perhaps because Joseph K. does not have in himself a corresponding selflessness, a realization that his ego participates in a vast structure that it cannot conquer and should not want to conquer. Therefore this aspect of man dies "like a dog" and the shame of his death will "outlive him"—that is, it will pass into us, be inherited by us, if we cannot isolate Joseph K.'s sin.

The experience of enlightenment or grace, or the psychological equivalent of what Kierkegaard meant by the leap of faith, is always possible and, like guilt itself, is never to be doubted. Though Kafka was deeply interested in ancient Chinese philosophy, especially Lao Tzu's *Tao Te Ching*, few critical studies have related his work to Taoism; yet it is in Taoism that we come across the very spirit of Kafka himself, the awareness of a dominion of absolutely impersonal and incomprehensible Being over the efforts of individuals to influence it, or even to influence their own lives. Foreign to the West, because it is completely unscientific, committed to a metaphysics that scorns any expectations of causality, the Tao is experienced as parable, or paradox; but it transcends language entirely, just as it transcends any individual's grasp of it. Kafka obviously brought to Lao Tzu's writing a sensibility predisposed to this way of thinking, though he is characteristically modest in saying that he cannot quite understand it. According to Gustav Janouch in his *Conversations with Kafka*, Kafka owned nearly all the volumes of the German translations of Taoist writings. He spoke of having studied them " 'fairly deeply over a long period of time,' " though in Lao Tzu's *Tao Te Ching* "I only discovered the hopeless shallowness of my own intellectual categories, which couldn't define or accommodate Lao Tzu's. . . ."[4] To Janouch he read the following passage by a follower of Lao Tzu's, Chuang Tzi: "Death is not brought to life by life; life is not killed by dying. Life and death are conditioned; they are contained within a great coherence." He spoke of this insight as fundamental to all religions and all wisdoms about life, and it is illuminating to see how the "great coherence" resolves —though without language—the predicaments of Kafka's various heroes.

According to tradition, Lao Tzu, an older contemporary of Confucius, taught that "the Tao that can be told is not the eternal Tao." The *Tao Te Ching* (The Book of the Way) consists of eighty-one brief, enigmatic chapters and represents a mysticism foreign even to Western mysticism, because it is totally without emotion; it is so foreign to Western empirical thought that it is probably unreadable by men committed to rationalism and the "active principle." The teachings of Lao Tzu are always

277

simple: "Yield and overcome." "He who stands on tiptoe is not steady. He who strides cannot maintain the pace." In Chapter Twenty-nine, it is said that the universe cannot be improved: ". . . if you try to change it, you will ruin it. If you try to hold it, you will lose it." Chapter Thirty-two:

> Once the whole is divided, the parts need names.
> There are already enough names.
> One must know when to stop.
> Knowing when to stop averts trouble.
> Tao in the world is like a river flowing home to the sea.

Lao Tzu says in another verse that "the ten thousand things are born of being; Being is born of not being," and, in three lines remarkably similar to lines of Kafka's from *Reflections on Sin, Suffering, Hope, and the True Way,*

> Without going outside, you may know the whole world.
> Without looking through the window, you may see the ways of heaven.
> The farther you go, the less you know.[5]

Evidently Kafka did not read Buddhist writings, which would surely have intrigued him—the denial not only of a God, but of an existing self!—though he dramatizes with nightmarish detail the "Great Doubt" that overcomes the ego when it is about to be precipitated into enlightenment. This experience of soul-shattering doubt, of which Zen Buddhists write in detail, is the "sickness unto death" of Kierkegaard, but viewed with characteristic Eastern detachment, it is not emotional; it is psychological. It is only a mental experience, a phenomenon of the human mind, and therefore not very significant. Kafka, unlike Kierkegaard, attempts to describe this experience not in terms of pre-existing religious language (in which it must necessarily be obscured or distorted) but as psychological, secular experience. Not for Kafka the fastidious puritanism of an Augustine, who divides the universe into realms of God and Man; Kafka declares that the City of Man *is* the City of God, just as hell is paradise and paradise hell. One of the paradoxes of Zen is the belief that one's "ordinary mind" is his "Buddha-mind," which Kafka would have understood perfectly. Just as paradise is a continuous event, a continuous loss and a continuous gain, so in Oriental mysticism "the wisdom of Nirvana and the Ignorance of the Sangsāra illusorily appear to be two things . . . [but] cannot truly be differentiated."[6]

Basic to any understanding of Kafka's work is his sympathy with this kind of thinking; otherwise his writing is hopelessly despairing, incomplete, self-pitying. Many of the entries in the Octavo Notebook for 1918 are illuminating in this regard, but that of February 5 is especially direct:

Destroying this world would be the task to set oneself only, first, if the world were evil, that is, contradictory to our meaning, and secondly, if we were capable of destroying it. The first seems so to us; of the second we are not capable. We cannot destroy this world, for we have not constructed it as something independent; what we have done is to stray into it.
. . .

For us there exist two kinds of truth, as they are represented by the Tree of Knowledge and the Tree of Life. The truth of the active principle and the truth of the static principle. In the first, Good separates itself off from Evil; the second is nothing but Good itself, knowing neither of Good nor of Evil. The first truth is given to us really, the second only intuitively. That is what it is so sad to see. The cheerful thing

279

is that the first truth pertains to the fleeting moment, the second to eternity; and that, too, is why the first truth fades out in the light of the second.[7]

By "active" he meant "striving," by "static" he meant "without striving." The first truth is given "really"—that is, objectively or scientifically, so that others may verify it; the second is given "only intuitively"—that is, only from within. This is the same distinction that Pascal makes between *l'esprit de géométrie* and *l'esprit de finesse* —though Pascal seemed to believe that it was possible to be neither mathematical nor intuitive, and Pascal, of course, lived in a time in which one side of the psyche had not been overdeveloped.

In Kafka's secular age, the unmiraculous age of the penal colony in which guilt is not acknowledged, let alone punished, and which therefore denies redemption for the sinner, the intuitive has been suppressed. (For this reason Kafka is a little skeptical of Pascal's sincerity; he says in one of his diary entries:

Pascal arranges everything very tidily before God makes his appearance, but there must be a deeper, uneasier skepticism than that of a man cutting himself to bits with—indeed— wonderful knives, but still, with the calm of a butcher. Whence this calm? this confidence with which the knife is wielded? Is God a theatrical triumphal chariot that (granted the toil and despair of the stagehands) is hauled on the stage from afar by ropes?[8])

Both Pascal and Kafka affirm, however, the superiority of the "intuitive" over the "mathematical," the truth of eternity over the truth of time. In Kafka's analysis of this problem there is an awareness of the simultaneity of both truths, as if they were, perhaps, uses or techniques of the

280

mind rather than permanent states of "personality." That is, the "two kinds of truth" of which Kafka speaks are fluctuating, always in motion, not poles of being so much as possibilities of existential experience. What Kafka calls the truth represented by the Tree of Knowledge is a pragmatic, calculating, operative mode of adapting the environment to oneself, initially in order to survive but gradually, in civilization, in order to conquer the environment: to press forward, like Faust, hoping for immortality. The "truth of the active principle" immediately dissociates what Kafka calls Good and Evil, though it could also be called self and object—for the self always assumes that it is in possession of what is good (self-realization and self-aggrandizement) and that its environment, in so far as it resists this "Good," is Evil. That Kafka should assign these ethical terms to a problem that is really psychological or epistemological indicates the degree to which he was shaped by his Judaeo-Christian culture, which is characterized, like Western philosophy in general, by a need to divide the world into opposites. Yet Kafka goes on to say that the rational mind is, in itself, that which *separates good from evil*; in the beginning, then, good and evil are not separated, self and object are not separate entities but one process, one event, one experience—like the Tao itself, beyond language and never experienced by the part of the mind that has invented language.

In his "Homage" to Kafka, which is the introduction to the 1954 edition of *The Castle*, Thomas Mann says that Kafka is not a mystic because he lacks the "hot and heavy atmosphere of transcendentalism" and the transformation of the "sensual" into the "super-sensual." In Kafka there is no "voluptuous hell," no "bridal bed of the

281

tomb," nor the rest of the "stock-in-trade of the genuine mystic." Mann characterizes him as a "religious humorist." It is understandable that Mann, who investigated the dangers of the irrational and what he saw as the mystical (the "folk" in *Dr. Faustus*), should draw back from any admiration of a vision that lies outside of civilization; but at the same time, one can doubt whether all mysticism is characterized by these clichés and whether transcendentalism—surely not Kantian transcendentalism?—is "hot and heavy" and "voluptuous." Even so, one can see in Kafka this voluptuous hell, in the perverse ecstasy of the hunger artist, in the "transfiguration" and "radiance" of the victim's sixth hour on the torture instrument of "In the Penal Colony," and in any number of other frightening, surrealistic transformations of the "sensual" into the "super-sensual." But Kafka's mysticism is primarily one that intuits unity (though it experiences—or seems to experience—only fragments); it makes a distinction between the unifying mind and the mind that reasons this very distinction between self and object. As Kafka says in the aphorism from the Octavo Notebook, the truth of the static (or timeless) principle is "nothing but Good itself, knowing neither of Good nor of Evil."

The anguish we read of in Kafka's diaries and journals evidently grew out of his conviction that he must come to terms with his mysticism in a rational manner; he seemed to believe, guiltily and miserably, that he should continually "explain" himself to others. There is no doubt but that he did experience guilt—overwhelming, sickening, paralyzing guilt—but he seems to have felt it because he was cutting himself off from that "bliss of the commonplace" that so fascinated Thomas Mann as well. For, as long as we assign the terms "good" and "evil" to an experience that is psychological, and only psychological, we are forever trapped, like the Hunter Gracchus, between two worlds; we are always in motion. Kafka is forever drawing away from people who love him, especially women—and then he is drawn back to them, violently, helplessly—then, detaching himself from them, he suffers immeasurable guilt,[9] as the letter written to Milena Jesenská make clear. However closely one studies Kafka, however intimately one seems to know him, there is always the ambiguity: Does the art grow out of the guilt, or the guilt out of the art?

It does not lessen Kafka's value as a visionary artist to note, as have Max Brod and others, the amazing ways in which Kafka transmuted difficult emotional experiences into fiction (how Milena "becomes" Frieda, for instance[10]), and the process by which he imagined his father as an archetypal presence, absorbing the various floating anxieties of the era—as the Victorians did as well, expressing the war between ways of life as symbolic contests between fathers and sons; which is hardly an expression of private father-son feuds, but the expression of an entire civilization's neurotic burden. Certain kinds of art are cathartic, exorcizing, magical; not always for the artist, but perhaps for his audience. Like dreams, artistic creations transmute private, undifferentiated emotions or impulses into actual images that can be dealt with, but it is problematic whether these images are equivalent to their sources or whether, in some way, they constantly fall short and do not attain for the artist the liberation of a rebirth. There is a passage in one of Kafka's letters to Milena in which he speaks of the two of them standing "side by side, watching this creature on the ground which is me; but I, as the spectator, am then non-existent"[11]—a

vision that grows out of his despair, however, since he is
very sick at this time, nearing death, and realizes that he
and Milena can never live together. Only in isolated moments, only when he is operating as an artist, does Kafka
seem to experience the liberation from his own emotions
that so cripple him ordinarily. Yet he must have seen his
art as an artistry of "hunger" that would lead inevitably
to his death by starvation—emotional starvation. The falling short of the artist's attempts to objectify his own
unique, curious psychological experience does, in a way
that would be quite disturbing to most artists if they understood it, make certain the fact that he will keep on
writing and that he will, exhausted or penniless or love-
sick, put into recognizably coherent forms certain primordial images or experiences that his era requires. But why
does his era require *him* to give shape to these shapeless
dreams?—Why not someone else? A question not to be
answered and, indeed, to be uttered only at the risk of
releasing a psychic disturbance, or rather the awareness of
one; for it is the rare artist, like Blake or Whitman, who
acknowledges happily his total dependence as an artist
(an impersonal instrument) upon a ground of Being that
cannot be comprehended by him, to which his intellect
has no access whatsoever and for which, unceasingly, his
personal life must be sacrificed if it threatens to use up
too much of his energy. Unsettling as his remarks must be
for the artist, and perhaps for most modern men, Jung is
quite correct in stating so bluntly that every creative person is a synthesis of ostensibly contradictory aptitudes: on
the one side he is a human being with a personal life; on
the other, an impersonal, creative process. In the essay
"Literature and Psychology" of 1933, Jung says that the
artist's work has very little to do with his personal life,

284

except as the circumstances of his life allow it to be released; there is a distinction between the human being and the artist, who is "objective and impersonal—even inhuman—for as an artist he is his work, and not a human being."[12] Though Jung does not speculate about whether the economic use of one's energy determines his personal "happiness" or "unhappiness," it might be that in the case of such physically weak artists as Kafka and Kierkegaard unhappiness is inescapable—for in order to create the work they are evidently destined to create, they must sacrifice the expenditure of energy in normal human relations. Thus they experience their isolation as both gift and punishment, an inheritance they have no choice but to accept, yet for which they must—ironically—suffer guilt over.

Not all artists, of course, find themselves in this situation, of knowing with one part of their minds that they are fulfilling their destiny and have no need to explain or defend it, yet of feeling with another part of their being a terrible anxiety, an alienation from the norms of their era—sensing, as Kafka did, that he is in both paradise and hell and that to realize the former one must simply erase his self-inflicted perception of the latter. The artist-as-neurotic is by no means a universal phenomenon but, since the artist must conserve and direct his energy *into* his art and *away* from human relations, and will suffer if he fails to do this, the chances of his achieving a fluid, sane equilibrium between inner and outer worlds are much less than are those for other people. Consider the deathly aphorism in Kierkegaard's *Either/Or* about the poet, that

. . . unhappy man who conceals profound anguish in his heart, but whose lips are so fashioned that when sighs and

285

groans pass over them they sound like beautiful music. His fate resembles that of the unhappy men who were slowly roasted to death by a gentle fire in the tyrant Phalaris' bull— their shrieks could not reach his ear to terrify him, to him they sounded like sweet music. And people flock about the poet and say to him: do sing again; which means, would that new sufferings tormented your soul. . . .

Obviously, such an art is not cathartic for the artist; he is possessed, and resents his possession; he is capable of small, temporary victories, but generally he acknowledges his fate. In this parable of Kafka's, given here in its entirety, the melancholy acceptance of this strange fate is made clear:

The Sirens

These are the seductive voices of the night; the Sirens, too, sang that way. It would be doing them an injustice to think that they wanted to seduce; they knew they had claws and sterile wombs, and they lamented this aloud. They could not help it if their laments sounded so beautiful. (Parables)

We do get the feeling, however, in reading Kafka's personal writings, that he really felt, unlike the Sirens, he could help it; he felt somehow responsible for his sterility, his otherness, made all the more seductive because his song is so beautiful. (Kafka did not doubt his talent as a writer: he knew he was inspired, that he was "capable of everything," and that if he simply wrote the first sentence that came into his head it would possess "perfection"— an incredibly confident statement for a twenty-seven-year-old to make.[13]) This may be one of the reasons he left his most ambitious works unfinished, and even requested that Max Brod burn those manuscripts he had not yet published. He was conscious of himself as seductive, as

286

powerful, as possibly deadly to those who might not understand him because they were not equal to his vision. He spoke of the "fall into sin" in his conversations with the seventeen-year-old Gustav Janouch, then asked the boy not to brood on his words: "My seriousness might act like poison on you. You are young."[14] At the same time he believed that his art was far more than the transformation of Franz Kafka's agonies into objective images; it is the ecstasy of "[raising] the world into the pure, the true, and the immutable."[15]

Like the Hunter Gracchus, he can neither ascend nor descend.

But though the expulsion from paradise is a permanent fact, it is also a permanent fact that we are in paradise. The analytic mind is a "chain . . . long enough to give [man] the freedom of all earthly space"; the world is by this time filled with men's eager rationalizations about the "fall" and their relationship to it. But it may be argued—madly, brilliantly—that the "whole visible world is perhaps nothing more than the rationalization of a man who wants to find peace for a moment" (from "Paradise"). What is the visible world, then, in Kafka's own life but the continual building of towers of Babel (or the hypothesized, comic erection of this tower upon the Great Wall of China)—that is, his own books? K., exhausted by his aggressive maneuvers to win recognition from the Castle's officials, will finally be allowed to live in the Castle community as he had so desperately desired—*not* in consideration of his own efforts, of course, but only owing to "certain auxiliary circumstances." Kafka's writings, like K.'s strategies, are both what he must do and what is, at the same time, not enough to save him. Salvation comes from a higher source: it cannot be demanded.

The Castle, like the more dramatic, more tightly constructed *The Trial*, is not a tragic work unless one identifies with the confused hero. It is a brilliant expression of the helplessness with which the conscious mind fights the unconscious, the comic-grotesque struggle of the intellect to know its soul; that it is so puzzling a work to many readers, and so unsatisfying, attests only to the fact that its basic assumptions are foreign to the assumptions of our era. Yet the Castle, imagined as Kafka's European, historical, vaguely sinister expression of the same primordial force that Lao Tzu calls the Tao, is clearly that static or purposeless truth that rests in eternity and is realized only within the stilled, unstriving mind:

When K. looked at the Castle, often it seemed to him as if he were observing someone who sat quietly there gazing in front of him, not lost in thought and so oblivious of everything, but free and untroubled, as if he were alone with nobody to observe him, and yet must notice that he was observed. . . . (p. 128)

What K. wants from the Castle, most specifically from the official Klamm, is, in his own words, "difficult to express": there is no reason, really, for his meeting Klamm, any more than there is any reason for Klamm's wanting to meet him. Klamm and K. are united, and not simply in the body of Frieda; they are united already, but K.'s perpetual motion of the intellect will not allow him to see this. However grotesque Klamm may seem—and the forms that the unconscious may take are far, far more grotesque than those Kafka usually chooses—he is yet divine, he is beyond reproach. It is pointless for K. to ask questions about the unfathomable Klamm. He is warned when a woman tells him, " 'Where is the man who could hinder me from running to Klamm if Klamm lifted his little finger? Madness, absolute madness; one begins to feel confused oneself when one plays with such mad ideas' " (p. 108). But he ignores this warning, and the entire novel is a way of confusing us, a way of demonstrating that this is what life is, this is truly what life is for most people, these small spurts of activity, these trivial, abortive events, delusive emotions, misunderstandings that grow into ever more complex misunderstandings, then fade abruptly, only to be replaced by new worries. K. creates his own problem, then tries to solve it. The problem-solving mechanism of the human mind will begin to create, spontaneously, its own objects of perception, its own problems, if the deeper, more human, more natural aspect of existence is suppressed. K. says, in effect, "Where the Castle is, there shall I be." Freud, in declaring, "Where Id is, there shall Ego be," articulates most clearly the Western concept of the "id" as a negative and perhaps even unhuman part of the psyche, and implies that the ego's task, its very destiny, is to conquer the id, to know it. But once the very basis of life is feared—once the relationship between conscious and unconscious mind is seen as a combative one—sanity itself is no longer possible, though men may keep going for generations without collapsing, except as collective units. To make war against one's own self is suicidal; at the very least, it is ludicrous.

In a passage deleted from the manuscript of *The Castle*, K. learns of Barnabas' initial excitement over K.'s arrival as the Land-Surveyor, for *he*, Barnabas, has been fighting for his appointment for three years, ". . . all in vain, [with] not the slightest success, only disgrace, torment, time wasted . . ." (p. 467). K.'s arrival, then, seen from Barnabas' and Olga's point of view is, in a masterly piece of Kafkan comedy, a kind of salvation. How mad! K. tells her that hearing this is like "listening to stories about your misery as if it were my own. . . ." Which of course it is, exactly. Kafka could have then invented a character subordinate to Barnabas and Olga, who took heart at Barnabas' evident success (his appointment as Castle messenger); and a character subordinate to that one, and so on to infinity. There is no writer who has dramatized so well the basic hopelessness of the logical, empirical, fact-accumulating method, not even Lewis Carroll; only Proust, in his brilliant choice of social life as *the* metaphor for spiritual degradation, outdoes Kafka in terms of needless confusion and ennui.

The Castle is a parable, and one is always defeated in parable. But not in reality. Therefore K. is "saved" outside the confines of the novel as it exists, in its unfinished form; Kafka intended to allow him some measure of happiness, however small, since he is to be informed on his death bed that the castle officials have decided he may remain in the Castle community after all, owing to circumstances that have nothing to do with his efforts. As Lao Tzu expresses it:

> Returning is the motion of the Tao.
> Yielding is the way of the Tao.
> The ten thousand things are born of being.
> Being is born of not being.
> (Chapter Forty, complete)

Ultimately K. knows no more of the Castle than we know; he only knows the Castle community and its people—the "ten thousand things" that are born of and supported by a mysterious structure they cannot know, except to know that it is "madness, absolute madness" to go

290

against it. Is there a mystery about the Castle? Where is the mystery? Kafka said, in explanation of his dislike for detective fiction, that in real life mystery isn't hidden in the background: "On the contrary! It stares one in the face. It's what is obvious. So we do not see it. Every-day is the greatest detective story ever written. . . ."[16] If the world is denuded of spiritual significance, as many modern writers seem to feel, what remains?—matter? Yet "matter," or what is meant by the word *matter*, is as mysterious as spirit ever was; the term itself is only a way of pointing toward another mystery, in the pretense that it is somehow not a mystery but, being named "matter," is solved. In creating a dark, comic, upside-down epic in which the hero never gets any closer to his goal yet is granted his wish as he lies dying, Kafka was expressing a timeless truth; but he had to express it in images suitable to his era. The artist, however anxious he may feel about being misinterpreted or even "poisonous," cannot do other than shape his vision according to the specific time in which he lives—as Kafka said of Picasso, seeing some cubist still lifes and paintings of deformed women, such art is not willful distortion but a registering of the deformities that have not yet penetrated our consciousness. "Art is a mirror, which goes 'fast,' like a watch—sometimes."[17] Thomas Mann, whom Kafka admired (he especially liked "Tonio Kröger," for obvious reasons), created in *Death in Venice* that doomed, solitary artist, Aschenbach, the brook fouled by ashes, who is "so busy with the tasks imposed upon him by his own ego and the European soul" that his joyless life is best symbolized by a clenched fist, never a relaxed open hand.[18] Unable to integrate the first (the active principle) with the open hand (the static principle), as K. of *The Castle* is unable to integrate the effortless peace represented by Frieda with his own masculine, combative personality, Aschenbach, suddenly released from the burden of history and civilization, discovers in himself an affinity with the beast, a bliss in pure abandon that extends the "no little innocent bliss" hoped for by Tonio Kröger to its logical psychological conclusion.

Both Mann and Kafka registered the deformities of the era that had not yet penetrated the general consciousness, but in Kafka we find a possibility of transcendence not granted Mann; Mann seems to us a historical novelist, then, a genius who analyzed the breakdown of civilization in Europe from the point of view of a European to whom that civilization—in its highest accomplishments—was unparalleled. Kafka, however, perhaps because of his Jewishness, perhaps because of his own temperament, seemed to identify with the ahistorical, the timeless, the spiritual; for him the drowning of the ego was a necessary experience in order that something beyond the ego might emerge. For Mann, the failure of the ego unleashes violent, shameful, nightmarish, and basically sexual activities, both in fantasy and in "real life," and the tragic problem for him—as it was for Freud—is that civilization and its restraints are necessary, therefore its discontents are necessary, so that individual neuroses may be absorbed in a larger neurosis. But where is the human spirit in all this? Safest, most secure only in the unimaginative, hard-working, role-directed world of the bourgeois, which exhausts men's energies both for good and evil. Kafka, as we know, did not fear the abyss—like Nietzsche, he was willing to pay the price of staring into it, of inviting it to stare back into him:

The truth is always an abyss. One must—as in a swimming pool—dare to dive from the quivering springboard of trivial everyday experience and sink into the depths, in order later to rise again—laughing and fighting for breath—to the now doubly illuminated surface of things.[19]

For Kafka loss of ego was the only way into this abyss, and the abyss—in Oriental terms, the "Void"—is not necessarily nightmare, not necessarily Aschenbach's feverish erotic dreams, but the undifferentiated primary paradise itself. There we cannot experience what is "good" because "good" and "evil" are not yet separated into opposing forces; nor does human language exist, let alone habits of civilization. Consciousness cannot be primary because it grows out of a prior condition of unconsciousness, into which it must someday return; and when consciousness sinks into sleep, this primary world rises, triumphant, incontestable. No activity of the ego, however ingenious and arrogant, can really erase from the memory the knowledge of an original, undifferentiated mind, which perhaps accounts for the desperation with which the ego attacks it when it is objectified by the poet, the artist, the mystic. The demand that a work of art be intelligible is one that can be made only by those to whom art itself is a threat and not a way of participating in an ineffable experience. All of Kafka's writings are poetic expressions of the necessity of surrender to the soul's transformation, however terrifying it may be. The point is made graphically in "In the Penal Colony" that one already *is* his ultimate self, his fate, though only by contemplating the specific words tattooed upon his body can he know himself, can he be realized as a unique individual; or was the experiment with individuality in the West a failure, symbolized by the comically disintegrating torture machine? Does the explorer leave the penal colony in order to explore another part of the world?

The typical Kafka hero's end is in his beginning: Joseph K. is arrested on the morning of his thirtieth birthday and executed a year later. But the execution—the annihilation of his ego—begins on that morning when his landlady's cook fails to appear as usual with his breakfast, and, in a sense, it is already complete. Each defeat that follows the initial defeat is merely a temporal intensification of it, and the more hopeless one's case appears, the more grasping one becomes. In paradise without knowing it, one is in hell and there one is insatiable—one carries inside one one's own mortal hunger, which can never be satisfied by anything that is mortal. A number of Kafka characters are accused of being "insatiable"—the hunger artist, ironically, who cannot get enough of fasting; the man from the country who waits for so many fruitless years at the doorway to the Law; Joseph K. himself, who demands a definite release, a final pardon for all time, but is told by the priest (the "prison chaplain") that "the verdict is not suddenly arrived at, the proceedings only gradually merge into the verdict" (p. 264, *The Trial*). Joseph K. never realizes that his verdict, his sentence, his execution *are* himself, and that there is no self, no Joseph K., outside this. He cannot discover himself because he will not surrender to losing himself; refusing to make the human effort of a self-annihilation, he dies like a dog.

In his diary entries Kafka expressed the idea that this "ego-annihilation" might be possible through what he saw to be ordinary, uncomplicated life, that is, "normal" marriage. This too seemed to him a kind of abyss, a way of salvation, of stopping the fast-running clock. He speaks of the "infinite, deep, warm, saving happiness of sitting beside the cradle of one's child opposite its mother. . . ." And:

There is in it also something of this feeling: matters no longer rest with you, unless you wish it so. In contrast, this feeling of those who have no children: it perpetually rests with you, whether you will or no, every moment to the end, every nerve-racking moment, it perpetually rests with you, and without result. Sisyphus was a bachelor.[20]

Yet the crossing over to this state of mind necessitates an abandonment of the senses, in which the body of another somehow provides "salvation" for one; and Kafka cannot accept this. Like one of Flannery O'Connor's demented saints, Kafka is really too pure to consider anything not "spiritual"—even obscenity must be spiritual in order to have value. K. of *The Castle* makes love to Frieda on the tavern floor, amidst puddles of beer and piles of refuse, and he cannot even resist a triumphant shout for Klamm's benefit—a needless, self-destructive taunt, though certainly a futile one; what does Klamm care if the Land-Surveyor has stolen his mistress? By now he has forgotten her, though not as ordinary people "forget"; her existence is erased in his memory, she does not exist for him at all. One cannot acquire salvation through the efforts of another, not even through the willing, warm, maternal bodies of the mistresses of Castle and Court officials, since salvation comes only from within: a psychological experience only. Kafka did not seem to believe, and perhaps for him it was quite true, that the experience of erotic love can create another "self," a personality that is the result of the lovers' spiritual unity. It may also be that Kafka's religious and cultural background forbade any spiritualization of physical love; for women, perhaps, are not quite equal to men:

Women are snares, which lie in wait for men on all sides in order to drag them into the merely finite. They lose their dangers if one voluntarily falls into one of the snares. But if, as a result of habit, one overcomes it, then all the jaws of the female trap open again.[21]

This is not Saint Paul or Augustine, but Kafka himself, speaking frankly to the boy, Janouch, after he had happened to see him with a girl.

In Kafka's imagination it cannot be through erotic love, then, that one can find his liberation from the ego; Kafka must consciously set out to explore the infinity within. He spoke, in a much-quoted remark, of books as axes wielded against the "frozen sea within," and it is clear from his diary entry for January 16, 1922, that he quite deliberately approached what he called an "assault upon the last earthly frontier." Unlike Rimbaud, who threw himself into activities that might assure a "systematic derangement of all the senses," Kafka seems to have let go: to have stopped struggling. In a curious passage at the beginning of *The Castle*—curious because Kafka is not writing naturalistic fiction and has no need to substantiate a character's previous existence—K. remembers when, as a boy, he climbed a churchyard wall and seemed to experience it as a "victory for life" (p. 38). The victory is there, inside; it sinks beneath the surface of consciousness, but is not extinct by any means. The "victory" is a kind of initial baptism, a baptism of the ego that restores its innocence and allows Kafka the artist (though not Kafka the man) the secret knowledge that he has perfection within his grasp, that the simplest sentence he writes is "already perfect." At such moments Kafka is not Kafka, but his art; he *is* the sentence he writes, and the sentence he writes is an expression of Kafka's own perfection—as an artist, that is. What of the external world, what of "normal" life? It must be abandoned, finally. On that day in January, 1922, Kafka allowed his introspective energies full release so that the inner and outer worlds drew apart and their separate times could no longer coincide. "The clocks are not in unison," he writes; "the inner one runs crazily at a devilish or demoniac or in any case inhuman pace, the outer one limps along at its usual speed." The two worlds then threaten to split apart. Kafka saw the agony of life as the ego's fear of the future, and not the future itself, which cannot be experienced; an imagining of the future without that self. It is not the higher life that knows good or evil or dread, but only the self in its fear of ascending to the higher life, as if, in releasing itself even from fear, it would suffer a tremendous loss.

In spite of Kafka's interest in Chinese philosophy, he seems to have been unable, for most of his life, to reconcile the inner and outer worlds. He remained preoccupied with guilt until the last year or two of his life when, according to Max Brod, he experienced an awakening of his energies and a desire to live that contrast sharply with the Kafka of the years before; ironically, his experience parallels K.'s of *The Castle*. His works, however, reflect the anguish of his constant struggle to synthesize the Tree of Knowledge and the Tree of Life; to realize himself, Kafka, in terms of life. Perhaps it was a fear of losing language, of losing the means by which he defined his soul, as he hints in this diary entry of 1922:

297

Evil does not exist; once you have crossed the threshold, all is good. Once in another world, you must hold your tongue.[22]

Either a continual self-destroying "assault" upon the earthly frontier, or a transformation into the Void, into silence. How else was Kafka to reconcile himself to so unhuman a universe, except to imagine himself continually as a parable?—his life as a series of parables in which the logically incompatible are wedded so beautifully?

NOTES

Notes to Chapter 1

1 From two letters of William James, addressed to Henry. Quoted in Margaret Knight's *William James* (London, 1954), p. 60.
2 In her frank, valuable essay "Professions for Women" (included in *The Death of the Moth and Other Essays*), Virginia Woolf says that one of the adventures of her professional life, the telling of "the truth about my own experiences as a body," she did not believe she had solved satisfactorily; she goes on to express doubt that any woman has solved it. With the publication of Doris Lessing's *The Golden Notebook* in 1962, however, this particular aspect of the feminine literary adventure was "solved."

Notes to Chapter 2

1 Quoted in John Paterson's *The Novel As Faith* (Boston, 1973). pp. 198–99. Perhaps because Woolf quite consciously desired "less life and more poetry" in her novels, she made the creative act a strangely perverse doubling back upon itself—as if the artist, like the Puritan, *must* not enjoy his activity for fear of its being somehow wrong.

2 See this eloquent, passionate statement in *A Propos of Lady Chatterley's Lover:* "Sex is the balance of male and female in the universe. . . . Oh, what a catastrophe, what a maiming of love when it was made a personal, merely personal feeling, taken away from the rising and the setting of the sun, and cut off from the magic connexion of the . . . equinox!" (p. 110, Penguin Books, 1961)

3 Calvin Bedient, *Architects of the Self* (University of California Press, 1972), p. 179. The book is about the "ideal self" as imagined by George Eliot and E. M. Forster, in addition to Lawrence. Forster emerges as the most reasonable of the three—but perhaps the least exciting.

4 Some critics, among them Graham Hough in *The Dark Sun* (London, 1968), see in Lawrence a "doctrinaire cruelty" in such stories as "The Princess," "None of That," etc., not taking into account how Lawrence imaginatively divided himself into the characters in his stories, both male and female. Lawrence's critical stance, which is often savage, must be understood in terms of the entire organic structure of the story, not simply its apparent "theme." If one sees that Lawrence *is* the white women he appears to be revenging himself upon, that he *is* "the Princess," whose father's ethic of the cold, locked-in ego dooms her to frigidity, the story comes alive as drama and does not seem so flat and polarized in its elements of "consciousness" and "instinct." Most novelists divide themselves up lavishly in their novels—it is an error to believe that Lawrence *is* Mellors any more than he *is* that strange, complex, and rather mad Lord Chatterley (who in one of his roles is a successful writer).

5 *Reflections on the Death of a Porcupine* (London, 1934), p. 6.

6 This dissolving of subject into object is a feat that few poets—especially those passionately involved with their own emotions—can achieve. The extraordinary empathy that James Dickey feels for nature has allowed him to create poems like "The Movement of Fish," "The Dusk of Horses," "Winter Trout," and many others, in which he

gives us the sense of a magical transformation of the human ego. Western poetry, however, is generally dense with thought-out emotions, and even imagism develops into a self-conscious aesthetic technique. Had I space, I would like to discuss poems like "Fish" in relation to Zen enlightenment poems, especially those that concentrate on realizing the absolute uniqueness of a single moment in nature, when poet and subject fuse together.

Notes to Chapter 5

1 Since completing this essay I have come upon Roy Fuller's complex consideration of Nietzschean "tragedy" and its relationship to the literature of the present day, "Professors and Gods," in *The Times Literary Supplement*, March 9, 1973. He acknowledges that poetry in our time has lost much to the novel, but that it need not surrender entirely what the art of the novel forces upon the novelist—"a viewpoint not always his own and a regard for the situation of others." Fuller's distinction between the dramatized "tragedy" of the individual and the higher, more formal, and far more idealistic "tragedy" of the community is an important one, helping to explain why tragedy as an art form is so difficult and, in execution, so often disappointing in our time.

Notes to Chapter 6

1 Eliseo Vivas, *Creation and Discovery* (New York, 1955), p. 42.
2 Lewis A. Lawson, "Flannery O'Connor and the Grotesque: *Wise Blood*," *Renascence*, XVII (Spring, 1965), pp. 137–47.
3 Quoted by Lewis A. Lawson, *loc. cit.*, p. 139.
4 Philip Rahv, Introduction, *Eight Great American Short Novels* (New York, 1963), p. 15.
5 Flannery O'Connor, "The Violent Bear It Away" in *Three by O'Connor* (New York, 1964), p. 357.
6 O'Connor, *op. cit.*, p. 151.
7 Pierre Teilhard de Chardin, *The Phenomenon of Man* (New York, 1959), p. 262.
8 Flannery O'Connor, *Mystery and Manners* (New York, 1969), p. 68.

9   *Ibid.,* p. 44.
10 Teilhard, p. 291.
11 *Ibid.,* p. 290.
12 *Ibid.,* p. 289.
13 Gustav Janouch, *Conversations With Kafka* (New York, 1971), p. 90.
14 Teilhard, p. 309.
15 In the essay "The Fiction Writer and His Country," she declares that "for me the meaning of life is centered in our Redemption by Christ. . . ." *Mystery and Manners,* p. 32.
16 See John Hawkes's essay, "Flannery O'Connor's Devil," *Sewanee Review,* LXX (Summer, 1962), p. 400.
17 Quoted by Robert Fitzgerald in his introduction to *Everything That Rises Must Converge* (New York, 1965), p. xiii.
18 Teilhard, p. 256.
19 Flannery O'Connor is a remarkable synthesis of what Jung would call the personality characterized by *participation mystique* and the personality that "suffers only in the lower stories, so to speak, but in the upper stories is singularly detached from painful as well as joyful events." "Commentary on *The Secret of the Golden Flower,*" in Jung's *Psyche and Symbol* (New York, 1958), p. 340.

Notes to Chapter 7

1   See Mailer's well-known essay "The White Negro: Superficial Reflections on the Hipster," in *Advertisements for Myself,* pp. 281–302. This rapid cataloguing of totally disparate types of human beings is typical of Mailer, and unfortunately it is a tendency in his thinking that has discouraged many serious readers; that Mailer should neglect to see the primary difference between "mystics and saints" on the one hand and "psychopaths, existentialists, lovers, and bullfighters" on the other testifies to his total immersion in time, in the stimulus-response rapidity of *time* as measured by a slightly fast-running clock. The crucial distinction between these two categories of human beings is, of course, the transcendence by the former of the "existentialism" of the temporal world.
2   One can only be puzzled by the general reluctance of critics to take the novel seriously, as if such aggressive psychopathic wit as D.J. displays were not a significant poetry for our time. Even the advertising for the English edition of the novel degrades it, and might well have

been written by D.J. himself: ". . . the zaniest, funniest, most pene-
trating, fizziest novel of the year." Mailer's own advertisement for
The Deer Park (published in the *Village Voice* back in 1955) is more
dignified.

3   An error of oversimplification, perhaps. The highest forms of art,
including the mystic's experience, all soar beyond the brain's capacity to record in simple linguistic terms. One has to possess a language in order to *define* an experience, not to have it; visual art,
music, even our personal sketchy dreams, rely minimally or not at all
upon language. Einstein evidently "felt" his complex intellectual
theories for some time before translating them into any language at
all.

4   As when he classifies himself as a "Left-Conservative-revolutionary,"
or calls our attention to his increasingly peripheral relationship to the
events he writes about, with the title *Existential Errands*.

5   In *The Eye-Beaters, Blood, Victory, Madness, Buckhead and Mercy*
(Garden City, New York, 1970), p. 55.

6   Richard Poirier, *Norman Mailer* (New York, 1972), p. 124.

7   In "Last Advertisement for Myself Before the Way Out" Mailer
analyzes his private dilemma and that of the era's in these frank lines:
"When I come to assess myself, and try to measure what chance I
have of writing that big book I have again in me, I do not know in all
simple bitterness if I can make it. For you have to care about other
people to share your perception with them, especially if it is a perception which can give them life, and now there are too many times
when I no longer give a good goddam for most of the human race"
(*Advertisements*, p. 411). Mailer's art is an autobiographical dramatizing of his interior war, the conflict of "selves," the murderous self
in perpetual pursuit of the creative self, which he cannot help but
project outward upon the rest of us. Hence, the dynamic concentration of father-son murderers or twin killers in *Why Are We in Vietnam?* and its mysterious exclusion of feminine "evil" (Mailer's deepest fear). If the mystic cannot integrate his many voices, his fate is
to swerve sideways or down, not to ascend.

Notes to Chapter 8

1   *The Suspect in Poetry* (Madison, Minnesota: The Sixties Press,
1964), p. 47.

Notes

2   Lewis Thomas, M.D., "Information," in the *New England Journal of Medicine*, December 14, 1972, pp. 1238–39.

3   Dickey either literally or figuratively puts on masks in any number of poems—notably "Armor," "Drinking from a Helmet," and "Approaching Prayer" (in which he puts on a "hollow hog's head").

4   Dickey's perfect vision singled him out for training in night fighters in the Army Air Corps. Throughout his poetry there is a concern, not just imagistic or metaphorical, with vision—eyesight—that makes doubly poignant his conclusion in "False Youth: Two Seasons" (from FALLING) that his youth was "a lifetime search/For the Blind." Also, the conclusion of "The Eye-Beaters" shows us the poet "in perversity and the sheer/Despair of invention" taking his "double-clear bifocals off"—then succumbing to a fantasy of regressive madness.

5   *The Suspect in Poetry*, p. 77. The word "helplessness" is repeated several times in connection with Jarrell, and in an essay on Howard Nemerov (a review of Nemerov's *Selected Poems*, 1960), Dickey praises Nemerov for what seem to me the wrong reasons: ". . . the enveloping emotion that arises from his writing is helplessness: the helplessness we all feel in the face of the events of our time, and of life itself: the helplessness one feels as one's legitimate but chronically unfair portion in all the things that can't be assuaged or explained" (p. 67). Throughout *Self-Interviews*, which seems the work of a different James Dickey, one who cannot do justice to the excellence of the essential Dickey, there is a reliance upon an inner, moral "helplessness," as if certain emotional prejudices were *there*, in human nature, and one might as well acquiesce to them; though elsewhere does Dickey take on as rigorously combative a tone as Nietzsche in feeling that the true artist would not tolerate the world as it is even for one instant.

6   From Dickey's account of his growth as a poet, in *Poets on Poetry*, edited by Howard Nemerov (New York, 1966), pp. 225–38. It is ironic that Dickey should so distrust and mock his own reflective, intellectual nature, since he knows himself a poet of the "Second Birth" —one who has worked hard at his craft. Yet his finest poems give the impression of having been written very quickly; one feels the strange compulsion to read them quickly, as if to keep pace with the language. Dickey's poems are structures that barely contain the energies they deal with. That "agent" in the poem known as the "I" is unpredictable, at times frightening, for he may lead us anywhere. Dickey might have written extraordinary short stories had he not chosen to develop himself as a poet almost exclusively. In an excellent essay, "The Self as Agent," from *Sorties*, Dickey says that the chief

glory and excitement of writing poetry is the chance it gives the poet to "confront and dramatize parts of himself that otherwise would not have surfaced. The poem is a window opening not on truth but on possibility . . ." (p. 161).

7 Dickey's reviews of *Howl* and *Kaddish* are both negative. He says that Ginsberg's principal state of mind is "hallucination" and that the poetry is really "strewn, mishmash prose." Yet Dickey allows that, somewhere, in the Babel of undisciplined contemporary poets, "there might one day appear a writer to supply the in-touch-with-living authenticity which current American poetry so badly needs, grown as it has genteel and almost suffocatingly proper." From *The Suspect in Poetry*, pp. 16–19. When a poet-critic speaks in these terms, one may always assume he is talking about himself, whether he knows it or not.

8 Raymond Smith, "The Poetic Faith of James Dickey," *Modern Poetry Studies*, Vol. 2, No. 6, pp. 259–72. Masculine response to Dickey's poetry probably differs inevitably from a woman's response.

9 Dickey has granted a number of interviews, all of them characterized by an extraordinary frankness. In a recent one, the poet William Heyen asks him to discuss the violent "morality" of *Deliverance*, and Dickey states that there is a kind of "absolutism" about country people in his part of the world: "Life and death . . . are very basic gut-type things, and if somebody does something that violates your code, you *kill* him, and you don't think twice about it. . . . the foremost fear of our time, especially with the growing crime rate, crime in the cities and so on, . . . the thing that we're most terrified of is being set upon by malicious strangers. . . ." He therefore agrees with the decisions his characters make in the novel, and it is clear from his discussion of Ed Gentry's decision to kill and Gentry's growing realization that he is a "born killer" (Dickey's words) that the novel, like much of the poetry, is an attempt to deal with an essentially mystical experience. That it is also brutal and dehumanizing is not Dickey's concern. Murder is "a quietly transfiguring influence" on the novel's hero. "A Conversation with James Dickey," ed. by William Heyen, *The Southern Review* (Winter, 1973) IX, 1, pp. 135–56.

Notes to Chapter 9

1 Franz Kafka, *Dearest Father: Stories and Other Writings*, ed. by Max Brod, trans. by Ernst Kaiser and Eithne Wilkins (New York, 1954), pp. 48, 41.

Notes

2 *Parables and Paradoxes* (New York, 1961), p. 11.

3 In "Kafka's Distorted Mask," from *Creation and Discovery* (New York, 1948).

4 Gustav Janouch, *Conversations with Kafka*, trans. by Goronwy Rees (New York: New Directions, 1971), p. 153. In addition to the *Tao Te Ching*, Kafka had in his possession the following books: Kung-Futze's *Conversations*, Tzchung Yung's *The Great Doctrine of Measure and Mean*; Lao Tzu's *The Book of the Ancients Regarding Sense and Life*; Liä Tze's *The True Book of the Spring of the First Cause*; Chuang Tzi's *The True Book of the South Land of Blossom*. These works, he said, "are a sea in which one can easily drown." To my knowledge, Kafka never came across the *Bardo Thödol* (The Tibetan Book of the Dead)—fortunately for him, since it would have substantiated some of his most terrifying visions and provided a means by which his interest in Freudian thought might have been synthesized with his interest in Chinese philosophy.

5 All these quotations from the *Tao Te Ching* are from the excellent new translation by Gia-Fu Feng and Jane English (New York, 1972).

6 From "The Yoga of Thatness' of Tibetan Buddhism, in *World of the Buddha*, ed. by Lucien Stryk (New York, 1969), p. 315.

7 *Dearest Father*, pp. 90–91.

8 Diary entry for August 2, 1917. *The Diaries of Franz Kafka: 1914–1923*, ed. by Max Brod (New York, 1965), p. 173.

9 "Sometimes I believe I understand the Fall of Man as no one else"— from a letter to Milena Jesenská. *Letters to Milena*, ed. by Willy Haas, trans. by Tania and James Stern (New York, 1953), p. 167.

10 Max Brod, *Franz Kafka: A Biography* (New York, 1960), pp. 219–22.

11 *Letters to Milena*, p. 197.

12 Carl Jung, "Literature and Psychology," in *Modern Man in Search of a Soul* (London, 1933), p. 194.

13 *The Diaries of Franz Kafka: 1910–1913*, ed. by Max Brod (New York, 1948), p. 45. Martin Greenberg in his *The Terror of Art* (New York, 1968) begins his detailed and illuminating study of Kafka as an artist with this quotation.

14 Janouch, p. 127.

15 Diary entry for September 25, 1917. *Diaries 1914–1923*, p. 187.

16 Janouch, p. 133.

17 *Ibid.*, p. 143.

18 *Death in Venice and Other Stories* (New York, 1958), p. 6.

19 Janouch, p. 155.

20 *Diaries 1910–1913*, p. 7.

21 Janouch, p. 178.

22 P. 205. Kafka's own division of worlds allows us to interpret his
writing as both negative (in terms of history) and positive (in terms
of the human spirit). If one believes himself trapped in history, in
matter, then "Count Westwest" of *The Castle* is an extinct God for
all time and the Castle is no more than a delusion, the tomb of
God as Nietzsche saw the churches of his time to be the "tombs and
sepulchers of God." However, Kafka certainly believed in the individual's ability to detach himself from history and to achieve a transcendence of the merely historical. Though the individual is always *in*
paradise, he is not always aware of the fact, and this failure to be
aware of his own participation in the divine, this failure to *see* the
illusory nature of his own ego, constitutes the only hell (its high-
lights sensationally recorded as history!) possible. Kafka, more than
any of the writers considered in this study, is the true Rorschach test
of literature, that mirror held up to us that reflects only the precon-
ceived expectations we bring to it. But though one is told repeatedly
that Kafka dramatizes "existential anguish," a thorough, systematic,
and deeply contemplative study of his work over a period of time
reveals another Kafka altogether—one who even knew, and grieved
over, the "Kafka" of all the clichés.

FEB 18 1975